The Beginning Translator's Workbook

or the ABC of French to English Translation

Michele H. Jones

University Press of America, Inc.
Lanham • New York • Oxford

Copyright © 1997 by
University Press of America,® Inc.
4720 Boston Way
Lanham, Maryland 20706

12 Hid's Copse Rd.
Cummor Hill, Oxford OX2 9JJ

Library of Congress Cataloging-in-Publication Data

Jones, Michèle H.
The beginning translator's workbook : or the ABC of French to
English translation / Michele H. Jones.
p. cm.
Includes index.
1. French language--Translating into English--Handbooks, manuals,
etc. I. Title.
PC2498.J66   1997   428'.0241--dc21   97-24809 CIP

ISBN 0-7618-0836-1 (cloth: alk. ppr.)
ISBN 0-7618-0837-X (pbk: alk. ppr.)

⊖™The paper used in this publication meets the minimum
requirements of American National Standard for information
Sciences—Permanence of Paper for Printed Library Materials,
ANSI Z39.48—1984

Table of Contents

Chapter 9   **Modulation**

Chapter 10   **Equivalence**

Chapter 11   **Adaptation**

Chapter 12   **Applying Translators' Devices to Literary Texts**

Preface

Why a textbook on translation?

Necessity is the mother of invention. This book was born of the need for adequate material to be used in a translation course for beginners with a proficiency in French ranging from intermediate to advanced level. Contrary to most books on the subject which either focus on the theory and method and are aimed at professionals, or focus on the practice and only provide texts with their finished translation without indicating the means of reaching such an art, this manual combines methodology and practice by offering both concurrently.

Each of the beginning eleven chapters defines a particular translation problem, introduces a method of dealing with it, provides numerous examples to illustrate the point, and concludes with practice exercises consisting of short sentences designed to make the student think about the difficulty and decide on the appropriate translation strategy. The advantage of this methodological approach is that even a novice translator will quickly learn how to sense and to identify the various pitfalls of translation and will react with the proper response.

It has been my experience as a translation instructor that neophytes have a sort of primary aversion to idiomatic translation which they display by sticking stubbornly to the text word for word. The proposed method, through a progressive framework, will enable them to move beyond literal translation to a fluid and idiomatic rendition of the source text by building up confidence and savoir-faire.

After students become familiar with the translation environment, and attain a solid level of proficiency through the use of the various devices put at their disposal, the final chapters are intended to provide a global application of the principles taught by guiding them through the actual translation of literary and non-literary excerpts. Suggested translations are offered alongside the texts as illustrations of what a finished translation can be, but by no means as the one and only solution and model.

Throughout the book, particular care has been taken to provide material for both literary and business or technical translation, in order to make the apprentice translator aware of the semantic and structural differences involved. Guidelines have also been provided delineating the different approaches to follow and the different expectations to be met on both counts.

A selection of texts to be translated on one's own has not been included, so as to leave freedom of choice to the course instructor, for the reason that everyone has particular favorites in that regard.

Translation is both an art and a skill, a discipline with rules, with dos and don'ts. The newly coined words of "traductique" and "traductologie" in French emphasize the scientific aspect of modern translation. It is difficult and demanding. To attain a high proficiency level will require years of practice. But it is a wonderful exercise for the mind and yields great intellectual benefits: from the sharpening of analytical powers and the sheer enjoyment of being able to convey a message by watching thoughts take shape in different words, right down to the thrill and sense of accomplishment which accompanies the finding of solutions to puzzling semantic or structural problems.

Translation can be a discipline as well as a pastime. And even though computer scientists and linguists have been working for some fifty years now on "robot translators' or automatic translation in the hope of one day replacing the human translator, technology is still light years away from being able to produce the software which will translate Molière, Baudelaire or Proust. Let's be thankful for that, for it would deprive us of using and developing that great machine of ours, our brain.

Lastly, I would like to add a word of thanks to my students, who have provided the experimental field without which this book would not have been possible, and particularly to Walter Schaap for allowing me to reproduce the poem translations found in this book. I also thank the weekly magazine Evènement du Jeudi, and the newspapers France Amérique and Journal de Genève-Gazette de Lausanne for their gracious permission to reprint the articles found in chapter 17.

The Would be Translator's Basic Terminology

Source language (S.L.): language from which one translates (Fr. langue de départ, L.D.)

Target language (T.L.): language into which one translates (Fr. langue d'arrivée, L.A.)

Sign versus concept: a linguistic sign is formed of an acoustic sound (in speech) or a visual image (in writing) representing a concept, i.e. *arbre* and *tree* are two signs and one concept.

Translation Unit (T.U., Fr. unité de traduction, U.T.): a unit of thought in the language, the smallest portion of a message whose elements cannot be translated separately without resulting in mistranslation or even nonsense, i.e. *faire un clin d'oeil* (*to wink*), or *to put on weight* (*grossir*).

Delineation of translation units: structural analysis of the text to be translated in order to determine the translation units it encompasses.

Mistranslation: erroneous or incorrect translation which may or may not make sense in the TL and results from a lack of sufficient knowledge or a misinterpretation of the SL; can occur in one word or a whole sentence.

Barbarism: the use of words or expressions not in accordance with the classical standard of a language, especially such as are of foreign origin. A mistake sometimes made in translation by inventing a word or a grammatical structure by copying the SL; i.e. the use of the definite article for general terms and concepts being the rule in French, but not in English, a barbarism in English would be incurred by saying: *The beauty is fleeting* to translate *La beauté est éphémère.*

Solecism: a specific type of barbarism involving a violation of the rules of grammar or syntax.

Overtranslation: occurs when the translator sees several translation units when only one exists. Elements absent from the source text are added and the translation is longer than it should be; i.e. *petits pois* constitutes one translation unit rendered as *peas* rather than *small peas,* which would be the equivalent of *petits pois extra fins.*

Undertranslation: occurs when the translator overlooks one or several of the elements of the original message and fails to translate them.

Retranslation: is a checking device in translation. The translator retraces his steps from the TL back to the SL and then compares this retranslation with the original text to verify translation accuracy.

Deficiency versus compensation: a deficiency occurs when a particular semantic or grammatical concept does not exist in either the SL or the TL.   A compensation, on the other hand, is an attempt to make up for that deficiency through some other means;   i.e the lack of the *tu* form of address in English can be compensated with the use of the person's nickname to indicate familiarity;   or the lack of phonetic emphasis in French can be compensated by stylistic emphasis: *I told you, not he* may be rendered as *C'est moi qui te l'ai dit, ce n'est pas lui.*

Loss versus gain: a loss in translation results from a semantic or structural deficiency in the TL which cannot be compensated for, while a gain adds something which did not exist in the SL whenever the TL is semantically richer.   When the sentence *Le taux de chômage est passé à 5,8 pour cent en avril de 5,5 pour cent en mars* is translated as *The unemployment rate jumped to 5.8 per cent in April from 5.5 percent in*

March, we have a gain in English with the verb *jumped* indicating a sudden upward trend absent from the SL word *est passé*.

Saving versus padding: saving is when the S.L. message can be translated in fewer words, and padding when it has to be expressed in more words. An example of saving in English: *Il a prit sa retraite, He retired*; an example of padding: *Tu es insortable, You cannot be taken out because you have no manners*.

Language levels: they determine the type of language to be used in translation: poetic versus prosaic, literary versus colloquial, refined versus vulgar, ancient versus modern, aesthetical versus functional, philosophical versus technical etc. The translator has to adopt the tone of the SL and target the audience targeted by the SL. One does not translate *Je vous prie de bien vouloir quitter ces lieux* and *Foutez moi le camp!* quite in the same language register in the TL.

Literal versus figurative sense: many words have both a concrete meaning and an abstract one, i.e. Fr. *ivresse*: (literal sense) *drunkenness*; (figurative sense) *rapture*.

False cognates (Fr. faux amis): words with the same linguistic origin in the SL and TL whose meanings have evolved differently over the years. i.e. Fr. *actuellement*: *at present*, and Engl. *actually*: *en réalité*.

Translation devices: translation strategies at the disposal of a translator when confronted with structural, semantic or metalinguistic obstacles.
There are three literal translation devices: borrowing, calque and word for word translation, and four non literal devices: transposition, modulation, equivalence and adaptation.

Borrowing: when a concept first exists in the SL but not in the TL it is often borrowed in its original form by the TL.without any form of translation. Example of English borrowing from French: *mayonnaise*; of French from English: *steak*.

Calque: occurs when instead of being borrowed in its original form a new concept from the SL is translated literally, "copied" by the TL; i.e. from English to French: *the cold war, la guerre froide*; from French to English: *secrétaire général, secretary general.*

Word for word translation: when there are no structural or semantic obstacles for doing so, the words in the SL and in the TL can be translated word for word and in the same order, i.e. *Où est le chat? Where is the cat?*

Transposition: is a change in grammatical categories between SL and TL so as to surmount a structural obstacle and remain idiomatic, i.e. *Maison à vendre: House for sale* (in this case the change is from a verb to a noun).

Modulation: occurs when the SL and the TL see the same concept from different angles. There can be word modulations (found in dictionaries), i.e. *un logiciel* (abstract viewpoint): *software* (concrete); preposition modulations (found in grammar books), i.e. *J'ai vu une émission intéressante à la télé, I saw an interesting show on TV*; or message modulations, i.e. *On m'a appris la nouvelle, I was told the news*.

Equivalence: when the translation unit is an idiomatic expression, a cliché, a reflex formula, a greeting formula, slang, a proverb or saying, a cultural reference, the translator must from the context first understand the situation and then give the appropriate equivalent expression used in a similar situation in the TL. For instance, in the situation of a child asking another about what has been going on during his absence: *Quoi de neuf?, What's up?* would be the equivalent in English.

Adaptation: when there are obstacles to translation resulting from cultural differences, i.e. different institutions, customs or traditions which the readers in the TL cannot well comprehend for lack of a ready equivalent, the translator must resort to adaptation. One form of adaptation is compensation, another might be an explanatory periphrasis, yet another some similar concept in the TL, for example: *Le musée se trouve à 200 mètres d'ici, The museum is about 200 yards away.*

Preliminary Remarks
Linguistics and Metalinguistics

Reality, in the creative process required to give a language its vocabulary and syntax, can be seen under many different angles. In apprehending a particular concept each language tends to focus on different aspects of the same reality, and to see things slightly or even very differently from what other languages may perceive. This is true at the semantic level, in the creation of vocabulary and idioms. It is also true at the syntactic and grammatical level, in the delivery of the message.
A few examples:

Semantically
Where Anglophones see: Francophones see:
- a goldfish   a red fish (un poisson rouge)
- a fireman   a (water) pumping man (un pompier)
- a keyhole   a lockhole (un trou de serrure)
- a mountain range   a mountain chain (une chaîne de montagne)
- a life threatening disease   a mortal disease (une maladie mortelle)

Grammatically
Whereas English favors the passive voice in certain constructions, French favors the active voice:

I've been told that he is feeling better

translates best as   *On m'a dit* qu'il va mieux.

Modulation can occur in the use of the auxiliary verb in common expressions:

"She *is* 20 years *old*"   becomes   "Elle *a* 20 *ans*"

Syntactically

Syntax is yet another field in which variations are frequent. English has a propensity to be more synthetic and to favor the use of compound words, French more analytic and to favor the use of articulations:

business French	le français *des* affaires
a customer oriented company	une firme tournée vers le client/
	qui donne la priorité au client

Importance of culture and civilization in the formation of languages

Metalinguistics (from the Greek meta, beyond), i.e. all the elements which beyond the language encompass the civilization and culture of a particular linguistic group, has a profound influence over the formation of the language.

Concepts as French as the 14th of July, cafés, croissants, the baccalauréat, the legion of honor are steeped in history and culture. A serious translator must therefore have a very good knowledge of the culture and civilization of the language from which he or she is translating in order to be able to pick up historical and literary references which would elude a less informed amateur. Expressions such as *l'homme du 18 juin*, a reference to De Gaulle, the man responsible for the famous London broadcast of June 18th 1944 which called for a rally of all the forces of Free France to continue fighting the Nazi regime which had just overtaken France; or *Revenons à nos moutons*, a saying taken from a popular medieval play, *La Farce de Maître Pathelin*, in which a judge, overwhelmed by the imbroglio of complaints made deliberately so as to confuse him, pleads to have the plaintiff stick to one complaint at a time: the loss of some sheep. The expression has eventually passed into everyday speech with the meaning of *Let's stick to the point.*

Differences in concept focus between English and French in the creation of words

The following are sample categories in which metalinguistics and different perceptions of the world resulted in diverging messages for the same concept. The list is by no means exhaustive.

Greetings and salutations
Different ways of dividing the day:
Good morning!/ good afternoon!   Bonjour!

Reflex formulas
Different perspectives.   The English exclamation below is concrete and involves the eyesight while the French one is abstract and involves the mind:
Look out!   Attention!

Public signs
Different approaches in the delivery of the message. Here is an informal communication in English and a more formal and authoritative French counterpart:
Keep off the grass   *Défense* de marcher sur les pelouses

Idioms and clichés
Different priorities and values in life. The importance of sports and the outdoors in the English speaking world versus the importance of anything having to do with cooking in French speaking countries are reflected in these two equivalent clichés:
Let's not beat around the bush   Ne tournons pas autour du pot

Vocabulary related to architecture
Different ways of defining space:
a first floor (U.S.)   un rez de chaussée (= G.B.ground floor)

Vocabulary related to measures
Different ways of visualizing measuring units:
a yard
un mètre (a unit created during the French Revolution in a concerted effort
to improve on the confusing measure system then existent throughout France)

Vocabulary related to professions
Different ways of delineating areas of specialization in professions.
A lawyer (U.S.) who may specialize in litigation, tort law, deeds etc.is the
equivalent of two French professions:
avocat (G.B. barrister) and notaire (G.B. sollicitor)

We will see more of these metalinguistic divergences as we go along, for metalinguistics cannot be dissociated from the creative process involved in linguistics.

Chapter 1 Translation Units

What are translation units and what is their use?

After reading the text to be translated, the basic task of the translator, in the transcoding process from the source language to the target language that follows, is to go beyond words to the concepts behind those words. In that particular phase of translation and for a split second, the translator is actually transcending words, languages, navigating in a world of pure thought, before giving back the message in a new shape, a new code.

Literal or word for word translation occurs whenever there are no semantic or grammatical obstacles, i.e. when one noun in the S.L. corresponds to one noun in the T.L., one verb to one verb, one grammatical construction to a structurally similar grammatical construction and when the word order also is identical. Needless to say, such ideal conditions generally do not exist, except perhaps in sister languages originated from a common tongue with a similar grammar and syntax such as Romance languages, which are derived from Latin.

In the case of English and French however, we cannot speak of sister languages, for, although they are often close semantically due to a common vocabulary stock derived from Latin, ancient Greek, old French, and mutual borrowings over the centuries, they both differ considerably in grammar and syntax, English belonging to the family of Germanic languages and French to the Romance language group. Between English and French, therefore, literal translation may occur in very simple and short sentences, sentences such as: *The cat eats the mouse, Le chat mange la souris,* but never in complex structures. In French, or in English, a concept may not always coïncide with one word, and so one word in one language may correspond to several words in the other and vice-versa.

Both languages have different characteristics. French tends to be more analytical and to expand its concepts with the use of articulations. English tends to be more synthetic, using concise compound expressions. A translation into English from the French will typically run much shorter than the original without any loss in the global message.

The translator must then learn what constitutes a concept, a unit of thought in the S.L., delineate the message to be translated into as many translation units as there are concepts, and finally translate them into their T.L. counterparts.

This is how we may therefore define a translation unit:

> A translation unit is the smallest portion of a sentence whose words cannot be translated separately without resulting in nonsense or mistranslation.

A. Lexical translation units

These translation units may be lexical, based on words or expressions which can be found in a good dictionary.

Overtranslation is a common mistake made by beginners: several translation units are seen where only one exists and the end result is either nonsense or mistranslation, that is to say an erroneous interpretation of the SL

Let's take two examples:

> 1. **the adverbial phrase** *de bonne heure*: if the translator does not see a single translation unit there, it will be divided into 3 parts and translated literally as *of good hour*, which would result in total nonsense in the T.L., or as *at a good hour* which would be a mistranslation instead of the correct meaning *early*.
>
> 2. **the nominal phrase** *poids lourd* in the context *Ce poids lourd me barre la route*: again, if the translator, due to lack of semantic knowledge, sees two units of translation where in fact only one exists, the concept will be translated as *heavy weight*, also a mistranslation,

since the message in the T.L. would read *heavy weight* as in *heavy weight champion* instead of *truck*.

The following are representative examples in both languages of what may constitute a lexical translation unit:

French (group of words) to English (one word):

Nominal phrases: un hôtel de ville: a townhall; un chef d'orchestre: a conductor

Verbal phrases: montrer du doigt: to point (at); donner un coup de pied: to kick

Adverbial phrases: à toute vitesse: speedily; quand même: anyway; dans tout le pays: nationwide

Adjectival phrases: mal à l'aise: awkward/ uncomfortable

Prepositional phrases: le long de: along; au dessus de: above

Conjunctional phrases: au fur et à mesure que: as; du temps où: when

French (one word) to English (group of words):

Nouns: une standardiste: a (female) switchboard operator; un percepteur: a tax collector; l'équitation: horse back riding; un bilan: an outcome assessment

Verbs: vieillir: to get old; rentabiliser: to make profitable; déconseiller: to advise against; s'immobiliser: to come to a standstill

Adjectives: influençable: easily influenced; fragilisé: rendered more precarious

Adverbs: péniblement: with difficulty; dorénavant: from now on

Standard expressions:

Global expressions which are standard and idiomatic in the language also constitute units of translation. They involve for instance a verb and a direct object, such as:

établir une comparaison: **to draw** a comparison; **faire face** à une obligation: **to meet** an obligation; **faire** une objection: **to raise** an objection; **réaliser** un bénéfice: **to make** a profit etc...

or a nominal group, such as:

un cas de force majeure: circumstances beyond one's control; un délit d'initié: insider trading; un travail de longue haleine: long and hard work, etc...

or even a group adjective-noun:

un **pauvre** type: a loser; une **belle** américaine: an American **car**; un **gros** rhume: a **bad** cold, etc...

B. Grammatical translation units

These translation units may also be grammatical, based on different grammatical or syntactical structures between the two languages, structures giving cohesive unity to a global concept.
For example:

Verbs followed by prepositions:
Verbs whose construction requires that they be followed by a special preposition before a noun or another verb constitute translation units:

Cela ne *dépend* pas *de* moi: that does not *depend on* me.

Sometimes the prepositions coïncide in the two languages; but sometimes also they can be different, or there can be a preposition in one language and none in the other. Good grammars will offer lists of such prepositional constructions. Otherwise, check in your dictionary.

Examples of prepositional structures which coïncide:
s'habituer *à*: to get used *to*; voter *pour*: to vote *for*
Which do not coïncide:
commencer *par*: to start *with;* décider *de*: to decide *to*
Instances in which there is a preposition in English but none in French:
to look *at*: regarder; to ask *for*: demander
A preposition in French/ none in English:
assister *à*: to attend; discuter *de* : to discuss

Active/ passive voice:
Very often an active voice in French will be translated as a passive voice in English. The corresponding structure constitutes a translation unit.

On nous avait prévenus: *We were forewarned*. Instead of an awkward literal rendition contrary to English usage (one had forewarned us...) the use of the passive voice will yield an idiomatic translation.

Articulated expressions/ Compound expressions:
French like all Romance languages is an analytic language, that is to say one which often makes use of connective prepositions between the various components of a concept, whereas English is a synthetic Germanic language which tends to juxtapose these same elements without connectors. Therefore articulated expressions in French will constitute units of translation often to be rendered as compound expressions in English with an accompanying change in word order:

> Ces jeans *serrent au corps*: these are *tight fitting jeans*.
> Les territoires *d'*outremer: overseas territories.
> Notre compagnie est *une compagnie en plein essor*:
> Ours is a *fast growing company*.

C. Extended translation units

Translation units are not necessarily limited to phrases, small groups of words, or different grammatical constructions: they can encompass entire sentences or even entire messages. Idioms and slang, greetings and reflex-formulas, clichés, proverbs and sayings, public signs and regulations, all constitute complex translation units whose elements cannot be translated separately:[1]

> *A la prochaine*! *See you soon*!
> *Non mais alors*, vous ne pouvez pas faire attention! *Look here*, can't you be *more* careful!
> J'étais *dans mes petits souliers*: I was *on tenterhooks*.
> Votre fils est *sage comme une image*: Your son is *as good as gold*.
> Tandis qu'il parlait, *j'avais la moutarde qui me montait au nez*: As he spoke, *I was getting miffed*.
> *Comme on fait son lit on se couche: As you sow, so shall you reap*.
> *Sens interdit: One way street*.

D. Delineation of translation units

---

[1] We will deal with these at length in the chapter on equivalence.

It is good practice for the student translator to learn how to delineate translation units, i.e. make a semiological analysis of the text, by cutting out and pairing the words which constitute single concepts in order to translate them with their proper counterparts. Experienced translators will automatically do a quick mental delineation of translation units before a translation, and after some practice this procedure should become second nature.

Make sure that all nominal, verbal, adverbial, prepositional and conjunctional phrases are correctly recognized, as well as grammatical TUs such as active/passive constructions, prepositions attached to verbs, and all the idiomatic expressions which we grouped under the heading *Extended T.U.s.*

Examples:

Tout le monde me dit que je ressemble comme deux gouttes d'eau à mon grand père.
[1   ] [2] [3] [4] [5] [6   ] [7]
[8   ]
Everyone tells me that I   am the spitting image of my grand father.
[1   ] [3] [2] [4] [5] [6   ] [7] [8   ]
The difficulty here lies in the proper recognition of *ressembler comme deux gouttes d'eau à* as one concept, therefore as one TU.

On nous a demandé de repasser dans une semaine.
[1] [2] [1   ] [3] [4] [5] [6] [7] [8   ]
We were asked to come back in one week.
[2] [1   ] [3] [5] [4] [6] [7] [8]
The active construction *on nous a demandé* and the verb *repasser* have to be understood as two TUs.

Ça par exemple, tu as encore fait la grasse matinée!
[1   ] [2] [3] [4] [3   ]
My goodness, you've been sleeping late again!
[1   ] [2] [3   ] [4]
Ça par exemple has to be recognized as a fixed expression, therefore as one TU, and so does the idiom *faire la grasse matinée* even though it is interrupted by the adverb *encore* which has to be repositioned in English.

Défense de stationner.
[1   ]

No parking.
[1   ]

Aide-toi le ciel t'aidera.
[1   ]
Heaven helps those who help themselves.
[1   ]
Public signs and regulations, proverbs and sayings, which are fixed in the language, constitute one TU each.

Overtranslation and undertranslation are standard translation mistakes resulting from improper TU delineation:

- **Overtranslation** occurs when the translator sees more TUs in the source text than actually exist.
- **Undertranslation**, when the translator sees fewer TUs than actually exist.

> **Example one: Que veux-tu dire?**
> If the translator sees two TUs in the verb *vouloir dire* (to want to say) instead of only one (to mean), as is correct, the result will be an overtranslation: *What do you want to say?* instead of *What do you mean?* The first translation is erroneous because it introduces an intent absent from the source text, and would be more the equivalent of *Tu veux dire quelque chose?*

> **Example two: Quand vous reverrai-je?**
> If the translator fails to recognize that the verb *revoir* actually constitutes two TUs (to see/ again) the result will be an undertranslation: *When shall I see you?* instead of *When shall I see you again?*

In summary, the main purpose behind the delineation of a text into translation units is to remind the novice translator to work with concepts rather than words: you must rise to the message behind the signs in order to avoid error, nonsense or just plain unidiomatic translation.

Exercices: Les Unités de Traduction

Une unité de traduction est le plus petit segment d'une phrase dont les éléments ne peuvent être traduits séparément sans tomber dans le non-sens ou le contresens (synonyme: unité de pensée, concept) Dans l'unité de traduction le concept peut être un mot, un groupe de mots ou même une phrase .
Un mot dans la langue de départ (LD) peut coïncider avec un groupe de mot dans la langue d'arrivée (LA) ou vice versa.

A. Les unités de traduction lexicales

I. Les locutions suivantes en français constituent des unités de traduction qui se traduisent par un mot simple en anglais. Retrouvez en le sens.

1. Locutions nominales:
Un ancien combattant; un ancien élève; un chef de gouvernement; un exploitant agricole; un franc tireur; un homme politique; un metteur en scène; une personne du troisième âge; un sans abri; un sans emploi.
Un animal domestique; le bout des doigts; un chef d'oeuvre; un chemin de fer; un coup de pied; un courant d'air; le cuir chevelu; un grand magasin; une grande surface; un hôtel de ville; la main d'oeuvre; des petits pois; un poids lourd; un point de vente; une pomme de pin; une pomme de terre; une tenue vestimentaire; une vente aux enchères.
Un chiffre d'affaire; une expression idiomatique; un fil de fer; un jour férié; une manchette de journal; un manque de considération; une matière plastique; une mise au point; un mode d'emploi; une pension alimentaire; un point de repère; un titre de propriété; une tranche horaire.

2. Locutions verbales:

Avoir affaire à; donner une autorisation; donner des leçons particulières; donner sa démission; être en mesure de; faire allusion à; faire appliquer (une loi); faire confiance à; faire état de; faire mention de; faire peur à; faire de la publicité; faire un procès; jouer un mauvais tour; lancer des représailles; mettre en cause; mettre en question; mettre (une lettre) à la boîte; montrer du doigt; prendre sa retraite; remettre (quelquechose) à plus tard; traduire en justice; tirer un coup de fusil; vouloir dire.

3. Locutions adverbiales:

(Battre) à coups précipités; (comparer) à l'échelle mondiale; (prendre) au sérieux; (se lever) de bonne heure; (se comporter) d'une façon désinvolte; (parler) en connaissance de cause; (regarder) en silence; (faire quelquechose) tout de suite.

4. Locutions adjectivales:

(Etre) à bout de forces; (être) transporté de joie; (un produit) sans matière grasse.

5. Locutions prépositionnelles:

A côté de; à destination de; à la différence de; au dessus de; au lieu de; dans la direction de; de la part de; en ce qui concerne; en provenance de; en raison de; le long de; par le moyen de; pour ce qui est de.

6. Locutions de conjonction:

A l'endroit où ; à l'époque où; au fur et à mesure que; au moment où; de telle sorte que.

II. Les mots français suivants correspondent à des groupes de mots en anglais: traduisez.

1. Substantifs:

Un charcutier; une fermière; une pâtissière; une correspondante; un particulier; une standardiste; un récidiviste; un vieillard; un arriéré (de paiement); la cohabitation; la conjoncture; une gentilhommière; un trafic.

2. Verbes:
Arrondir; élargir; grossir; lâcher; maigrir; rajeunir; culpabiliser; rentabiliser; sensibiliser; redémarrer; refaire; revoir; s'aggrandir; s'assouplir; se désintéresser; s'entendre (avec quelqu'un).

3. Adjectifs:
Influençable; insortable; indissociable; frileux; travailleur.

B. Les unités de traduction grammaticales

> *Les verbes auxquels sont rattachées des prépositions constituent des unités de traduction. Parfois les prépositions coïncident dans les deux langues, parfois elles sont différentes, et parfois il y a une préposition dans une langue mais pas dans l'autre.*

Traduisez.

1. Il faut téléphoner *à* la compagnie aérienne pour confirmer notre retour.
2. Le résultat ne dépendra que *de* toi.
3. Dans une dissertation on doit toujours commencer *par* une introduction.
4. Pourquoi étais-tu en colère *contre* moi?
5. Il vient de se faire opérer *d'*un kyste.
6. Etudions pour éviter *d'*échouer *à* cet examen.
7. Quand t'intéresseras-tu *à* quelquechose qui en vaille la peine?
8. Le commandant de la milice donna l'ordre de tirer *sur* la foule.
9. Il me semble que je commence à m'habituer *à* ma vie d'étudiant.
10. Attends-moi!
11. Je cherche mes lunettes.
12. Mais je n'ai pas ri *de* toi, seulement *de* ton chapeau!
13. *A* quels cours vous êtes-vous inscrits ce semestre?
14. Il tient ses talents d'homme à tout faire *de* son père.
15. Nous préférons écouter de la musique classique.
16. Il serait désormais difficile de se passer *d'*électricité.

C. Les unités de traduction: découpage

Découpez les phrases suivantes en unités de traduction.

1. Le succès de l'entreprise ne dépend que de toi.
2. De temps à autre je me fais des idées noires, ce que mon petit ami met en question avec désinvolture.
3. Le jeune homme eut tout de suite l'idée qu'il s'agissait d'un piège.
4. Bien qu'elle eut très peur, la petite fille ne poussa pas un cri.
5. Je n'avais pas le coeur serré à la pensée de quitter l'endroit qui m'avait vu naître.
6. On nous montra du doigt le musée qui se trouvait juste en face de l'hôtel de ville.
7. Au fur et à mesure que la soirée avançait les invités s'éclipsaient jusqu'à ce qu'il ne reste plus que nous.
8. Le président directeur général va prendre la parole pour établir une comparaison entre le chiffre d'affaire de cette année et celui de l'année dernière.
9. Tout le monde s'attend à ce que l'inculpé soit traduit en justice dans les jours qui viennent.
10. Une fois par an nous faisons une grande fête de famille qui commence par un banquet et se termine par des embrassades.

D. Les unités de traduction: le contexte

> *La distinction entre les groupes de mots qui constituent des locutions, donc des unités de traduction simples et les groupes de mots qui n'en sont pas est quelquefois difficile à faire. Elle dépend du contexte, ou bien encore de petits indicateurs morphologiques, syntaxiques ou lexicaux, tels les changements d'articles ou de prépositions, mots composés, sens propre contre sens figuré, etc..*

Dans les phrases suivantes indiquez si les groupes de mots similaires constituent une seule U.T. (en tant que locutions) ou plusieurs U.T (en tant que concepts séparés).

1. Please set out the tea cups.
2. Would you like another cup of tea?
3. Come to morrow morning at 9 without fail.
4. I won't fail this exam.
5. They are not in the know.
6. They are not to know.
7. Concerning this matter, we are all in the same boat.
8. The same boat took them to the other side of the lake.
9. There's a man in the street standing in front of our door.
10. How does the man in the street feel about this issue?
11. Serves you right!
12. Guests must be served first.
13. One can never tell you anything for fear of having it broadcast everywhere.
14. You never can tell!
15. That takes the cake!
16. Take the rest of the cake with you, we're on a diet.
17. I got this antique chest for a song at a flea market.
18. For this song you'll get a kiss.
19. There's no need to rub it in.
20. The instructions say: first rub the paste in, let it dry, then buff it to a polish.
21. You are going about it the wrong way.
22. We drove up the street the wrong way.
23. There you go again: you spilled the beans!
24. Be careful not to spill any beans on the floor.
25. The prisoner was shot in the arm while trying to escape.
26. Lower interest rates have given the economy a shot in the arm.

E. Les unités de traduction complexes

Les formules-réflexes, les salutations, les clichés, les expressions idiomatiques et argotiques, les affiches officielles, et les proverbes et dictons sont des cas particuliers d'unités de traduction.

Retrouvez les équivalents anglais des unités suivantes.

1. *Bon appétit*!
2. *Comment ça va*?
3. *Dites donc*, comme votre fils a grandi!
4. *Tant pis pour toi*!
5. *Allons*, tu ne vas pas me faire croire ça!
6. *Voyons*, ce n'est pas sérieux!
7. *Défense de marcher sur les pelouses.*
8. *Attention: travaux.*
9. *Défense de stationner.*
10. Elle est jolie *comme un coeur.*(très)
11. Tu fumes *comme un pompier.*(beaucoup)
12. *J'ai pris mes jambes à mon cou.*(J'ai vite couru)
13. *Ne va pas chercher midi à quatorze heures!*(Ne fais pas de difficultés)
14. *Occupe-toi de tes oignons!* (Occupe-toi de tes affaires)
15. *22, v'la les flics!* (Attention voilà la police!)
16. *L'habit ne fait pas le moine.* (Il ne faut pas juger les gens sur l'apparence)
17. *Plus on est de fous, plus on rit.* (Plus il y a de gens, plus on s'amuse)

F. Traduction de texte

Le dialogue suivant contient un certain nombre d'expressions idiomatiques et de clichés (en gros caractères dans le texte) qui constituent des unités de traduction, et, de ce fait, ne peuvent pas être traduits littéralement. En voici les équivalents (dans le désordre) en anglais.

if you think I'm gonna fall for this	*buddy*
for goodness sake	*a booby trap*
you must be kidding	*nothing doing*
a strange thing happened to me	*to be busy reading*
sweepstakes	*congratulations*
that's it, I get it	*speaking*

Traduisez le passage ci-dessous en choisissant les expressions équivalentes en anglais.

Il m'est arrivé une drôle d'histoire l'autre jour. J'étais **plongé dans la lecture de** mon journal juste avant de partir pour le bureau, quand le téléphone a sonné. "**Ça par exemple**, qui peut bien téléphoner de si bonne heure?" J'ai décroché. Une voix à l'autre bout du fil s'est fait entendre:

-Allô, ici Jean Dupont de la firme Bouquins et cie, j'aimerais parler à M. Jacques Legrand.

-**C'est lui-même à l'appareil**.

-Monsieur, j'ai le grand plaisir de vous annoncer que vous êtes l'heureux gagnant de notre **tirage au sort**. **Toutes mes félicitations**!

-Que voulez-vous dire?

-Vous avez gagné l'un de nos premiers prix: un magnifique baladeur d'une valeur de 500 francs.

-**Vous voulez rire**!

Ce type me prenait par surprise, je n'avais jamais rien gagné de ma vie auparavant.

-Mais pas du tout! Il n'y a qu'une petite condition pour que vous puissiez recevoir ce prix exceptionnel: vous engager à souscrire à un abonnement de 3 ans au magazine...

-**Ça y est, je comprends**. **Un attrappe-sot**, ai-je pensé, **mon vieux**, si tu crois que **je vais me laisser prendre comme ça, tu peux toujours courir**!

Et j'ai raccroché.

Chapter 2   **Words in Context**

Polysemy: Words and their Semantic Range

Words cannot be separated from their context. Far from being separate entities, they are flavored by their surroundings. The context will give a word a particular twist, a particular shade of meaning. The span of meaning of most words offers a certain number of variations, and different contexts will highlight anyone of these variations, for instance the concrete versus the abstract meaning of the word, or the standard meaning of the word versus its meaning in a specialty context, etc...

One important problem in translation arises from the fact that words in the S.L. and in the T.L. generally have semantic ranges which do not exactly coïncide: a word in the S.L. may have one (or several) of its shades of meaning covered by one counterpart in the T.L., while other extensions or variations of meaning of the same S.L. word require the use of totally different counterparts in the T.L.

The following diagram tries to illustrate how the semantic range of two words may coïncide:

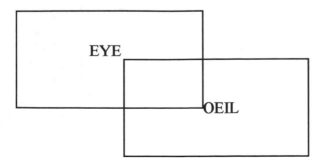

Two examples.

Looking up the French equivalent for the word *eye* in a bilingual dictionary will yield:

eye:	1. oeil	as in the eye of the master:	l'oeil du maître
	2. chas	the eye of a needle:	le chas d'une aiguille
	3. en vue	to be in the public eye:	être en vue (idiom).

Conversely, looking up the English equivalent for the French word *innocent* also gives diverse translations:

innocent: 1. pure, sinless, blameless as in le massacre des Saints *innocents,* the slaughter of the Holy *Innocents*

2. simple, guileless, simpleton as in l'*innocent* du village: the village *idiot.*

In both examples only the first meaning of the word coïncides in the S.L. and in the T.L. The other meanings, being an extension of the first, no longer coïncide in the T.L. and have to be rendered by the equivalent required by the context.

Literal vs. figurative meaning

Due to extended semantic ranges many words have both concrete and abstract meanings. It may happen that the two coïncide in the SL and TL. One can speak of a *hole* in the sleeve of a sweater and a *hole* in the budget, *un trou dans la manche d'un chandail* and *un trou dans le budget,* but such coïncidences are rather rare. Here are a few examples taken from different grammatical categories which illustrate differences between literal and figurative meanings, with the former requiring one word and the latter a different word in the TL:

literal:	se mordre *la langue*	to bite one's *tongue*
figurative:	être une mauvaise *langue*	to be a *scandalmonger*
literal:	*faire face à* une foule en colère:	*to face* an angry crowd
figurative:	*faire face à* une obligation:	*to meet* an obligation
literal:	être *ivre:*	to be *drunk*
figurative:	être *ivre de joie*	to be *ecstatic*

Language levels

Language levels are an example of the importance of the context in determining word significance. Words are chosen in function of the public they are destined for. Other than standard French or standard English there are many other language levels: technical, poetic, or slang, to name just a few.

Thus a word may mean one thing in standard French and quite another in a language of specialty. In theatrical jargon for instance *la douche* does not refer to a *shower* but to the spotlight focusing on the actors on the stage, and *le torchon* not to any rag but to the curtain. Likewise in the language of oil drillers *une carotte* is no longer a vegetable but a core sample.

Whereas the word *les méninges* anatomically refers to the meninges, the colloquial expression *se creuser les méninges* means *to think hard*. *La peau* may signify *the skin* in standard French. In slang, however, *une vieille peau* has more of the connotation of the English expression *an old bat*.

Poetic language is yet another one of these levels: *les palmes d'un arbre* refers to the branches of a tree, *l'azur* to the sky and not just to the color blue, while *the main* in English designates the sea.

Gender problems

French being a language which assigns genders to all nouns, some specific problems in translation may arise from overlooking the gender of words identical in everything but gender:

le chèvre (goat cheese)	la chèvre (goat)
le critique (the critic)	la critique (criticism)
le livre (book)	la livre (pound)
le manche (handle)	la manche (sleeve)
le mode (mode)	la mode (fashion)
le parti (party)	la partie (part/ game)
le poste (position/set)	la poste (post office)
le tour (tour)	la tour (tower)
le voile (veil)	la voile (sail)

Let's examine the following sentence:

> A l'horizon un petit vapeur est passé et j'en ai deviné la tache noire au
> bord de mon regard.   (Albert Camus, L'Etranger)

A mistranslation would arise should the gender of *vapeur* be overlooked and the word taken in its usual meaning of *steam*, a feminine word in French (*la vapeur*), instead of the masculine *le vapeur*, the *steamboat*.

> On the horizon a small steamboat went by and I could make out its
> dark patch from the corner of my eye.

Dictionaries and thesauri

Given the prevalent importance of the context in determining the exact significance of a particular word, here is one piece of advice: beware of dictionaries, especially small dictionaries which do not show the various meanings of a word in a sentence. And even the best of dictionaries will not always give you the exact equivalent required by the context, since they can only provide a limited number of illustrations. In this respect a thesaurus, which lists synonyms and the subtle nuances encompassed by one concept, will prove of more help in your search for the right word. For certain semantic fields in which the English language is richer, such as the field of sensorial perceptions, having recourse to a thesaurus will enable you to select the proper word in light of the context.

In conclusion, remember this rule:

> **There is no single permanent equivalent for any given word.**

Exercices: **Les Mots en Contexte**

Il est assez rare qu'un mot puisse être traduit d'une seule façon. Le sens des mots est influencé par le contexte dans lequel ils se trouvent. Un mot peut ainsi avoir des traductions tout à fait différentes selon son contexte.

A. Les mots en contexte

Traduisez les phrases suivantes en changeant la traduction des mots en italique en fonction de leur contexte.

1. **Aller:**
   Ça *va*? -oui, ça *va*.
   Nous *allons* déjeuner dans 10 minutes.
   Ce pull te *va* à ravir!
   Ne te trompe pas: les fourchettes *vont* dans le tiroir de gauche.
   Mon père *va* sur la quarantaine.
   Allons, dépêchez-vous, sinon nous serons en retard!

2. **Faire:**
   Il *fait* beau aujourd'hui, vous ne trouvez pas?
   Pour rester en forme il faut *faire* du sport.
   Tu *as fait* quelquechose d'intéressant hier?
   Ma soeur *fait* mieux la cuisine que moi.
   Cette robe te plaît? C'est moi qui *l'ai faite.*
   Il est assez grand, il *fait* un mètre 80.
   Je prends une livre de pommes. Combien ça *fait?*
   Tu devrais aller te *faire* couper les cheveux.
   Elle ne dormait pas. Elle *faisait* seulement semblant.

3. **Lever:**
   Levez la main lorsque vous aurez la réponse.
   Il est 10 heures du matin; il est grand temps de *vous lever.*
   Levez-vous lorsque le principal entrera dans la classe.

La séance *est levée.*
Un corps d'armée de 50 000 hommes *a été levé.*
L'O.N.U. cherche à faire *lever* le siège de Sarajevo.

4. Mettre:

C'est l'heure du dîner. *Mets* vite la table!
L'hôtesse *avait mis* sa plus belle robe pour faire impression sur ses invités.
On ignore qui *a mis* le feu au bâtiment.
Mettez-vous dans ce fauteuil, il est beaucoup plus comfortable que la chaise.
Mets-toi là pour arrêter la balle!
Jeanne d'Arc *mit* le siège à la ville d'Orléans pour la délivrer de l'emprise anglaise.
Son patron vient de le *mettre* au courant de la situation.

5. Passer:

Il faut que je *passe* un examen de chimie.
Quand on s'amuse le temps *passe* vite.
Par mesure de sécurité personne n'a le droit de *passer.*
Que *passe*-t-on au cinéma du quartier cette semaine?
Le docteur Girod *passe* pour être le meilleur cardiologue de la région.

6. Tenir:

Il *tient* le coup (idiomatique).
Votre fils *tient* de vous, c'est frappant!
Elle *tenait* beaucoup à ce collier qui lui venait de sa grand-mère.
Les chiens doivent être *tenus* en laisse dans le parc.
Vous voulez que je *tienne* tête au P.D.G.?
Tenez, vous ne savez pas ce que vous dites!

7. S'agir:

Dans ce film, il *s'agit* d'un homme et d'une femme qui tombent amoureux l'un de l'autre.
Ne faites pas de bêtises, c'est de votre intégrité professionnelle qu'il *s'agit.*

Il *s'agit* de faire attention, si nous ne voulons pas être grondés
par nos parents. (colloquial)

8. **Chez:**

Les Durand m'ont invité à venir passer le week end *chez* eux à
la campagne.

On retrouve souvent *chez* Balzac les mêmes personnages d'un
roman à l'autre.

Chez un animal qui doit fuir ou combattre, le coeur s'accélère et
la tension artérielle s'élève.

9. **Plein:**

As-tu fait le *plein* d'essence?

Ce devoir est *plein* de fautes d'orthographe!

La nuit de la Saint Jean, en Scandinavie, il fait clair comme en
plein jour.

En *plein* milieu du concert quelqu'un s'est mis à éternuer.

10. **Coup:**

Passe moi un *coup* de fil demain!

L'homme donna un *coup* de pied au chien.

Ils furent réveillés dans la nuit par de grands *coups* à la porte.

Pouvez-vous me donner un *coup* de main pour changer cette
table de place?

11. **Ennui:**

L'*ennui* est source de bien des maux.

Qui ne connaît actuellement des *ennuis* financiers?

Je voudrais bien t'aider. L'*ennui* c'est que je n'ai pas beaucoup
de temps.

12. **Etat:**

"L'*état*, c'est moi" aurait dit Louis XIV.

Tu es fort enrhumé: tu n'es vraiment pas en *état* de sortir.

Ces vêtements sont encore en bon *état*. Il ne faut pas les jeter.

Un propriétaire, avant de louer son appartement, fait en général
faire un *état* des lieux.

Le tiers *état*, groupe auquel appartenait la bourgeoisie, participa activement à la révolution française de 1789.

B. Sens propre ou figuré?

Déterminez si le sens des mots en italique est concret ou abstrait en fonction du contexte, puis traduisez les phrases dans lesquelles ils se trouvent.

1. Des champs de tournesol *s'étendaient* à perte de vue.
2. Il n'est pas assez de toute une vie pour *étendre* son savoir.
3. Les enfants s'étaient amusés à *jouer* aux gendarmes et aux voleurs.
4. Il *joue* régulièrement de grosses sommes dans l'espoir de devenir un jour millionnaire.
5. La porte du café *s'ouvrit* et un inconnu s'avança vers le zinc.
6. Si tu as des craintes au sujet de ce traitement, *ouvre-t-en* à ton médecin traitant.
7. Connaissez-vous l'expression "*doux* comme une peau de bébé"?
8. En dépit des prédictions pessimistes l'hiver s'est révélé très *doux*.
9. Vous êtes *assez* perspicace pour comprendre la difficulté de la situation.
10. A l'heure actuelle le choix d'un métier est une chose *assez* difficile.
11. Il est interdit de parler à *voix* haute dans la salle de lecture de la bibliothèque.
12. Le candidat donné comme favori par les sondages n'a été élu qu'à quelques *voix* de majorité.
13. Le développement des *transports* en commun serait une solution pour soulager la congestion urbaine.
14. Dans un *transport* de colère je me saisis du vase et le lançai violemment à terre.
15. Sa *démarche* était horriblement bancale, ce qui lui avait valu le surnom de Bamban (Alphonse Daudet, Le Petit Chose)
16. Le gouvernement ne sait quelle *démarche* adopter pour désamorcer les tensions sociales.

17. Ses *freins* ayant lâché, la voiture dévala la pente et alla s'écraser contre un arbre.

18. En France le coût du licenciement est longtemps demeuré un *frein* à l'embauche.

19. *L'étau* de l'ennemi se resserrait autour de la ville assiégée.

20. Nous devrions nous mettre d'accord pour ce qui *touche* à cette question.

C. Les champs sémantiques

Pour les champs sémantiques tels que les perceptions sensorielles, la langue anglaise se révèle plus riche que le français. Utilisez un thésaurus anglais[1] pour trouver les mots qui rendent au mieux le sens des mots en italique dans les phrases ci-dessous.

***Champ sémantique des sons** (consultez: sound, sonance, faint sounds, loud sounds, explosive sounds, resonance).*

1. Au loin une cloche *tinte* dans l'air du soir.

2. Je pensais à la source fraîche derrière le rocher. J'avais envie de retrouver *le murmure* de son eau. (Albert Camus, L'Etranger)

3. Seul *le murmure* des conversations d'élèves parvenait au professeur derrière sa chaire.

4. C'était une magnifique journée de printemps. Les oiseaux *chantaient* dans les arbres.

5. Nous entendîmes *un bruit sec,* semblable à celui d'un coup de fusil.

6. *Le bruit* des vagues lui parvenait à intervalles réguliers.

7. Aimes-tu *le bruit* de la pluie sur les toits?

8. Il y eut deux *coups brefs* à la porte, puis plus rien.

***Champ sémantique de la lumière** (consultez: light).*

9. Après que le soleil eut disparu à l'horizon, une *lueur rouge* continua à embraser le ciel.

---

[1] See Appendix pp.264-5 for a list of thesauri.

10. Seule *la lueur* d'une chandelle éclairait la chambre où il travaillait.

11. Il y a peut-être encore *une lueur* d'espoir.

12. J'aperçois *une lueur* de malice dans tes yeux.

13. La surface du lac *miroitait* sous la lune.

14. Vois-tu l'étoile polaire qui *brille* là-haut dans le ciel?

15. Toute la maison *brillait* de propreté.

Champ sémantique de la chaleur (consultez: heat, hotness).

16. La plage était *brûlante* de soleil.

17. Le soleil *avait complètement brûlé* les récoltes.

18. Attention, tu risques de *te brûler* avec cette eau chaude!

19. Ces petits pains sortent du four: ils sont *brûlants*.

20. *La chaleur* de l'été nous engourdissait.

21. Ce qui frappait le plus chez lui, c'était *la chaleur* de son regard.

Champ sémantique des vibrations (consultez: vibration, shaking).

22. Sous le coup de la peur, mon coeur se mit *à battre à grands coups* dans ma poitrine.

23. On pouvait voir ses veines qui *battaient* à fleur de peau.

24. L'oiseau *battit* des ailes, puis s'envola.

25. *Un tremblement* nerveux au coin de l'oeil trahissait son agitation intérieure.

26. La voix de l'enfant *tremblait* d'émotion.

27. Sur le chemin de la guillotine, Bailly, le maire de Paris déclara: "Si je *tremble*, c'est de froid et non de peur."

28. Son image *dansait* devant mes yeux.

Chapter 3   **Deceptive Cognates**

Faux amis

> **Deceptive cognates are what French linguists refer to as "*faux amis*", that is to say words which you think you might trust to mean exactly the same thing as similar looking target language words, but should not.**

Cognates and deceptive cognates

Cognates in English and French are words of similar origin, usually derived from a common Latin, ancient Greek or old French source, which carry the same meaning: words such as nation, classicism/ classicisme, biography/biographie, beauty/beauté, clear/clair, to descend/ descendre etc. Due to a long history of political interaction and cultural exchanges between the English and French speaking world, these are many.

However, over centuries of use, some of these cognates have evolved in different semantic directions, to the point of yielding such divergent meanings as *achever* (to finish) and *to achieve* (accomplir), English, in this instance, having focused on what remains after the task is finished while French left it at that; or *hasard* (chance) and *hazard* (danger); *malicieux* (mischievous) and *malicious* (méchant), English in both cases having retained only the negative elements of the concept.

Occasionally cognates can be so deceptive as to carry diametrically opposed meanings. Be the judge:

Fr. chiffon (rag)	**Engl**. chiffon (gauze material as in "chiffon" dress)
clinique (hospital for private patients)	clinic (hospital for the indigent)

Partial Faux Amis

To confuse the translator further there are, in addition, so-called "partial false cognates" which occur in the case of polysemous words (words carrying several meanings). In such words, one meaning might coïncide with its French or English cognate while others do not.

For example:
French to English
faculté: 1. faculty, ability, as in *Il a la faculté de voir clairement les choses*
2. faculty, college, as in *Ses enfants vont à la faculté de lettres de la ville*

However the French word never assumes the meaning of *faculty* in the sense of *a teaching body at a school or college*. This last meaning is a false cognate, and a different counterpart, *le corps enseignant*, must be resorted to in translation.

English to French
to assume: 1. assumer, as in *assumer une fonction, to assume a function* (cognate)
2. supposer, as in *Qu'allez-vous supposer? What are you assuming?* (false cognate)

The word is a partial false cognate due to the second meaning of the English word which has a different French counterpart.

Unrelated similar looking words

Not to be confused with true or false cognates are a certain number of words of totally unrelated origin which only look the same out of sheer coïncidence. Such words can easily be spotted due to the fact that they usually belong to different grammatical categories.
Let's mention:

une *averse*: shower (noun)	**and**	*averse*: opposé à (adjective)
fond (m.): bottom (noun)		*fond*: affectueux (adjective)
if (m.): yew tree (noun)		*if*: si (conjunction)
lame (f.): blade (noun)		*lame*: boiteux (adjective)
legs (m.): legacy (sg noun)		*legs*: jambes (plural noun)
lent: slow (adjective)		*Lent*: le Carême (noun)
or: now (adverb)		*or*: ou (conjunction)
sale: dirty (adjective)		*sale*: vente; soldes (noun)

but also, belonging to the same grammatical category, we may list:

bride (f.): bridle	*bride*: mariée (f.)
dot (f.): dowry	*dot*: point (m.)
nappe (f.): tablecloth	*nap*: sieste (f.)
pin (m.): pine tree	*pin*: aiguille (f.)
pain (m.): bread	*pain*: douleur (f.)
rein (m.): kidney	*rein*: rêne (m.)
ride (f.): wrinkle	*ride*: promenade (f.) (à cheval, à bicyclette ou en voiture)

Never underestimate the importance of learning about false cognates. Failure to do so may put you in some very embarrassing situations. Suppose for a minute that you are at a dinner table in a French speaking country and wish to convey to your hosts that you appreciate fresh, natural food in which there are no *preservatives*. If unaware that the term is a "faux ami", you will be tempted to use the French cognate *preservatif,* only to find out after the company has burst out laughing, with much damage to your dignity, or worse, stiffened into a deadly silence, that you have been speaking about food in which there are no *condoms* instead of using the correct term, *agent de conservation*!

The following is a list of some of the most common deceptive cognates:[1]

---

[1] Entries marked (part.) are partial false cognates. For a more comprehensive study refer to any of the dictionaries of false cognates listed in the appendix, p.265.

French

English

achever: to complete, to finish

accommoder: to accomodate, (part.)
to arrange (food)

actuel: present, current, up to date

actuellement: at present, now

agenda: memo book

agréable: pleasant

amateur: fan, lover

ancien: ancient, (part.) former

antique:(adj.) ancient

anxieux: worried

apologie: apology, defence

application: application, (part.)diligence

argument: raison, justification

arrêt: stop

assister à: to attend

assumer: to assume, to take on

attendre: to wait for

attirer: to attract

audience: hearing, session

avertir: to inform, to warn

avertissement: warning

avis: opinion, notice

bachelier: holder of the baccalaureate

blesser: to wound, to hurt

bribe: fragment, scrap

caractère: character, personality

brigadier: corporal

caméra: movie camera

canapé: couch, sofa

to achieve: accomplir, réaliser

to accomodate: (part.) loger

actual: réel, véritable

actually: en réalité

agenda: ordre du jour

agreeable: consentant

amateur: non-professionnel,
dilettante

ancient: ancien, antique

antique: (noun) antiquité

anxious: désireux

apology: apologie, (part.) excuses

application: (part.) demande (sur
formulaire)

argument: forte discussion,
querelle, dispute

arrest: arrestation

to assist: aider

to assume: (part.) présumer,
supposer

to attend: assister à (an event),
fréquenter (a place)

to attend to: s'occuper de

to attire: vêtir

audience: auditoire, assistance,
public

to avert: prévenir, empêcher

advertisement: réclame, publicité,
annonce

advice: conseil

bachelor: holder of college
degree, (part.) célibataire

to bless: bénir

bribe: pot de vin

character: (part.) personnage (in a
play)

brigadier: général de brigade

camera: appareil-photo

canopy: dais, baldaquin, voûte

candide: ingenuous

candid: franc, sincère

canot: rowboat

canoe: pirogue

cap: cape (i.e of Good Hope)

cap: (with visor)casquette, (without) bonnet

car: coach, intercity bus

car: automobile, voiture

caution: bail

caution: précaution

cave: cellar

cave: caverne, grotte

chance: luck

chance: occasion

chandelier: candlestick

chandelier: lustre

charte: charter

chart: carte, graphique

collège: junior high school

college: faculté, université

complainte: lament (poetry, music)

complaint: plainte, réclamation

complexion: disposition, constitution

complexion: teint

conducteur: driver

conductor: chef d'orchestre, chef de train, receveur

confection: making, ready to wear

confection: confiserie

conférence: lecture, speech

conference: congrès

confidence: secret

confidence: confiance

confus: embarrassed

confused: embrouillé

contrôler: to check, to verify

to control: diriger, maîtriser

copie: copy

copy: (part.) exemplaire (of magazine etc.)

courrier: (part.) mail

courier: messager, courrier (person)

courtier: broker

courtier: courtisan

crier: to scream, to shout

to cry: pleurer

décade: ten days

decade: décennie

décevoir: to disappoint

to deceive: tromper

défendre: to defend, (part.) to forbid

to defend: défendre, protéger

délai: delay, (part.) time limit

delay: retard

demander: to ask

to demand: exiger

député: (U.S.) assemblyman, (G.B.) M.P.

deputy: sous-chef, suppléant,délégué

dérober: to steal

to disrobe: se dévêtir

déterrer: to unearth

to deter: dissuader

dévotion: piety

devotion: dévouement

disposer de: to have at one's disposal

to dispose of: se débarrasser de

dresser: to set up (sthg), to train (animals)

to dress: habiller

éditeur: publisher

editor: rédacteur

ennuyer: to bore, to trouble, bother

to annoy: irriter

étiquette: etiquette, (part.) label,

etiquette: étiquette, protocole

éventuellement: possibly

eventually: finalement, tôt ou tard

évidence: obvious fact

expérimenté: experienced, skilled

fabrique: factory

faculté: faculty, college

faillir: (to) almost (do)

faute: fault, (part.) mistake

figure: face

filer: to spin,(coll.) to run away

formel: definite, strict

formidable: formidable, (part.) great

fournitures: supplies

glace: mirror, ice, ice cream

grief: grievance

grand: big

habit: costume

hasard: chance

heurter: to knock

humeur: mood

hurler: to yell

ignorer: not to know, to be unaware of

inconvénient: (noun) disadvantage

informations (pl.): the news

inhabité: uninhabited

injure: insult

intoxiqué: poisoned

issue: end, exit

joli: pretty

journée: whole day

labourer: to plough

large: wide

lecture: reading

librairie: bookstore

evidence: preuve, témoignage

experimented: testé

fabric: tissu, étoffe

faculty: faculté, (part.) corps enseignant

to fail: échouer

fault: fault, (part.) défaut

figure: silhouette, personnage, chiffre

to file: limer (nails), classer (documents)

formal: cérémonieux, de cérémonie

formidable: formidable, redoutable

furniture: mobilier, meubles

glass: verre

grief: chagrin

grand: grandiose

habit: habitude

hazard: danger, risque

to hurt: blesser, faire mal

humor: humour

to hurl: lancer violemment

to ignore: ignorer, faire semblant de ne pas voir (person), (part.) ne pas tenir compte de, négliger (facts)

inconvenient: (adj.) gênant, incommode

information: renseignement

inhabited: habité

injury: blessure, dommage

intoxicated: ivre

issue: résultat, question, émission (banknotes), numéro (magazine)

jolly: enjoué

journey: voyage, trajet

to labor: travailler péniblement

large: grand, gros

lecture: conférence

library: bibliothèque

licence: permis, (part.) bachelor's degree

license: licence, permis

licencier: to lay off, to dismiss

to license: accorder un permis

limonade: lemon soda

lemonade: citron pressé

location: rental

location: situation, emplacement

lunatique: moody, fickle

lunatic: fou

malicieux: mischievous

malicious: méchant

mémoire:(f.) memory, (m.) memoir

memory: mémoire (f.), (part.) souvenir

messe: mass (religious office)

mess: désordre

misère: extreme poverty or misfortune

misery: souffrance, détresse

monnaie: currency, (small) change

money: argent

note: note, (part.) (school)grade, bill

note: note, (banknote) billet

nouvelle: piece of news, short story

novel: roman

ombrelle: parasol, sun umbrella

umbrella: parapluie

opportunité: timeliness

opportunity: occasion

or: gold

ore: minerai

pair (m.): peer

pair: paire

passer: (exam) to sit for, to take

to pass: (exam) réussir à

pâte: paste, (part.) dough

paste: colle

patron: boss

patron: mécène

part: share, portion

part: partie

pasteur: shepherd, (protestant) minister

pastor: prêtre, curé

peuple: nation, people

people: peuple, (part.) les gens, on

photographe: photographer

photograph: photo(graphie)

phrase: sentence

phrase: locution, expression

physicien: physicist

physician: médecin

place: seat, (town) square

place: endroit, lieu

plat: dish

plate: assiette, plaque

préjudice: damage, wrong

prejudice: préjugé, parti pris

préservatif: condom

preservative: agent de conservation

prétendre: to claim

to pretend: faire semblant

prévenir: to warn

to prevent: empêcher

procès : trial

process: procédé, processus

propre: clean, own

proper: comme il faut, convenable

prune: plum

prune: pruneau

questionner: to question (someone)

to question: (part.) mettre en question, contester (sthg)

raisin: grape

raisin: raisin sec

réaliser: to realize, (part.)to achieve

to realize: se rendre compte

récupérer: (coll.) to recover (health),

to recuperate: se rétablir

(part.) to recover (sthg)

recycler: (part.) to retrain (s.o.); to recycle

regard: look, glance

relaxer: to free (prisoner)

relief: (geographic) surface

rente: unearned income

reporter: to postpone

(se) résigner à: to be resigned to

rester: to stay, to remain

résumer: to summarize

résumé: summary

réunion: meeting

révoquer: to revoke (decree), (part.) to fire, to dismiss (s.o.)

schéma: diagram, sketch

sensible: sensitive

sensiblement: appreciably

sentence: sentence, judgment

souvenir: (part.) memory, souvenir

spirituel: spiritual, (part.)witty

store: shade, venitian blind

supplier: to beg, to beseech

supporter: to support, to prop, (part.) to tolerate, to bear

sympathique: likeable, personable, nice

trafic: traffic (goods), (part.) illicit trade

transpirer: to transpire (news), (part.) to perspire

unique: sole, single, only

usage: custom

user: to wear out

voyage: trip (by sea, air, or land)

vent: wind

veste: jacket

wagon: (railroad) car

to recycle: recycler, récupérer

regard: considération, égard

to relax: se détendre

relief: soulagement, secours

rent: loyer

to report: rapporter

to resign: démissionner

to rest: faire reposer, se reposer

to resume: continuer, reprendre

résumé: curriculum vitae

reunion: retrouvailles

to revoke: révoquer, annuler

scheme: agencement, intrigue

sensible: sensé, raisonnable

sensibly: raisonnablement

sentence: sentence; (part.) phrase

souvenir: souvenir

spiritual: spirituel, de l'esprit

store: magasin, boutique

to supply: fournir

to support: soutenir (sth or s.o.), faire vivre (s.o.)

sympathetic: compréhensif, compatissant

traffic: circulation (road)

to transpire: transpirer, (part.) se passer, avoir lieu (events)

unique: sans pareil, seul en son genre

usage: emploi

to use: utiliser

voyage: voyage en bateau

vent: passage, trou d'aération

vest: gilet

wagon: charrette, chariot (in supermarket)

36. Avec la chute des taux d'intérêt les personnes vivant de leurs *rentes* sont les plus touchées.

37. La firme garantit la réception de la marchandise dans un *délai* d'une semaine.

38. Le *patron* est *actuellement* en congé de maladie à la suite d'une opération chirurgicale.

39. L'entreprise a dû *licencier* du personnel en raison de la crise économique.

40. La banque exige que toutes les transactions soient *régulières*.

41. Le projet a été *sanctionné* par le conseil des ministres.

42. L'administration va l'*affecter* à un nouveau poste en province.

43. Le chef du gouvernement a fait une *grande* faute en n'acceptant pas de dialoguer avec les représentants des grévistes.

44. Il est *formellement* interdit d'apposer des affiches dans les endroits publics.

B. Vrai ou faux ami?

Donnez le mot français qui correspond au mot anglais.

1. I am still a novice at this game but I will *eventually* get the hang of it.

2. Oil painting is *actually* easier than you might think.

3. Must you always *pretend* to have the answer to everything?

4. The driver *realized* too late that he had taken the wrong turn.

5. I *assume* that you know what you are doing.

6. Do you plan to *attend* the lecture?

7. As soon as he gets better, the patient may *resume* all his former activities.

8. The chairman of the board was forced *to resign* after the scandal.

9. How do you intend to *achieve* your proposal?

10. Eight hours of sleep a night are generally *regarded* as necessary for the body's equilibrium.

11. Running out without a raincoat in this weather, is that *sensible*?

12. There was *malicious* intent in this so-called accident.

13. Do you have any *relevant* material to show me?

14. Experts seem very *confident* that the economy is on an upturn.

15. Pride and *Prejudice*, S*ense* and Sensibility are two of Jane Austen's best loved novels.

16. Do not add insult to *injury*!

17. To prevent any mishap please put the *camera* back in its case.

18. Only a *lunatic* could reason in this way.

19. A compromise was reached to settle the *argument*.

20. *Figures* do not lie: the budget is not balanced.

21. January 1st is the deadline for filing all *applications*.

22. During the holidays a *delay* in the processing of packages is inevitable.

23. We need some *information* about train schedules.

24. Staff loyalty, for *decades* a matter of immense pride, has been shaken.

25. A research *executive* for the company was dispatched to a second tier job in Asia.

26. The candidate's *accomplishments* are *significant*.

Chapter 4   **Translation Devices**

What strategies do translators have at their disposal?

When faced with problems in the transcoding process of the message, the translator can resort to a certain number of devices which will help yield an idiomatic and fluid rendering, one which will not "smack" of translation. Remember that among the worst criticisms which can be levelled at you, as a translator, is the following kind of reaction: "I understand what you are trying to convey, but it sounds too much like a translation. No one speaks like that in good English." In other words, you have not been idiomatic enough and here are the tools at your disposal to help redress the situation.

> Problems in translation stem from one of three things:
> semantic, structural or metalinguistic obstacles standing in the
> way of a word for word translation.
> A translation device is a specific strategy to help translators
> find a solution.

The following examples are representative of the seven translation devices described by J.P. Vilnay and J. Darbelnet in their groundbreaking work *La Stylistique Comparée du Français et de l'Anglais,*[1] which are generally accepted as standard by linguists and translators.

---

[1] Paris: Didier, 1958.

They are at the word level in the first column, and at the message level in the second column, while the various devices (from borrowing to adaptation) are listed in order of increasing remoteness from the S.L. original.

Borrowing	
French-English: mayonnaise	French-English: C'est la vie
English-French: un steak	English-French: Okay
Calque	
A.I.D.S:	used cars:
S.I.D.A.	chars usagés (Canada)
Literal translation	
un jeune homme	Où sommes-nous?
a young man	Where are we?
Transposition	
faillir:	Comment vous appelez-vous?
(to) almost (do)	What is your name?
Modulation	
une pomme de discorde:	On m'a embauché
a bone of contention	I've been hired
Equivalence	
Aïe!: ouch!	L'habit ne fait pas le moine
	You can't tell a book by its cover
Adaptation	
1 kilogramme	Nous nous tutoyons
2.2 lbs	We are on a first name basis

Three of these devices will yield a literal translation:

- borrowings
- calques
- word for word

And four, a non literal translation:

And four, a non literal translation:
- transpositions
- modulations
- equivalences
- adaptations

We are going to examine all seven of these devices in detail in the following chapters. Meanwhile, here is a general word of advice for a faithful and good translation:

> **Be as literal as possible and as idiomatic as necessary.**

Therefore stick to literal translation whenever meaning and structure allow it, but do not be afraid to resort to a non-literal translation when needed.

> **Resort to non-literal translation whenever the message if translated literally into the T.L.:**
> 1. **makes some sense but does not sound idiomatic.**
> 2. **is structurally impossible to translate word for word.**
> 3. **gives a meaning different from the one in the S.L.**
> 4. **makes no sense.**
> 5. **cannot be translated as such, due to lack of equivalent concept, custom or institution in the T.L.**

Chapter 5   **Borrowings**

What is a borrowing and what is its purpose?

> A linguistic borrowing is a translation device born of a deficiency in the T.L.
> This deficiency may result from one of two factors:
> * cultural
> * technological

When a particular concept, which is the result of a way of life or of a technological advance, be it expressed as a noun, verb, adjective or even phrase, exists in one linguistic group only, and then through communications and exchanges is introduced to other lands, an immediate need for a sign to convey it arises in the target languages. Through lack of an immediate and ready equivalent, it is often borrowed from the S.L. in its original form without incurring any change in spelling. However, when the borrowing goes against the etymological characteristics of the T.L. (as in the case of English and French), modifications usually occur in pronunciation, and over the years significant changes may even develop in spelling and meaning.

Let's take two examples, one from the field of culture and the other of science:

> **A café,** a public place where one may order alcoholic or non-alcoholic beverages and even snacks while sitting out on a terrace watching other people stroll by, is a concept developed in Mediterranean lands where the sun shines and outdoor public life plays an important role.

When at the onset of mass tourism northern Europeans and Americans discovered the café and started enjoying its obvious benefits they borrowed both the institution and the word.

A pacemaker, on the other hand, is a 20th century American invention, a technological advance which, when it came out, revolutionized the field of health and therefore was immediately accepted worldwide. At any rate, for lack of linguistic creativity no French word was available and so the S.L. word was adopted in its foreign form (although since then, the more gallic sounding word of *stimulateur cardiaque* has been substituted).

French and English: a history of mutual borrowings

Ever since the fateful date of 1066 which marks the Norman conquest of England by the duke of Normandy William the Conqueror, the two linguistic groups have been borrowing extensively one from the other.

The Norman conquest indeed changed for ever the character of the English language, and from that time it is roughly estimated that half of the English vocabulary has evolved from the French. This explains the richness of the English language: a bilingual English to French dictionary is typically twice as big as its French to English counterpart. Often two terms coexist, one of Anglo-Saxon origin and the other of French origin, as in *to come in* and *to enter* (from the French *entrer*), *lovely* and *pleasant* (from *plaisant*), *tastily* and *deliciously* (from *délicieusement*), *by the side of* and *along* (from *le long de*) etc.

French, on the other hand, only started borrowing heavily from English in the mid 19th century when an appeasement took place after centuries of bitter political rivalry and anglomania first hit the affluent classes during the reigns of Louis Philippe and Napoleon III. But it has since made up for lost time and the trend started to accelerate right after the first World War as English began to be considered the world's most influencial language. Since World War II fashionable but indiscriminate borrowing in many fields, even where at times a perfectly good French equivalent already existed, has given alarm to the formidable French Académie, the long time cultural watchdog over French language and grammar. Fearing irretrievable damage to the tongue of Molière, Voltaire and Victor Hugo, and in an effort to prevent it from turning into unrecognizable "franglais", a special branch has been created at the Ministry of Culture, a *Délégation Générale à la Langue Française* whose function is to come up with a new nomenclature of French equivalents to English concepts based on roots closer to French etymology.[1] The linguists who comprise this delegation have indeed been responsible for various strikes, such as *ordinateur, logiciel* and *matériel* which have managed to supercede *computer, software* and *hardware,* no small feat in a world dominated by American computer terminology. But ultimately the public will remain the final judge, as some replacements are easily accepted while others continue to be scorned in favor of English borrowings, and only time will tell. In any case, after twenty years of research, an official dictionary was published in 1994 listing 3,500 terms or technical expressions which are to replace common English borrowings,[2] and a very controversial law was passed, the Toubon law, named after the minister of culture who suggested it, in order to impose their use by administrative public services.

Here is a representative sample, with some clever replacements and a few potential flops:

brainstorming: un remue-méninges
cameraman: un cadreur
compact disk: un disque audionumérique
design: la stylique
fast food restaurant: un restovite
jumbo jet: un avion gros porteur
hit parade: le palmarès

one man show: un spectacle solo
play back: un rejeu
preventive medicine: la prévento-
-logie
scoop: une primeur
speakerine: une annonceuse
to sponsor: parrainer

---

[1] Since most of the French government's main divisions have their own terminology commissions to deal with anglicisms, a Commission générale de Terminologie et de Néologie was recently created (decree of July 3rd, 1996) which answers directly to the prime minister. Its purpose is to harmonize the findings, and, after approval by the French Academy, publish them in the Journal Officiel.

[2] Dictionnaire des termes officiels de la langue française, Journal officiel, 1994.

hot money: des capitaux fébriles
leader: un meneur
leasing: voiture louée avec option d'achat
marketing: la mercatique

tennisman: un joueur de tennis
tie-break: un jeu décisif
walkman: un baladeur

Lexical fields of borrowing

Borrowing occurs when one linguistic group proves culturally more creative or technologically more advanced than another. For instance when, in the seventeenth century, France was the number one military power in Europe and its army a model for other nations, many of its military terms were borrowed. But by the eighteenth century, French supremacy had switched to the fields of art, philosophy and social life, which in turn led to borrowings by England in those domains. Today most borrowings are one way, from English into French, and pertain to the fields of sports, entertainment, finance and above all technology.[3]

Some examples of borrowings in a list that is far from exhaustive:

English from French
army: general, brigadier, colonel, lieutenant, major, sergeant (sergent), corporal (caporal), grenadier, cavalry (cavalerie), artillery (artillerie), infantry (infanterie), battalion (bataillon), canteen (cantine), bivouac, reconnaissance, corps, legionnaire, maneuver (manoeuvre), surveillance, camouflage, fatigues
gastronomy: cuisine, restaurant, café, hotel, chef, gourmet, maître d', hors d'oeuvre, sauce, casserole, dessert, champagne, eau de vie, mayonnaise, omelette, soufflé, mousse, sorbet, filet mignon, à la carte, (to) sauté
politics and diplomacy: diplomat, attaché, envoy (envoyé), vice-roy, aide, partisan, informant, protégé, coup (d'état), détente, impasse, communiqué, accord, clause, laissez-faire
economy and finance: financier, entrepreneur, millionaire, arbitrage, franchise
architecture and fine arts: architect, arcade, façade, balustrade, cornice (corniche), frieze (frise), niche, bas relief, dome, suite, apartment, garage, baroque, rococo, palette, crayon, pastel

---

[3] For a more exhaustive study please refer to dictionaries on borrowings from English to French and French to English listed in the appendix p.265.

fashion: haute couture, boutique, béret, culotte, lingerie, négligé, brassiere, chic, elegant, coiffure, brunette, blond, beige, ecru, rouge

society: étiquette, savoir faire, flair, finesse, expertise, gaffe, faux pas, malaise, routine, penchant, liaison, affair, tête-à-tête, rendez-vous, matinée, soirée, encore, salon, élite, bourgeois, cachet, cliché, connaisseur, amateur, fiancé, divorcé, chauffeur, habitué, clairvoyance, osé, risqué, grotesque

medicine: curettage, ligature, malaise, massage

and many phrases: au courant, c'est la vie, la crème de la crème, coup de grace, tour de force, pièce de résistance, double entendre, mot juste, carte blanche, déjà vu, ménage à trois, fait accompli, bête noire, en masse, bon voyage, bon appétit.

French from English

More than half of all borrowings from English to French are of Anglo American origin:[4]

sports and leisure: football, basketball, volleyball, rugby, tennis, golf, bowling, footing, aerobic, yatching, surf, camping, match, score, goal, shooter (verb), penalty, handicap, corner, tennisman, recordman, jockey, autostop, hobby

entertainment: night club, rock, swing, twist, bee-bop, blues, negro spiritual, jazz, folklore, film, western, script girl, camera, cameraman, travelling, suspense, star, cover girl, vamp, pin up, strip tease, sex, media, box office, hit parade, bridge, club

journalism: magazine, scoop, racket, hold up, revolver, reporter, free lance, flash, interview, copyright, best seller

everyday life: shopping, parking, motel, leader, stress, slogan, label, week end, design, living (room), baby sitter, shampoing (from shampoo), brushing, lifting

clothing: tweed, short, tee shirt, blue jeans, sweat shirt, pull over, cardigan, smoking, duffle coat, loden, tennis (sneakers)

food: cocktail, lunch, fast food, grill room, barbecue, steak, hot dog, hamburger, ketchup, chewing gum

technology: by far the largest and most active field of borrowing, most terms being the prerogative of specialists and having no impact on the general public. Let us just mention some terms in aviation: stewart, jet, cockpit; in heavy industries: pipeline, bulldozer, derrick, tank; in medicine: laser, pacemaker, by-pass; in economy and finance: dumping, cash flow, Dow Jones.

---

[4] Out of the 35,000 words considered representative of modern French, about 4,200 are of foreign origin, of which 25% or 1053 come from the English or American English language.

Creative borrowing

The term "creative borrowing" may seem like an oxymoron, but in the process of transfer from one language to the other it can happen that the original word undergoes slight or even appreciable variations in meaning.

What the French refer to as *le camping* (campsite), *le brushing* (blow drying), *le dancing* (dance hall) , *le shampoing* (shampoo) or *le smoking* (tuxedo) are nothing less than "faux amis". They are of the same order as the following English borrowings from the French: *citron* (cédrat), *chiffon* (voile), *clinic* (dispensaire), *amateur* (non-professionnel) and *boutonnière* (fleur à la bouton-nière).

Borrowing indeed does not preclude creativity. Nouns constitute the vast majority of borrowings due to problems presented by verb conjugation, but occasionally a language may coin other words from a borrowed stem. Thus French has patterned a few verbs after its first conjugation: *boycotter, loguer, shooter* (or *chouter),* *lifter* and *briefer*; and has created additional nouns with the standard French suffixes *-tion, -eur* and *-ine*: *gadgétisation, boxeur, speakerine.* It has even gone as far as to coin new terms with the English suffixes *-man* and *-ing*: *tennisman* (for tennis player), *recordman* (for record holder), *barman* (for bar tender), *footing* (for jogging), *parking* (for parking lot), *caravaning* (for going camping with a caravan or trailer) etc..; while English has coined verbs from French past participles, as in *to sauté*, or from nouns, as in *to camouflage.*

Some borrowings are even shuffled back and forth between the two languages. *Rail*, an English adaptation of the old French word *reille*, itself derived from the latin *regula* meaning a straight piece of wood, was borrowed back by the French in its English form in the second part of the nineteeth century with the advent of the railroad. *To flirt*, came from the French mediaeval word *fleuretter* or *conter fleurette*, and in turn gave *flirter* when it was borrowed back in the twentieth century with its English accent. *Chalenge*, another French mediaeval word, had become obsolete by the sixteenth century, but made it back to its homeland after World War II under the English spelling, *challenge*. And one of the most noteworthy examples is the linguistic history of *tennis*: the sport's English name, also returned after a lapse of about a hundred years to the land of its ancestor, the *jeu de paume*, a game originally played with the palm of the hand without a racket from the sixteenth century to the time of the French Revolution. One player would warn the other to catch at the call of "Tenez!", corrupted into *tennis* when the game took hold in England.

Unnecessary borrowing

The very purpose of a borrowing is defeated when a term already exists to designate a particular concept in the TL. And yet unnecessary borrowings do take place for reasons which may range from politics to snobism. We have already seen that, since the days of the Norman conquest, part of the English vocabulary is comprised of synonymous pairs consisting of one native term and one French borrowing (*to go down* and *to descend, fickle* and *versatile* etc.). As for French, in its long twentieth century borrowing phase, it has succumbed to snobbish appeal. Thus *une star* coexists with *vedette* which has given it its feminine gender, and *un smoking* with *habit de soirée*. Sometimes also, languages borrow to extend the semantic range of some existing words, as in the case of *réaliser* which, until around 1895 only signified *to accomplish* when the meaning of its English (false) cognate *to realize* was added to it, even though *se rendre compte* already served the purpose.

Use of borrowings

In conclusion be aware that borrowings are steeped in the civilization of the country they come from and therefore particularly reflect the culture of the SL.

Use them to add a touch of local color to your literary translations. A sentence like "C'était un *gentleman farmer*" replaces the story in its social British context, while in "After a arduous game of *pétanque* the players were resting in the shade at the terrace of the old *café*, sipping the local *pastis*" the borrowings help convey the atmosphere of a southern French village.

> **Use borrowings:**
>   **1. in case of semantic deficiency in the target language, especially in non-literary, technical translation.**
>   **2. for local color in literary translation.**

Exercices: Les Emprunts

A. Emprunts et faux amis

Traduisez les phrases suivantes en anglais en tenant compte du fait que les emprunts à la langue anglaise ont pu subir une variation de sens dans le processus de transfer. Essayez d'en retrouver le sens véritable.

1. J'ai laissé ma voiture au *parking* de la gare pour faire mon *shopping* en ville.
2. -Qu'est-ce que tu utilises? Un *shampoing* pour cheveux secs ou pour cheveux gras?
-Pour cheveux secs: mes cheveux sont devenus cassants avec tous ces *brushings*.
3. Tu ne trouves pas qu'il y a maintenant trop de *spots* publicitaires à la télé?
4. C'est ma *speakerine* préférée qui va annoncer le programme de ce soir à la télé.
5. Vous pouvez vous fier à ce *label* de qualité: il est reconnu par tous les *clubs* de consommateurs.
6. Avez-vous vu Mme Dubois récemment? Ne pensez-vous pas qu'elle a rajeuni? On dirait qu'elle s'est fait *lifter*!
7. L'invitation précise "tenue de soirée de rigueur". Ton *smoking* a besoin d'être nettoyé. Porte-le donc au *pressing*!
8. Après considération les jeunes gens ont décidé d'aller passer la soirée au *dancing* plutôt qu'au *night club*.
9. Le *barman* du Ritz se souvient encore d'un habitué célèbre: l'écrivain Ernest Hemingway.
10. Situé au bout d'une allée de tilleuls le terrain de *camping* était d'aspect accueillant.
11. Lors du *match* de *football* le *goal* de l'équipe locale a laissé marquer un but qu'il aurait pu arrêter.

12. Les *supporters* de l'équipe de France de *volleyball* étaient venus en masse assister au championnat.

13. Savez-vous qui est le *recordman* du monde pour le saut à la perche?

14. *Le dopping*, qui s'est révélé un problème majeur dans les courses de chevaux, fait désormais l'objet de contrôles très stricts.

15. Selon un récent sondage le *leader* socialiste a amélioré son *score* de 2% contre le candidat de la droite. Il recueillerait 38% des intentions de vote.

B. Les emprunts français

Choisissez l'emprunt français approprié pour traduire le mot en italique dans chaque phrase.

1. Le personnage principal du Bourgeois Gentilhomme de Molière est le type même du *parvenu* qui cherche à singer les belles manières.
a. bourgeois   b. nouveau riche   c. connaisseur

2. Ce paysage nous laissait une impression *familière*. C'était comme si, tant de fois reproduit et disséminé par les magazines et les cartes postales, nous le connaissions depuis toujours.
a. naïve   b. baroque   c. déjà vu

3. Selon le dernier dictat de la mode le beige sera *essentiel* pour le printemps et les fournisseurs de mode viennent de déverser des flots de khaki, écru et crème sur le marché.
a. de rigueur   b. chic   c. à la mode

4. Aux Etats Unis le nombre des femmes *chefs d'entreprise* s'élève à 6.5 millions.
a. concessionnaires   b. rapporteurs   c. entrepreneurs

5. Il est important que vous utilisiez toutes les *possibilités* qui s'offrent à vous en vue de résoudre ce problème.
a. avenues   b. echelons   c. cartes blanches

6. Avec la Mazda Miata, Honda a trouvé un *créneau*: celui des petites voitures de sport à prix abordable.
a. cache   b. sinecure   c. niche

7. La *maîtrise technique* de votre activité vous permettra d'évoluer de façon significative dans notre entreprise.
a. your technical tour de force   b. your technical expertise
c. your technical flair

C. Phrases originales

Faites des phrases originales en anglais avec les emprunts français suivants (consultez un dictionnaire pour les mots que vous ne connaissez pas).

Substantifs: amateur, protégé, élite, cliché, gaffe

Adjectifs: gauche, blasé, banal, risqué

Verbes: to sauté, to camouflage

Expressions figées: c'est la vie! bon appétit! savoir-faire, coup de grâce, rendez-vous

Chapter 6   Calques

What is a calque?

According to the Oxford English dictionary *to calque* (or calk) from the French *calquer* means "to copy a design by rubbing the back with a coloring matter and drawing a blunt point along the outlines so as to trace them in the color on a surface placed beneath." Or, if this definition seems a bit confusing, remember the game that children sometimes play: they take a coin, place a piece of paper over it and transfer the coin's design by rubbing a pencil over the paper. That's a calque. In other words, a copy of an original.

> A linguistic calque is also a copy of an original. It is a translated borrowing: the borrowing of a foreign word or group of words by literal translation of its components.

There are two sorts of calques:
- **semantic calques** which respect the structure of the T.L., i.e. its syntax and grammar.
    For example: *une conférence au sommet* (articulated group of words following French characteristics) for *summit meeting* (a typical English compound word)
- **structural calques** which even keep the structure of the S.L. by going against the traditional T.L. rules of syntax and grammar:
    For example: *ambassador extraordinary* which copies the French word order (adjective following noun) from *ambassadeur*

extraordinaire, or *surprise-partie* which copies the English compound word order.

Calques and neologisms

Like borrowings, calques are a particularly active device today in the creation of new words. And new words are coined almost daily in our era of technological and scientific discoveries, of global and instant communications. As a new concept emerges in one particular nation in the world, it is avidly borrowed or copied by the rest. The more trend-setting the nation, the less it will have to resort to borrowings and calques itself and the more others will try to borrow or copy its terminology. As we near the end of the 20th century, English, the predominant language in the world, is the original from which copies are presently being made.

We find calques in various fields, particularly in politics, science, and economics. And the media, which deal in the shuffling of concepts across countries, naturally play a very important role in their dissemination and acceptance by the general public.

Some of these calques are unwarranted, like *réaliser* calqued after *to realize* and used in the sense of *se rendre compte,* while prior to 1895, *réaliser* only had the sense of *to accomplish, to execute;* or *étoile* patterned after *star* when *vedette* would have done as well.

But in the field of nation terminology calques have proven very useful:

the United States of America:	les Etats Unis d'Amérique
the United Kingdom:	le Royaume Uni
the Commonwealth	la Communauté
of Independent States	des Etats Indépendants
the Middle East:	le Moyen Orient
the Third World	le Tiers Monde

As well as in politics:

the cold war:	la guerre froide
the iron curtain:	le rideau de fer
anti-ballistic missiles	les missiles anti-ballistiques

| D-Day | le jour J (a set term which allowed military planners during W W II to prepare and disseminate detailed plans much ahead of the date later decided upon: June 6, 1944). |

Calques and acronyms

We find calques in many acronyms, in an age when the acronym is king:

AIDS (Acquired Immuno Deficiency Syndrome)	SIDA (Syndrôme Immuno Déficitaire Acquis)
EMS (European Monetary System)	SME (Système Monétaire Européen)
WHO (World Health Organization)	OMS (Organisation Mondiale de la Santé)
WTO (World Trade Organization) etc.	OMC(Organisation Mondiale du Commerce).

Calque vs. borrowing

A calque, particularly a semantic calque, manifests a will on the part of the nation that resorts to it to keep the borrowing of foreign sounding words in check so as not to alter the characteristics of the native language.

Among French speaking countries the province of Quebec is particularly prone to resorting to calques from English, due to its linguistic isolation in the midst of English speaking lands and the overwhelming influence of English in the media. Only in Canada will you hear expressions such as *tomber en amour* (to fall in love) for *tomber amoureux*, *chiens chauds* for *hot dogs*, *chars usagés* (used cars) for *voitures d'occasion*, or *vivoir* (living room) for *salle de séjour*. Such calques give the language of Quebec a flavor all its own.

Exercices: Les Calques

Le calque est un emprunt de la L.D. traduit en L.A.
Il existe deux catégories de calques: les calques sémantiques qui
respectent la syntaxe de la L.A. c'est à dire l'ordre des mots et la
structure grammaticale, et les calques de structure qui conservent
la syntaxe de la L.D.

A. Calques sémantiques ou de structure?

Déterminez si les calques suivants sont sémantiques ou de structure.

1. Un cessez-le-feu; une conférence au sommet; une division aéroportée; une fin de semaine; une frappe aérienne; un gratte-ciel; la maladie des vaches folles; le papier-monnaie; les radicaux libres; la science-fiction; la Sécurité Sociale; le statut de la nation la plus favorisée; une surprise-partie; un char usagé (Québec); un chien chaud (Québec); compliments de la saison (Québec).

2. A chamber of commerce; an editor-in-chief; an envoy extraordinary; the Estates general; a head of state; a secretary general.

B. Les Sigles

Le procédé du calque est très employé actuellement dans la composition des sigles (acronyms). Essayez de retrouver les sigles anglais qui correspondent aux sigles français suivants.

L'A.D.N. (Acide Désoxyribo Nucléique)
L'A.G.E.T.A.C. (Accord GEnéral sur les TArifs douaniers et le Commerce)
L'A.L.E.N.A. (Accord de Libre Échange Nord Américain)

La C.E.I. (Communauté des États Indépendants)
Un D.A.B. (Distributeur Automatique de Billets)
L'E.E.E. (Espace Économique Européen)
Le F.M.I. (Fond Monétaire International)
L'O.M.S. (Organisation Mondiale de la Santé)
L'O.N.U. (Organisation des Nations Unies)
L'O.P.E.P. (Organisation des Pays Exportateurs de Pétrole)
L'O.T.A.N. (Organisation du Traité de l'Atlantique Nord)
Un P.D.G. (Président Directeur Général)
Le P.N.B. (Produit National Brut)
Le S.I.D.A. (Syndrome Immuno-Déficitaire Acquis)
La T.V.A. (Taxe à la Valeur Ajoutée)
L'U.E. (Union Européenne)

C. Traduction

Traduisez les phrases suivantes en essayant de retrouver les équivalents anglais des calques français indiqués en italiques.

1. Après les Etats Unis, la France lance le chantier des *autoroutes de l'information* pour faire circuler rapidement et facilement de grandes quantités d'images, de communication et de données informatiques dans des *cables en fibre optique* de l'épaisseur d'un cheveu. (France-Amérique, 5-11 mars 1994, no. 11334)

2. Avec une *souris*, l'utilisateur d'un ordinateur peut facilement *cliquer les icônes* de son écran pour avoir accès à différents *programmes d'application.* Il peut également souscrire à un *service en ligne* pour *se connecter* avec l'Internet et pouvoir *naviguer* de *site* en site dans *l'espace cybernétique.*

3. Pendant la *deuxième guerre mondiale* les *forces alliées* débarquèrent sur les côtes normandes au petit matin du *jour J* tandis que des *divisions aéroportées* américaines et britanniques étaient larguées à l'intérieur des terres.

4. Plus de trois cents hémophiles sont morts en France et plus de douze cents ont été contaminés par le *virus de l'immuno déficience humaine* entre 1984 et 1985. (France-Amérique, 25 juin-1er juillet 1994)

5. La France dont les soldats sont en première ligne face aux belligérants en Bosnie Herzégovine a ouvertement reproché à *l'O.N.U.* les hésitations et les retards dans l'emploi de *frappes aériennes* en risposte à des tirs contre les casques bleus. (France-Amérique, 19-25 mars 1994)

Chapter 7 Literal Translation
Structural Obstacles to Literal Translation

What is a literal translation?

> One may speak of a literal translation when the sentence or
> message of the SL can be translated word for word into the TL,
> without a change in the word order or grammatical structure,
> while remaining both correct and idiomatic.

Literal translation is possible when there are no structural
(grammatical and syntactical) obstacles and no metalinguistic
(cultural) obstacles. Such ideal conditions chiefly exist between
languages of the same linguistic family which share a similar syntax
and grammar but can hardly be the norm between languages
belonging to different backgrounds, as in the case of English and
French. However, a long history of mutual borrowing, both in
word formation and thought patterns, has brought them close
enough to warrant the occurrence of literal translation in very
simple sentences, sentences in the order of:

> Où est le propriétaire de ce chien? Where is the owner of that dog?
> Nous arrivâmes épuisés à l'hôtel après un pénible voyage. We arrived
> exhausted at the hotel after a taxing journey.

And even in a number of idiomatic expressions.

Some examples of identical verbal expressions:

> avaler la pilule: to swallow the pill
> avoir un mot sur le bout de la langue: to have a word on the tip of
> one's tongue

avoir un pied dans la tombe: to have a foot in the grave
chercher une aiguille dans une botte de foin: to look for a needle in a haystack
connaître toutes les ficelles: to know the ropes
donner le feu vert à quelqu'un: to give someone the green light
dorer la pilule: to gild the pill
envoyer en chute libre: to send into a free fall
être au septième ciel: to be in seventh heaven
être pris entre deux feux: to be caught between two fires
jouer avec le feu: to play with fire
jouer un jeu dangereux: to play a dangerous game
laisser quelqu'un mijoter dans son jus: to let someone stew in his own juice
mordre la poussière: to bite the dust
prendre le taureau par les cornes: to take the bull by the horns
remuer ciel et terre: to move heaven and earth
se casser le cou: to break on's neck
tenir sa langue; to hold one's tongue
trembler comme une feuille: to tremble like a leaf
verser des larmes de crocodile: to shed crocodile tears

Identical ways of looking at a concept in a verbal expression:

attacher de l'importance à: *to attach* importance to
courir un risque: *to run* a risk
être *en cours*: to be *in progress*
faire une scène: *to make* a scene
jouer un *sale* tour: to play a *dirty* trick
peser ses paroles: *to weigh* one's words
prêter l'oreille à quelqu'un: *to lend* someone an ear
savoir *par coeur*: to know *by heart*
tirer à sa fin: *to draw* to an end
voir rouge: *to see* red

Identical phrases:

avec de l'huile de coude: with elbow grease
sans l'ombre d'un doute: without the shadow of a doubt

Identical proverbs:

Il faut battre le fer pendant qu'il est chaud: you must strike the iron while it is hot
Pierre qui roule n'amasse pas mousse: a rolling stone gathers no moss

Nominal expressions: (most of them calques)

le libre échange: free trade

le prêt à porter: ready to wear
le tiers monde: the third world.

Sometimes the SL and TL words share their semantic range including figurative meanings which can be translated literally:
ex. un requin: a shark (1. fish, 2. swindler).

What are some structural obstacles to a literal translation?

Let us now examine some of the structural divergences which stand in the way of literal translation between the two languages.[1]

A. Differences in word order

The following will interfere with a word for word translation.

Respective position of adjectives and adverbs
Adjectives in French are generally placed after, not before, the noun they modify, except for a handful denoting Beauty, Age, Goodness, and Size (BAGS) and those which reflect the subjective opinion of the narrator, while adverbs of time, such as *bientôt, souvent, toujours, rarement, encore, enfin, déjà*, and manner, *bien, mal, vite* etc. are positioned after a verb in the simple tenses and between the auxiliary and the past participle in compound tenses:
Ainsi finit notre expérience *américaine*. Thus ended our *American* experience.
Ils manquent *souvent* leur train. They *often* miss their train.
Mange *vite* ta soupe! *Quickly* eat your soup!

Position of direct and indirect object pronouns
Before the verb in French, after in English:
Je *te l'*ai déjà donné. I already gave *it to you*.

Position of interrogative adverbs in a prepositional construction
In French the preposition must precede the interrogative adverb

---

[1] It is not our purpose here to list all diverging structures, which one can find in any good grammar, only to list the most representative ones.

whereas in English it has a tendency to be thrown to the end of the question:

> *Pour* qui as-tu acheté ça? Whom did you buy this *for?*
> *Par* quoi voulez-vous commencer? What do you want to start *with?*

Position of direct objects in relation to verbs

English does not like to separate a direct object from the verb it relates to. French does not mind interpolating adverbs, or adverbial phrases:

> Tu *fais* bien *ton travail.* You *do your work* well.
> Ma mère m'*offrit*, contrairement à mon habitude, *une tasse de thé.*
> (Marcel Proust). My mother, contrary to custom, *offered me a cup of tea.*

Inversion verb-subject with adverbs

In English and French literary texts certain adverbs may be placed in an initial position in a sentence for stylistic emphasis, but require an inversion verb-subject. Unfortunately these adverbs do not correspond between the two languages, and, with one exception, the order in translation will differ.

We find such a construction in French with adverbs *peut-être,* and *aussi* (bear in mind that these sentences are statements not to be confused with questions formed by inversion.):

> *Peut-être était-il* innocent. He *may* have been innocent.
> Nous travaillons dur, *aussi réussirons-nous.* We work hard, *therefore we will succeed.*

In English we find this inversion after adverbs such as *no sooner,* and *never:*

> *No sooner did we arrive* than the show began. Nous n'étions pas plus tôt arrivés que le spectacle commença.
> *Never have I seen* anything like this! Je n'ai jamais rien vu de tel!

No sooner ...than may be translated as *à peine...que,* in which case the order remains the same:

> *A peine se furent-ils rendu compte* de leur erreur, *qu'*ils s'excusèrent.
> *No sooner had they realized* their mistake *than* they apologized.

Analytic versus synthetic language

One of the basic causes of difference in word order between English and French is due to the fact that French is an analytical language which likes to make use of articulations (prepositions, conjunctions and even relative pronouns) in expressions, while English, a synthetic language like all Germanic languages, prefers juxtaposition.

Many French articulated nominal expressions will become nominal compounds in translation:

un lieu *de* travail:	a workplace
un mur *en* brique:	a brick-wall
un nid *à* poussière:	a dust nest
une assurance *contre* le vol:	theft insurance

French adjectival expressions may likewise become English adjectival compounds:

adepte en informatique:	computer savvy
tranchant comme un rasoir:	razor sharp

Nominal expressions involving past participles will be turned into multiple compounds:

des produits *destinés à l'exportation*:	*export oriented* merchandise
une grève *voulue par les syndicats*:	a *union driven* strike

And finally many short relative clauses in French can be rendered by a verbal adjective in the *-ing* form in English preceding the antecedent they refer to:

les mères *qui travaillent*:	*working* mothers
une tâche *qui prend du temps*:	a *time consuming* assignment
des facteurs *qui agravent la situation*:	*aggravating* factors

The English possessive case

This is another instance of the love of synthetic structures in English. The possessive case is essentially a genitive establishing a relation of possession between animate beings or animate beings and inanimate objects. French has no such structure and must articulate the possessive relation with the use of preposition "de":

le père *de* mon ami:	my friend's father
le dernier roman *de* Flaubert:	Flaubert's last novel
la maladie *de* Parkinson:	Parkinson's disease

B. Ellipses

Sometimes it is contrary to usage for the T.L. to translate all the
S.L. words (a case of economy in translation), and again sometimes
one must add to the message in order to remain idiomatic (a case of
amplification).

Ellipses in English are an example of economy in translation.

The French definite article in general concepts
Thus, the definite article which precedes all general concepts in
French is done away with in translation:

La vie est courte.	Life is short.

Other examples of ellipses in English:

invariable pronoun "le" which can replaces one or several
adjectives, or a direct object clause

pronoun of location "y" when refering to a place already
mentioned along with verb *aller*

indefinite pronoun "en" when used with an expression of quantity:

Les Français sont-ils *chauvins*?	En général, ils *le* sont.
Are the French chauvinistic?	Generally, they are.
La ligne est occupée.	Je te *l'*avais dit.
The line is busy	I told you (*that it is busy*).

On nous avait recommandé la rétrospective Matisse, alors, nous *y*
sommes allés. We had been told about the Matisse retrospective and
so we went.

Combien de revers ont-ils subis?	Ils *en* ont subi plusieurs.
How many set-backs have they had?	They have had several.

Ellipses of prepositions, conjunctions and possessive or demonstrative adjectives in a list:
Quand j'étais petit et *que* j'allais à l'école...*When* I was little and
going to school...

Elle l'a fait *par* devoir plutôt que *par* intérêt. She did it *out of* duty
rather than self interest.

La société a une responsabilité *envers ses* clients et *ses* actionnaires.
The company has a responsibility *towards its* clients and shareholders.

Il arriva avec toute *sa* famille: *son* père, *sa* mère, *ses* frères et soeurs.
He arrived with *his* entire family: father, mother, sisters and brothers

Optional ellipses in English: these occur in the case of relative pronouns which are direct objects, and conjunctions introducing an object clause:

> Voici l'article que j'ai lu. Here is the article (which/that) I read.
> C'est la personne à qui je fais le plus confiance. He/she is the person (whom) I trust the most.
> Je lui ai dit que je le rappellerais. I told him (that) I would call back.

Ellipses in French: these, on the other hand, are an example of amplification of the message in English.

Positive or negative answers to a question

> Tu n'as pas oublié notre rendez-vous? *-Non.*
> You did not forget our appointment? *-No, I didn't.*
> Ne préféreriez-vous pas prendre le dessert plus tard? *-Si.*
> Wouldn't you prefer to have dessert later? *-Yes, we would.*

C. Gallicisms and anglicisms

A gallicism is a mode of expression which is a characteristic feature of the French language and conversely an anglicism, one characteristic of the English language. Being idiomatic, they stand in the way of a literal translation.

Some examples of gallicisms

1. emphatic pronouns and emphatic constructions:

> *Moi,* ça m'est égal! *Personally,* I don't care!
> *C'est nous qui* sommes responsables. *We* are the real culprits.
> *C'est à toi que* je veux parler. *You are the one* I want to talk to.
> Où est-*elle, cette récompense*? Where *on earth* is that reward?

2. indefinite pronoun *"on"* which, when it does not stand for *"nous"*, is best rendered as an English passive, or alternately as an indefinite *"they"*, or even as a general *"you"* in sayings and axioms:

> *On ne le revit* jamais plus. *He was* never *seen* again.
> *On dit* que tu es dur avec les gens. *They say* that you are hard with people.
> *On* n'attrape pas les mouches avec du vinaigre. *You* can't catch flies with vinegar.

Some examples of anglicisms
Emphatic auxiliary verbs:

>We *did* send you a postcard. It must have gotten lost. Nous vous avons *pourtant* envoyé une carte postale. Elle a dû se perdre.
>
>You will close the door after you, *won't you?* Fermez la porte derrière vous, *vous voulez bien?*
>
>You wanted to go to see that movie? Well, *don't!* Vous vouliez aller voir ce film? *Gardez-vous en bien!*

D. Special problems with verb tenses

The English progressive form

The progressive form, which is used to express an action in progress, is a structural form specific to English. Present and future progressives find an equivalent in the regular French present and future while the past progressive finds an equivalent in the imparfait:

>Are we leaving?   *Partons-nous?*
>I *shall be working* all summer. Je *travaillerai* tout l'été.
>Il *neigeait*.   It *was snowing*..

As for the present perfect progressive, it translates the French present tense when the action started at some stated time in the past and is still going on:

>Il y a dix ans que j'*habite* ici. I *have been living* here for ten years.
>Voilà deux heures que nous vous *attendons*: We *have been waiting* for you for two hours.
>Il *pleut* depuis ce matin. It *has been raining* since this morning.

And the past perfect progressive translates a French imparfait under the same conditions:

>Cela *faisait* déjà longtemps que les gens *jasaient* sur l'origine de sa fortune.
>People *had* already *been gossiping* for a long time about the way he had acquired his fortune.

Translating a passé composé: simple past or present perfect?

Whenever the action is completed, the simple past is to be used. Whenever the verb conveys a past continuous action or situation which is still linked to the present, the present perfect is to be used. Compare:

J'*ai vu* ce film la semaine dernière. I *saw* this movie last week.
Je *n'ai pas* encore *vu* ce film. I *have not seen* this movie yet.
Hier, son état *s'est aggravé*. Yesterday, his condition *deteriorated*.
Son état *s'est aggravé* depuis hier. His condition *has deteriorated* since yesterday.

The iterative imparfait

Beside expressing a past progressive, the French imparfait can have an iterative or repetitive function rendered by "used to" or the more literary "would" of habit:

Quand j'étais petit je *faisais* de la bicyclette.
When I was young I *used to go cycling*/ I *would go cycling*.

Durative versus punctual aspects of French semi-auxiliaries

The imparfait expresses an action in its continuity or duration (the so-called durative aspect rendered by the English past progressive). This aspect stands in contrast with the function of the passé composé and the passé simple which is to express an action in its limitation, that is to say as a beginning and end without any notion of duration (the punctual aspect of the verb rendered by the simple past: the action is viewed as a point in time). However, some English verbs, particularly modal auxiliaries, cannot be expressed in the progressive form and, consequently, corresponding French verbs must be translated with different counterparts in the imparfait and passé composé to render these variances of aspect.

Il *savait* qu'il avait tort. He *knew* he was wrong (continuous).
J'*ai su* la nouvelle par Georges. I *heard* the news through George (limited).

Ils *se connaissaient* depuis longtemps. They *had known each other* for a long time.
Nous nous sommes connus en vacances. We *met each other* while on vacation.

Voulais tu m'accompagner? *Did you want* to come with me?
Je *voulus* m'arrêter mais les freins de la voiture lâchèrent. I *tried* to stop but the car brakes gave way.

Ne *pouviez-vous* pas faire attention? *Couldn't you be careful?*

J'ai pu dormir une heure ou deux dans l'avion. *I was able* to sleep for a couple of hours on the plane.

Tu devais être là à dix heures. *You were supposed* to be here at 10.
Elle a dû renoncer à son projet. *She had to* abandon her plan.

Nous *avions peur* que vous ne vous soyiez égarés. We *were afraid* that you had gotten lost.
L'enfant *eut peur* en entendant la grosse voix de l'homme. The child *became frightened* at the sound of the man's loud voice.

The future in temporal clauses
Don't forget that sometimes a French future has to be rendered as a present after conjunctions of time (quand, dès que, aussitôt que, tant que, pendant que):

Aussitôt que nous *serons* prêts nous partirons. As soon as we *are* ready, we will leave.

The subjunctive
The subjunctive mood, practically inexistent in English, presents special difficulties in translation. Strict rules govern tense sequence in the subordinate clause depending on whether there is a relation of anteriority, simultaneity or posteriority between the action in the main clause and the action in the subordinate clause. Consequently, a present subjunctive may correspond to an English future even though the verb in the main clause is present, and to a conditional present representing a future in the past even though the main clause verb is in the past; and since tense sequence also dictates the use of the present subjunctive in a subordinate clause when its action is concurrent with a past action in the main clause, a present subjunctive can, in addition, be the equivalent of a past tense.

Etes-vous sûr qu'il *vienne*? Are you sure that he *will come*?
Nous avions peur qu'ils ne *viennent* pas. We were afraid that they *would not come*.
Je craignais qu'ils ne *soient* en danger. I feared that they *were* in danger.

E. Problems with French pronominal verbs

Pronominal verbs are a feature specific to Romance languages. Most of the time translating them literally runs counter to an idiomatic translation in English. Here are various ways of dealing with them.

Pronominal verbs can be the expression:
1. of a reflexive action (done by an animate subject upon himself)
2. of a reciprocal action (when two or more subjects interact)
3. of an action suffered by an inanimate subject.

- In the first case, the French reflexive pronoun can be rendered by the equivalent English reflexive pronoun, although this is not necessary when the action is a customary one:
  Tu *t'es fait* mal? Did you *hurt yourself?*
  Le matin je *me lève*, je *me lave* et je *m'habille*.
  In the morning, I *get up*, I *wash* and I *get dressed.*

- In the second case, reciprocal pronouns are used, but sometimes the reciprocity is only implied in English:
  Ils *se téléphonent* tous les jours. They *phone each other* everyday.
  Nous nous sommes querellés. We *quarreled (with each other).*

- In the third case, a passive voice is often resorted to in translation:
  Ce vin *se sert* chambré. This wine *is served* at room temperature.

Many French pronominal verbs are therefore translated as simple verbs or as passive verbs in English.
Here is a representative list:

s'agir de: to be a question of, to concern
s'attendre à: to expect
s'accroître: to increase
se convaincre de: to become convinced of
se décourager: to become discouraged
se demander: to wonder
se déplacer: to travel
se dire: to think to oneself
se douter de: to suspect
se dérouler: to take place
s'engager à: to pledge to

se féliciter: to be very pleased
se mettre à: to begin to
se mobiliser: to rally
se moquer de: to make fun of
s'occuper de: to take care of
se passer de: to do without
se plaindre: to complain
se prononcer: to pass judgment
se réfugier: to take refuge
se rendre compte: to realize
se transformer: to turn into

s'ennuyer: to be bored   se tromper: to make a mistake
s'entendre dire que: to be bluntly told   se trouver: to be located

Further structural or linguistic obstacles shall be dealt with in the coming chapters.

Exercices: La Traduction Littérale

A. Les aphorismes

Traduisez en anglais les aphorismes suivants.

La Rochefoucauld
1. Tout le monde se plaint de sa mémoire, et personne ne se plaint de son jugement.
2. L'hypocrisie est un hommage que le vice rend à la vertu.
3. Nous pardonnons souvent à ceux qui nous ennuient, mais nous ne pouvons pardonner à ceux que nous ennuyons.
4. L'amour-propre est le plus grand de tous les flatteurs.
5. L'hypocrisie est un hommage que le vice rend à la vertu.
6. C'est une grande folie de vouloir être sage tout seul.
7. Nous avons tous assez de force pour supporter les maux d'autrui.
8. Si on juge de l'amour par la plupart de ses effets il ressemble plus à la haine qu'à l'amitié.
9. L'absence diminue les médiocres passions et augmente les grandes comme le vent éteint les bougies et allume le feu.

Boileau
10. Ce que l'on conçoit bien s'énonce clairement
    Et les mots pour le dire arrivent aisément.

Pascal
11. L'homme n'est qu'un roseau, le plus faible de la nature, mais c'est un roseau pensant.
12. Le nez de Cléopâtre, s'il eût été plus court, toute la face de la terre aurait changé.
13. -Pourquoi me tuez-vous? Je n'ai pas d'armes.
    -Eh quoi! ne demeurez vous pas de l'autre côté de l'eau? Mon ami, si vous demeuriez de ce côté, je serais un assassin et cela serait

injuste de vous tuer de la sorte, mais puisque vous demeurez de l'autre côté, je suis un brave et cela est juste.

La Bruyère
14. Les femmes sont extrêmes: elles sont meilleures ou pires que les hommes.
15. L'amour et l'amitié s'excluent l'un l'autre.

Vauvenargues
16. Les grandes pensées viennent du coeur.
17. La raison nous trompe plus souvent que la nature.
18. Pour exécuter de grandes choses, il faut vivre comme si on ne devait jamais mourir.

Lamennais
19. N'aimer que soi, c'est haïr les autres.

B. Articulation et juxtaposition

En vous référant aux explications des pages 62-3 (analytic vs. synthetic language) traduisez les phrases suivantes en anglais en utilisant le procédé de juxtaposition au lieu de l'articulation pour les expressions en italique.

1. Je préfère *les boissons sans caféine.*
2. C'est un sacrifice *qui en vaut la peine.*
3. Voilà *une personne à l'aspect qui n'augure rien de bon.*
4. Nous venons de vivre *une expérience à vous faire dresser les cheveux sur la tête.*
5. Je vous conseille de traiter avec *une société qui soit orientée vers le client.*
6. Il a *une voix aux sonorités jeunes.*
7. Le musée de la ville est fier de sa *collection de tableaux du XIXème siècle.*
8. *Un livre qui donne à penser,* voilà la qualité principale de cette critique de la société actuelle.

9. Grâce à la détection précoce *d'un cancer du colon*, le malade put subir *une opération qui lui sauva la vie*.
10. *Le domaine de l'industrie de la santé* a subi de fortes pressions en raison *d'une concurrence globale qui s'accentue*.
11. *Les maladies causées par le tabac* sont en nette progression dans tous les pays développés.
12. *Des augmentations de prix, prévues depuis longtemps*, viennent d'être mises en place.
13. *Des changements de fond en comble* vont être nécessaires pour l'assainissement des *finances de la société*.
14. Les obligations émises par l'état pour financer les travaux d'infrastructure du projet seront *exonérées d'impôts*.

C. Traduction littérale ou non-littérale?

Une traduction littérale des phrases suivantes est-elle possible? Sinon définissez le problème.

1. Pourquoi attacher tant d'importance à ce détail?
2. La guerre éclata vers le milieu de l'été.
3. Les syndicats avaient accusé la direction de chantage.
4. Dans les années qui viennent, le débat sur l'avenir de l'Europe va devenir crucial.
5. Le rouge est ma couleur préférée, et toi? Il l'est aussi.
6. Ce ne sont pas de vraies larmes que tu verses mais des larmes de crocodile.
7. La formule "L'existence précède l'essence" est au coeur de la philosophie de Sartre.
8. Comme nous n'étions pas sûrs qu'il fasse beau, nous avons reporté l'excursion que nous avions projetée.
9. Quand tu auras terminé ton rapport, montre-le-moi.
10. C'est lui qui veut démissionner, ce n'est pas moi qui l'y force.
11. Ne sait-on pas encore qui va gagner l'élection? Si.
12. Lorsque j'ai voulu expliquer ce qui s'était passé, on ne m'a pas cru.
13. Voilà deux heures qu'il joue le même morceau de musique!

14. Autrefois, en été, nous allions en pique-nique presque tous les dimanches.

15. Parce qu'il fait trop chaud et que tu es fatigué, nous allons nous arrêter pour nous reposer.

16. Par sa détermination, par son ambition et son énergie cette personne ira loin.

D. Les Verbes pronominaux

S'agit-il de verbes simples, réfléchis, réciproques ou de voix passive en anglais?

1. [Les années] *s'additionnent* si promptement...elles *s'évanouissent* si complètement qu'en *se retournant* pour voir le temps parcouru on n'aperçoit plus rien et on ne comprend pas comment il *se fait* qu'on soit vieux. (Guy de Maupassant, Contes du jour et de la nuit)

2. M. Seguin *se trompait.* Sa chèvre *s'ennuya.* Un jour, elle *se dit* en regardant la montagne: "Comme on doit être bien là-haut!" (Alphonse Daudet, La Chèvre de M. Seguin)

3. "Elle a toutes les griffes cassées, dit-il en *se parlant* à lui-même, elle *s'est retenue*, accrochée..." Il *s'interrompit*, prit sans un mot de plus la chatte sous son bras et l'emporta dans la salle de bains. (Colette, La Chatte)

4. Je *me mettais* quelquefois à penser à ma chambre. Je *me souvenais* de chaque meuble et, pour chacun d'entre eux, de chaque objet qui *s'y trouvait.* (Albert Camus, L'Etranger)

5. Il *se tuera*, pensa Kyo. Il avait assez écouté son père pour savoir que celui qui cherche aussi âprement l'absolu ne le trouve que dans la sensation. (André Malraux, La Condition humaine)

6. Mon père *se pencha* un peu vers lui et déclara: "J'ai une nouvelle, mon vieux. Anne et moi, *nous nous marions* le 5 octobre." (Françoise Sagan, Bonjour tristesse)

7. Mon grand père saisissait l'occasion de montrer sa faiblesse: il prenait parti contre sa femme qui *se levait* outragée pour aller *s'enfermer* dans sa chambre. (J.P. Sartre, Les Mots)

8. L'homme d'action ne *se conçoit* guère sans une forte dose d'égoïsme, d'orgueil, de dureté, de ruse. (Charles de Gaulle, Au Fil de l'épée)

9. Elle *se regarde*. Elle *s'est approchée* de son image, ne *se reconnaît* pas bien. (Marguerite Duras, L'Amant)

10. Il en est ainsi, Mademoiselle. Ça ne *s'explique* pas. Ça *se comprend* par un raisonnement mathématique intérieur. (Eugène Ionesco, La Leçon)

Chapter 8   Transposition

What is transposition?

Transposition is the first of the non literal translation devices. It is also the most used device in translation. Resort to it when an obstacle in the process of translation occurs due to different grammatical structures in the SL and TL. As we have seen in the chapter on literal translation, English and French have particular preferences for certain constructions which are at variance one with the other.

The following diagram will help you comprehend how a transposition works:

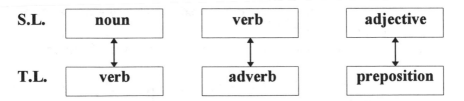

S.L.	noun	verb	adjective
T.L.	verb	adverb	preposition

A transposition is a translation device which involves a change between grammatical categories, i.e. nouns, verbs, adjectives, adverbs and prepositions, from the S.L. to the T.L.

It remains at the grammatical level without affecting the semantic level: the message stays exactly the same.

With a transposition, while the original and its translation remain literally close and semantically identical, a verb in the SL might become a noun in the TL; or a noun, a verb; a verb, an adverb or an adjective; a past participle, a preposition or an adjective etc. The possibilities are multiple, even though some transpositions are more commonly used than others, as with the change verb into adverb, or noun into verb.

> **When should you resort to a transposition?**
> **When the message, if translated literally, is either nonsensical, a mistranslation, or understandable to the TL speaker without sounding idiomatic or correct, while the cause of the problem is only structural.**

Some transpositions are absolutely necessary (i.e, when there is no other way of dealing with the structural problem), while others remain optional, as alternatives to a literal translation. In the latter case, a literal translation tends to be more literary whereas the use of a transposition will give a more colloquial flavor.

Some examples of necessary transpositions

1. **Est-ce que Jean est** *de retour*?
A literal translation has to be ruled out as being nonsensical. (Is John *of return*?)
Only a transposition will convey the elements of the original message:
Has John *come back*? transposition noun-verb
Or: Is John *back*?   transposition noun-adjective.

2. **Tu** *as raison* **de croire Marie.**
A literal translation (You have a reason to believe Mary) would result in a mistranslation, that is to say a mistake in the interpretation of the original message.
In this case only a transposition noun-adjective along with a change in auxiliaries will yield the correct translation:
You are right to believe Mary.

3. **Maison** *à vendre*

Here a literal translation would make sense (house to sell), but has to be dismissed for not being idiomatic.
House for sale is the expression sanctioned by usage, and we have a transposition verb-noun.

Examples of optional transpositions

1. *Réduction de* **25% sur tous les articles**
A literal translation (25% *reduction* on all articles) as well as a transposition noun-preposition (25% *off* all articles) are both correct.

2. *Après la reprise des combats* **la guerre parut s'éterniser.**
Both a literal and a noun-verb transposition are possible:
After resumption of the fighting the war seemed to drag on.
After the fighting resumed the war seemed to drag on.
However the two translations are not quite on a par stylistically: the first one, calqued after the French nominal expression, being more literary; and the second, which follows English preference for verbs, more colloquial.

Noun-verb transposition

This is one of the most common types of transposition between French and English, and it is due to the fact that French very often favors nouns in structures in which English uses verbs. Such structures include temporal clauses introduced by prepositions: *dès, au fur et à mesure de, après, avant, lors de, au moment de.*

Dès mon arrivée à l'hôtel, j'ai pris un bain, je me suis habillé et je suis sorti faire une promenade. *As soon as I arrived* at the hotel, I took a bath, got dressed and went out for a walk.
Nous nous trouvions à Paris *lors des grèves* des syndicats. We were in Paris *when* the unions *went on strike*.
Quelques jours *après sa mort*, la presse fit des révélations sur la vie privée du président. A few days *after he died*, the press leaked out information on the president's private life.

Mettez le fichier à jour *avant votre départ* en vacances. Bring the file up to date *before you leave* for your vacation.
A la vue des problèmes qui s'accumulaient, nous avons renoncé au projet. *When we saw* the problems accumulating, we gave up on the plan.
Au fur et à mesure de la montée du chômage, l'inquiétude s'accroît dans toutes les couches de la société. *As unemployment rises*, all strata of society become increasingly worried.

Transpositions with postpositional adverbs

As we have just seen, English is a dynamic language which often favors the use of verbs over nouns. As a result, it has developed verb structures which simply do not exist in French. One such structure involves the use of postpositional adverbs as mark of an incipient (*away, off*), gradual (*away, down*), continual (*on*), or final action (*out, up, off, through, down*). The English speaking translator must not forget to make use of their possibilities.

Continuons à marcher! *Let's walk on*!
Le bruit s'estompa, puis s'arrêta tout à fait. The noise *faded away* and *died out*.
La fabrique a fermé ses portes. The factory *closed down*.
Il faut *mettre fin* à ces fausses promesses. We must *break off* these empty promises.
Tu *te sortiras de cette situation*. You *will pull through*.

Cross transposition

A cross transposition is a special type of transposition. It is a double transposition with a change in word order, the two transposed words in the TL being switched around in relation to the order in the SL.

ex. **Je descendis l'escalier en courant**

A literal translation (I went down the staircase running) would fail to be idiomatic. Instead let's try a double transposition verb-preposition, and verbal adjective-verb in a cross pattern:

Je *descendis* l'escalier *en courant*

I *ran down* the staircase

Generally cross transpositions are de rigueur with actions involving motion when the means or manner of this motion are also expressed:

mean: *Nous nous rendrons* à New York *par avion.*
We will *fly to* New York.

manner: L'animal *s'éloigna en boitant.*
The animal *limped away.*

In this category, the manner or the means will be expressed as a verb in English, while the French verb of motion will be rendered as a preposition or adverb of motion (*up, down, to, across, by, on, off, out, through, away, forth etc.*).

Sometimes also cross transpositions are used when the end result of a situation is mentioned along with the reason for this result:

ex. Je suis *mort de faim*   I am *starved to death.*

The difference in word order between English and French which necessitates the use of a cross transposition in translation stems from a basic divergence of approach in apprehending reality:

- **French, a more abstract and intellectual language, favors the order:**

  results first, means or manner later.
- **English, more concrete and logical, follows the action through the visual order of events:**

  means or manner first, results subsequently.

Exercices: La Transposition

La transposition est un procédé de traduction non littérale par lequel un mot change de catégorie grammaticale en passant de la LD à la LA. Ainsi un verbe peut devenir un nom, ou un participe passé une préposition, ou un verbe un adverbe, ou encore un nom un adjectif, etc.

A. La Transposition

Traduisez les phrases suivantes en changeant la catégorie grammaticale des mots soulignés selon les directives.

Verbe en adverbe

1. Bien qu'on nous ait demandé de garder le secret nous *avons failli* tout révéler.
2. Si on le leur répète, ils *finiront* bien *par* comprendre.
3. Je *n'arrive pas à* vous entendre, la communication est brouillée, parlez plus fort!
4. Il *arrive à* tout le monde de se tromper.
5. Ça *va* faire un an que nous habitons ici.
6. Il *suffit* de lire ce livre pour se convaincre de l'originalité de son auteur.
7. Patientons un peu, les invités *ne vont pas tarder à* arriver.
8. Il *ne cesse de* pleuvoir depuis deux jours.
9. Le chien *n'arrêtait pas* d'aboyer.
10. Nous ne partageons plus les mêmes idées politiques mais je lui *conserve* toute mon estime.
11. Pendant que sa mère le grondait l'enfant *se contentait de* baisser la tête.
12. *Il paraît* que le premier ministre va démissionner.
13. En dépit de la baisse des taux d'intérêt l'affaire *demeure* rentable.

Nom en verbe

1. *Quelle est la date de votre départ?*
2. Il y a beaucoup à faire avant *la rentrée* des classes.
3. Le diner commencera dès *l'arrivée de* l'invité d'honneur.
4. La foule a applaudi *au passage du* cortège présidentiel.
5. Les animaux se sauvèrent *à l'approche des* chasseurs.
6. Le client est remboursé intégralement en cas *de non-satisfaction*.
7. Les hostilités cessèrent après *la signature du* traité d'autonomie.
8. *A la vue de* l'ampleur de la catastrophe les sauveteurs furent épouvantés.
9. *Par mesure d'économie* la société a décidé de licencier du personnel.

Verbe en nom

1. *Comment vous appelez-vous?*
2. Tiens, j'ignorais que la maison d'en face était *à vendre!*
3. *Il s'agit* maintenant de trouver une solution à ce problème.
4. Beaucoup de gens pensent que l'Europe peut aider *à lutter* contre le chômage en recourant au protectionnisme.
5. En politique le public exige *que cessent* les mensonges et la langue de bois.

Adverbe en verbe

1. Ils sont en retard: ils ont *peut-être* eu un accident de voiture.
2. *Certes*, les jeunes sont souvent égoïstes et intransigeants, mais ils sont l'avenir de la planète.

Verbe en adjectif

1. Le 34-25-69? Désolé, vous *vous trompez* de numéro!
2. *Ai-je réussi* à te faire changer d'avis?

Conjonction en verbe

1. *A force de* lire dans la pénombre tu vas finir par t'abîmer la vue.

Nom en adjectif

1. La séparation de l'Eglise et de l'Etat a eu lieu au *début du* XXème siècle.
2. Le mariage sera célébré à *la fin du mois de* juin.
3. Nous comptons prendre nos vacances *au milieu de* l'été.

Participe passé en adjectif

1. Le match est *annulé* en raison du mauvais temps.
2. Le four est-il *allumé* ou *éteint*?
3. Le voisin? Désolé, il est *parti* en voyage.
4. Non, Sabine n'est pas *sortie*. Elle n'est même pas encore *levée*.
5. Pierrot devrait bientôt être *rentré* de l'école.
6. Ces soldes d'hiver sont intéressantes: les prix sont *réduits* de 50%.
7. Le film *fini*, nous allâmes flâner le long des Champs Elysées.

Nom en préposition

1. Embarquement immédiat porte no 6 pour les passagers *à destination de* New York.

Adjectif en préposition

1. *Privé de* l'appui de la chambre des députés, le chef du gouvernement a dû démissionner.

Verbe en préposition

1. Son état empire. Il faut envoyer *chercher* le médecin.
2. N'as-tu jamais entendu *parler de* cette histoire?

B. L'adverbe postpositionnel anglais

Pour les traductions suivantes remplacez les mots en italique par un adverbe postpositionnel (voir p.80: transposition with postpositional adverbs).

1. Il a gaspillé *tout* son argent.

2. *Continuez de* lire!
3. **Tiens-toi** *à l'écart!*
4. J'ai usé ces vêtements *jusqu'au bout.*
5. Il faut *continuer à* suivre les évènements.
6. Nous nous sommes mis *en route.*
7. *Au commencement,* quand j'ai débuté dans cette carrière, j'étais très inexpérimenté.
8. Elle était gaie comme un pinson et chantait *sans s'arrêter.*

C. Transposition nécessaire ou facultative?

Déterminez si la traduction des phrases suivantes nécessite une transposition nécessaire ou facultative.

1. Ils sont toujours *en retard!*
2. Tu ne peux pas prendre de décision aussi importante sans *une consultation avec* le reste de la famille.
3. On me dit que je *ressemble* à ma soeur *de manière frappante.*
4. Je *viens* de rater mon train.
5. *Défense de stationner.*
6. Je vais trouver le temps long après *ton départ!*
7. Les spectateurs applaudirent *dès l'entrée* des joueurs de l'équipe locale sur le stade.
8. La petite grelottait de froid. Elle *ne* portait *qu'*un vieux châle élimé par dessus sa robe mince.
9. De la fenêtre de ma chambre j'entendais *le chant* des oiseaux.
10. *Il y eut un coup de sonnette* à la porte.
11. *Aidé de* ses proches, il put surmonter ses difficultés.
12. Le facteur est arrivé juste *au moment où* je partais.
13. Voilà la raison *pour laquelle* je me suis abstenu de donner mon avis.
14. *A l'arrivée de* la diligence il se fit un brouhaha dans l'auberge.
15. Les gens *qui en ont* les moyens peuvent s'offrir des vacances de neige.
16. *A chacun de nos voyages* en Italie, nous nous arrêtons à Venise.

17. Le chauffeur de la voiture *continua sa route sans s'arrêter devant* moi.

18. On a diagnostiqué *une rupture* de disque chez ce malade.

19. *Au sein de* l'Union Européenne l'unanimité n'est pas toujours de mise.

20. *Etant donné* vos capacités, vous ne devriez avoir aucun problème dans votre nouvel emploi.

21. De profondes réformes vont être *nécessaires* pour éviter une fracture du tissu social.

Exercices: La Transposition Croisée

> *La transposition croisée est un cas particulier du procédé de transposition.*
> *Dans une transposition croisée le changement grammatical est double et s'effectue par un changement d'ordre des mots entre la L.D. et la L.A. en forme de croisement.*
> *En général ce sont des actions indiquant des mouvements ainsi que le moyen ou la manière de ce mouvement qui nécessitent des transpositions croisées. Parfois aussi ce sont des résultats de situations lorsque la cause ou la raison en est mentionnée.*

A. Les verbes de mouvement

Traduisez les phrases suivantes en utilisant une transposition croisée pour les mots en italique.

1. Les enfants *sont entrés* dans la chambre *sur la pointe des pieds* pour voir si leurs parents dormaient encore.
2. Le chat *traversa* la rue *en courant* juste devant la voiture.
3. En été, les touristes *remontent* l'avenue de l'Opéra *en flânant* et en regardant les devantures des magasins.
4. Nous *avons chassé* les intrus *à coups de pied*.
5. Au lieu de prendre le train par l'Eurotunnel nous *irons* à Londres *par avion*.
6. Christophe Colomb fut le premier à *traverser* l'Atlantique *en bateau*.
7. Après les embrassades et les promesses de se revoir toute la petite troupe *disparut en voiture*.
8. Entendant un bruit étrange dans la chambre au-dessus il *monta* l'escalier *à toute vitesse* pour voir quelle en était la cause.
9. L'autre jour je *suis tombé par hasard* sur un de mes amis d'enfance.

10. Le jardinier doit *couper* la grosse branche du pommier *avec sa scie.*

11. Nous *avons longé* la rivière *à pied,* puis nous *avons continué notre chemin.*

B. Résultats de situations

1. Papa *a achevé de payer* l'hypothèque de la maison.

2. A la fin de la soirée les invités *étaient morts d'ennui.*

3. Si nous restons plus longtemps dans cet endroit glacé nous allons *périr de froid.*

4. Je *suis mort de peur* à l'idée de devoir parler en public.

Chapter 9   **Modulation**

What is modulation?

Two languages may view the same concept from different points of
view, different angles. When this happens we have a modulation.

> **A modulation involves a change, not in grammatical categories
> as with transposition, but in the way of thinking, in categories
> of thought.**

A change in categories of thought may mean a switch from
concrete to abstract, cause to effect, means to result. It may involve
viewing one part for the whole, and vice-versa, or one part for
another part. It may also involve a difference in the sensorial
perceptions of reality, a switch to opposites, the use of learned
terms for popular ones etc. A few modulations, at the message
level, do involve grammar with a change from positive to negative,
active to passive, or even singular to plural and vice-versa.

The underlying causes for such different points of view are to be
found in the characteristics of the language, in its particular genius.
We have already seen that English tends to be more logical, more
sensorial in its apprehension of reality, whereas French usually
manifests a more abstract and intellectual approach. In this chapter,
we will come across other specific traits of the two languages.

There are various types of modulations:
- **word modulations**, affecting one word or set of words which
  cannot be dissociated from each other, such as verbal or

nominal expressions. Such modulations are set in the language and found in dictionaries, and therefore, with the exception of newly coined words, pose no particular challenge to the translator.

- **preposition modulations**: also set in the language by grammatical usage (may or may not be found in dictionaries, but should be found in a good grammar).

- **message modulations**: which affect a whole phrase, sentence or message. These, like transposition, may be necessary, or optional as one solution among others. Since they will not be found in a dictionary, they are the real touchstone of a good and experienced translator, one who has learned to recognize when a change of focus is needed in order to give the message an idiomatic turn.

Word Modulations

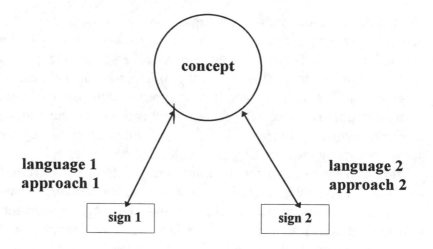

Perhaps one of the most striking examples of a word modulation is the tandem pompier-fireman mentioned by Vinay and Darbelnet in *La Stylistique comparée du français et de l'anglais*: the French word viewing the concept from the angle of the man whose task it is to pump water leaving out the eventual duty of extinguishing the fire, while English only sees the man who fights the fire. Between the two words the emphasis switches from the preparation for the task to the relation person-task.

Among the many word modulations which can be found in dictionaries, the following are worthy of note:

Concrete to abstract

la saison *creuse*:	the *off* season
un sans *abri*:	a *home*less
le siècle des *Lumières*:	the Age of *Enlightenment*
un *train* de vie:	a life*style*
les *verts*:	the *environmentalists*
des vacances *de neige*:	a *winter* vacation
donner *un coup de fil*:	to give *a call*

Abstract to concrete

un avant-*projet*:	a first *draft*
les heures *de pointe (peak)*:	*rush* hours
des *licenciements*:	*lay offs*
un *logiciel*:	*software*
des matières *premières*:	*raw* material
un tableau *d'affichage*:	a *bulletin* board
parler *haut*:	to speak *loud*
réduire les effectifs:	*to downsize*
rire *tout bas*:	to laugh *in one's sleeve*

Means–result

en venir *aux mains*:	to come to *blows*

Result–means

un cours de *rattrapage*:	a *remedial* class
un *libre* service:	a *self* service
un témoin *à charge*:	a witness *for the prosecution*

Cause–effect

un *bourreau* de travail:	a work*oholic*

(Fr.: one who is his own executioner through too much work. Eng.: patterned after the word "alcoholic", one who suffers the consequences of too much work)

Effect-cause

une maladie *mortelle*:   a *life threatening* disease

Part-whole

une maison *mère*:   a *parent* company
du *matin au soir*:   *all day* long
un *organe* executif: an executive *body*

Whole-part

le *billet* vert: the green *back*
de mon *temps*:   in my *day*
oublier son *texte*:   to forget one's *lines*
se laver *la tête*:   to wash *one's hair*

Part for other part

une brûlure d'*estomac*:   a *heart* burn
des *écouteurs*:   a *head*set
un *pied* de laitue: a *head* of lettuce
casser *les pieds* (à quelqu'un):   to be a pain *in the neck*
fermer la porte au *nez* de qqun   to slam the door in someone's *face*

Different images

une *pomme de discorde*   a *bone of contention*
(the first, a cultural allusion to Greek mythology: Paris's judgment, which, by awarding the apple to Aphrodite for her superior beauty aroused the jealousy of Athena and Artemis and led to the Trojan war; and the second, an evocation of the concrete and realistic image of a pack of dogs fighting over a bone)
avoir la *chair de poule*   to have *goosebumps*
faire chanter: to *blackmail*
un *dépliant* (which you unfold):   a *flier*
un *embouteillage* (bottle neck traffic flow): a traffic *jam*
un *rouge* à lèvres: a lip*stick*
une station *balnéaire* (where one goes bathing): a *seaside* resort

Different sensorial perceptions

avoir des idées *noires*   to have the *blues*
le fossé s'est *creusé*:   the gap has *widened*
un poisson *rouge*:   a *gold*fish
un repas *lourd*:   a *rich* meal

Different intellectual perceptions

une chance *sur deux*:	a *fifty-fifty* chance
j'ai dit *plus haut*:	I said *earlier...*
sans caféine:	caffein *free*
du jour au lendemain	*overnight*
le *troisième millénaire:*	the *twenty first century*

Opposites

une assurance-*maladie*:	*health* insurance
en chômage:	*out of work*
la *vente* par correspondance:	mail *order* business

Learned-popular

l'agriculture:	farming
un *auto*portrait:	a *self* portrait
une *congestion cérébrale*:	a stroke
un *infarctus du myocarde*:	a heart attack
un *oléoduc*:	a pipeline
*ostréi*culture:	oyster breeding
un *otorhinolaryngologiste*:	an ear throat and nose doctor
une *radiographie*:	an X-ray
un système *acoustique*:	a *sound* system

The following is a short list of some set word modulations found in common expressions:

Word modulations in verbal expressions

accuser réception:	to *acknowledge* receipt
avoir lieu:	to *take* place
avoir qqch à voir avec:	to have sth to do with
battre un record:	to *set* a record
céder le pas:	to *give* way
distribuer le courrier:	to *deliver* the mail
donner *la parole* à qqun:	to give so *the floor*
être en *pleine forme*:	to be in *great health*
faire face à une obligation:	to *meet* an obligation
lancer un emprunt:	*to float* a loan
lever une séance:	*to adjourn* a meeting
marquer un point:	*to score* a point
percevoir des impôts:	*to collect* taxes
poser une question:	to *raise* a question
poser un problème:	*to create* a problem
prendre *parti pour:*	to take *sides in favor of*

rallier des suffrages:	*to pick up* support
rattraper le temps perdu:	*to make up for* lost time
redresser un tort:	*to right* a wrong
régler une facture:	*to pay* a bill
remporter une victoire:	*to win* a victory
rendre hommage:	*to pay tribute*
répondre à un défi:	*to meet* a challenge
resserrer des liens:	*to strengthen* ties
se mettre au travail:	*to set* to work
se tailler la part du lion:	*to grab* the lion's share
suivre un cours:	*to take* a course
toucher un chèque:	*to cash* a check

Word modulations in nominal expressions

un *cheval de bataille*:	a *pet argument*
un *coup* de rouge:	a *shot* of red wine
la *fourchette* des prix:	a price *range*
l'*offre* et la demande:	*supply* and demand
des prix *cassés*:	*rock bottom* prices
la *société de consommation*:	*consumerism*
une *tranche* d'imposition:	a tax *bracket*
le *travail au noir*:	*working off the books*

Word modulations on adjectives and adjectival expressions

donner la *mauvaise* réponse:	to give the *wrong* answer
jouer un *mauvais* tour:	to play a *dirty* trick
un jour *ouvrable*:	a *working* day
un modèle *haut de gamme*:	a *top of the line* model
une phrase *affirmative*:	a *positive* sentence
un poste *vacant*:	an *open* position
des rapports *étroits*:	a *close* relationship

Word modulations on adverbial expressions

autrement dit:	*in other words*
en franchise:	*duty free*
expliquer *à fond*:	to explain *thoroughly*

Other word modulations

après réflexion:	*on second thought*
il n'en reste pas moins que:	*the fact remains that*

Clichés

Clichés theoretically belong in the chapter on equivalence. But an equivalence being an off-shoot of modulation, here are a few clichés which illustrate the principle of modulation:

joli comme un *coeur*:	pretty as a *picture*
laid comme un *pou*:	ugly as *sin*
sage comme une *image*:	as good as *gold*
avoir d'autres *chats à fouetter*:	to have other *fish to fry*
boire comme un *trou*:	to drink like a *fish*
couper *l'herbe* sous les pieds de quelqu'un:	*to pull the rug from* under someone's feet
fumer comme un *pompier*:	to smoke like a *chimney*
pleuvoir *des cordes*:	to rain *cats and dogs*

Preposition Modulations

Two languages may differ in the way they view things right down to the use of prepositions.

Let's examine the following sentence in French. Translating it literally without any modulation on prepositions would result in barbarisms:

L'homme *de* la rue qui voyage *dans* le métro se met en colère *contre* tout retard des trains.

In English one sees a man as being *in* the street rather than *of* the street, as travelling *on* the subway instead of *in* the subway and being angry *with* delays, certainly not *against* them!

A few other examples for good measure:

un enfant *aux* yeux bleus:	a child *with* blue eyes
une personne *sur* trois:	one person *out of* three
à l'émission de ce soir:	*on* to night's show
en moyenne:	*on* average
par chance:	*out of* luck
consulter *sur* rendez-vous:	to see (a patient) *by* appointment
envoyer *par* la poste:	to send *through* the post
être *en* vacances:	to be *on* vacation
ouvrir *sur* le jardin:	to open *into* the garden
parler *du* nez:	to speak *through* one's nose
regarder *vers* l'avenir:	to look *into* the future
sauter *de* joie:	to jump *for* joy

aller *chez* le dentiste: to go *to* the dentist
être *chez* le dentiste: to be *at* the dentist's
(Note that French here makes no difference between motion and non motion in
its use of the preposition.)

Most preposition modulations are lexical and can be found in
dictionaries. Many involve verbs which are constructed with one
sort of preposition in French and another, different from its literal
translation, in English:

> comparer *à* (to compare *with*), être intéressé *par* (to be interested *in*)
> être surpris *de* (to be surprised *at*), dépendre *de* (to depend *on*), faire
> feu *sur* (to fire *at*), remercier *de* (to thank *for*), remplacer *par* (to
> replace *with*), se détacher *sur* (to stand out *against*), substituer *à* (to
> substitute *for*), veiller *sur* (to look *after),* etc.

Message Modulations

Here are various categories of message modulation along with
some examples:

Positive-negative

> Le président *ne se rend pas compte* de la gravité de la situation. The
> president *fails to realize* how serious the situation is.
> Qu'il va y avoir une reprise de l'inflation *ne fait aucun doute.* That
> inflation is going to come back *is perfectly clear.*
> *Personne n'ignore* que ces mesures ne sont qu'un expédient.
> *Everyone is fully aware* that these steps are only a makeshift
> arrangement.
> *Tu n'arrêtes pas* de tousser: prends du sirop contre la toux! *You keep*
> coughing: take some cough syrup!
> Cet article est bon marché, *à la différence de* celui que tu as choisi.
> This article is cheap, *unlike* the one you chose.

Active voice-passive voice

> Ici *on parle français*:   *French spoken* here.
> Ce livre *se trouve* partout en librairie: this book *is found/ can be*
> *purchased* in all bookstores.

Singular-plural

> *La* police l'*a* appréhendé: the police *have* caught him.

Les hommes sont méchants: *Man is* wicked.
The news *is* alarming: *Les* nouvelles *sont* alarmantes.

Abstract-concrete

Nous *avons appris* qu'il allait y avoir un orage à la radio: We *heard* of the impending storm on the radio.
Parlez plus fort, je ne vous *comprends* pas! Speak louder I can't *hear* you!

Opposite points of view

Pouvez-vous patienter?   *Are you in a hurry?*
Comme vous avez la figure rouge! *How red your face looks!*
Tais-toi!   *Don't speak!*

Necessary and optional modulations

Message modulations   may be necessary or optional just like transpositions.

• **Necessary** when diverging structures or usage demand it.

Many message modulations involve a switch from the active voice (favored by French) to the passive voice (favored by English). Grammatically French is more limited in its use of the passive voice than English, since an indirect object may never become a passive subject. English, on the other hand, is reluctant to use the indefinite pronoun "one", contrary to French:

On lui promit de *prendre sa demande* en considération.
He was promised to *have his request taken* into consideration. (The modulation active to passive voice is the only possible solution.)

French use of pronominal verbs with an inanimate subject often has no counterpart in English except for the passive voice:

En France les télécartes *se trouvent* dans tous les bureaux de tabac.
In France telecards *can be found* in all tobacco shops.

Other modulations may involve metalinguistics, usage rather than grammar:

J'ai appris le résultat des élections *par* le journal.
I read the results of the election *in* the newspaper. (Abstract to concrete.)

L'hôtel *affiche complet*   The hotel *is booked out.*

- **Optional** when modulation is only one way of translating the message.

  Elle *n'a pas cessé* de me regarder pendant tout le trajet
  This sentence can be translated three ways:
  1. She did not stop looking at me during the whole trip   (literal)
  2. She *kept* watching me during the whole trip   (modulation)
  3. She looked at me *continuously/ incessantly/ without stopping* during the whole trip   (transposition).

Modulation and transposition

Modulation can be closely interrelated with transposition.

This is true of all expressions which take one auxiliary in one language and another in the second language (*avoir* chaud, froid, faim, soif, raison, de la chance etc.: *to be* hot, cold, hungry, thirsty, right, lucky etc.)

Ce chanteur *a* beaucoup de *succès*: This singer *is* very *popular.*
Vous *avez* de la *chance*: You *are lucky* (transposition-modulation)
as opposed to: *You're in* luck (modulation only).

Other examples:

Autrement dit, cela ne t'intéresse pas: *In other words* you're not interested.
Louis XIV vécut *jusqu'à un âge avancé*: Louis XIV lived *to be very old.*
Quelles que soient ses opinions politiques on ne peut rester insensible au problème du chômage: *Regardless of* your political opinions you cannot remain insensitive to the problem of unemployment.

Exercices: **La Modulation**

Lorsque deux langues expriment le même concept ou le même message selon un angle ou un point de vue différent, on parle de modulation. La modulation ne nécessite pas un changement de catégories grammaticales comme la transposition, mais plutôt un changement de catégories de pensée: par exemple la langue aborde le concept d'un point de vue concret ou abstrait, du point de vue de la cause ou de l'effet, du moyen ou du résultat. Elle considère une partie au lieu d'un tout, ou une partie à la place d'une autre partie, etc.

On trouve des modulations en anglais et en français à trois niveaux:

- *au niveau des mots et expressions nominales ou verbales dans des unités de traduction (groupes de mots qui ne peuvent pas être dissociés les uns des autres). Ce genre de modulation est figé et se trouve dans les dictionnaires bilingues.*

- *au niveau des prépositions (usage également figé et consacré par la grammaire).*

- *au niveau du message (ce type de modulation peut être nécessaire ou facultatif). Il est plus complexe et requiert la créativité du traducteur.*

A. La modulation de termes

Traduisez les phrases suivantes en faisant une modulation sur le ou les mots en italique.

1. Tu te trompes, ce n'est pas la *bonne* clé.
2. Mon patron est un *gros* fumeur.
3. Désirez-vous votre steak *saignant* ou *à point*?
4. Les exercices de notre livre de travaux pratiques sont d'un niveau *supérieur* plutôt que *moyen*.

5. Pendant la saison *creuse* il est possible d'obtenir des tarifs avantageux dans les grands hôtels de la Côte d'Azur.

6. Aux heures *de pointe* la circulation en ville est un véritable cauchemar.

7. L'usine utilise une technologie *de pointe*.

8. L'acteur avait oublié une partie de son *texte*.

9. Il n'y a de *distribution* de courrier ni le dimanche ni les jours fériés.

10. La *fraude fiscale* est un problème de nos sociétés modernes.

11. Quand nous avons fait cette suggestion au chef de service pour améliorer la productivité, il nous a ri *au nez*.

12. Avant l'utilisation du produit veuillez lire soigneusement *le mode d'emploi*.

13. La production se règle par la loi de *l'offre* et de la demande.

14. Le fournisseur n'ayant pas respecté les délais de livraison, le client a déclaré qu'il y avait *rupture* de contrat.

15. Les *droits* de douane ont été abolis entre tous les pays de l'Union Européenne.

B. La modulation de locutions verbales

Traduisez les phrases suivantes en faisant une modulation sur les verbes en italique.

1. Est-ce que tu *as* déjà *pris* une décision?

2. Si nous prenons cette route, nous *gagnerons* du temps.

3. Cette vieille photo ne lui *rend* vraiment pas justice.

4. Au lieu de *faire la queue* pour aller voir un film idiot, il vaudrait mieux *faire une promenade* dans le parc.

5. Pour le désarmer, *fais*-lui un joli sourire!

6. Dans le noir je heurtai quelquechose et *poussai* un cri.

7. L'orateur *prononça* son discours d'une voix monotone.

8. Le comité est chargé de *réunir* les fonds nécessaires pour le projet.

9. Le P.D.G. *a établi* une comparaison entre le chiffre d'affaire de l'année dernière et celui de cette année.

10. Les autorités compétentes vont vous *délivrer* un passeport.

11. Si vous avez été victime d'une agression, allez *porter* plainte au commissariat de police.

12. Les pays membres de L'Union Européenne veulent *resserrer* les liens qui les unissent.

13. Les représentants des syndicats et du patronat ont *jeté les bases* d'un accord durable.

14. Ces derniers temps un fossé *s'est creusé* entre les deux pays qui affecte de façon négative leurs relations diplomatiques.

15. Les politiciens *commettent* une grave erreur en ne tenant aucun compte de la majorité silencieuse.

16. Le service de publicité assure que le nouveau produit va *connaître* un gros succès.

C. La modulation de prépositions liées à des noms ou pronoms

Traduisez les phrases suivantes en faisant une modulation sur les prépositions en italique.

1. Les nouvelles *à* la radio sont catastrophiques.

2. Les trains en France sont toujours *à* l'heure.

3. C'est *à* moi de trouver une solution à ce problème.

4. Vous voyez la maison *aux* volets rouges là-bas? C'est la mienne.

5. Il y avait un tableau de maître *au* mur de la chambre.

6. Il lui a fait sa demande en mariage *à* genoux.

7. *A* l'avenir il faudra que tu fasses plus attention.

8. Il est exactement 10 heures et quart *à* ma montre.

9. Napoléon est resté *au* pouvoir pendant quinze ans.

10. Nous ne savons que faire: *d'*un côté nous ne pouvons pas demander au patron de s'arrêter de fumer et *de* l'autre nous ne voulons pas subir les effets nocifs de ses cigarettes.

11. Pouvez-vous m'indiquer le chemin *du* musée d'Orsay?

12. Il faut voir Paris *de* nuit.

13. Lis donc ce roman *de* Stendhal!

14. Son frère est plus âgé que lui *de* 3 ans.

15. Doit-on se fier à l'opinion de l'homme *de* la rue?

16. Entre 1939 et 1945 presque tous les pays du globe étaient *en* guerre.

17. La secrétaire est actuellement *en* congé de maladie.

18. Il lui semblait qu'elle avait le visage *en* feu.

19. La maison vend uniquement *sur* catalogue.

20. Nous n'avons qu'une chance *sur* plusieurs millions de gagner à la loterie.

21. J'aimerais attirer votre attention *sur* un détail.

22. Il fallut faire le trajet à pied *sous* la pluie.

23. Ne te dérange pas: j'ai le marteau *sous* la main.

24. Faisons-le *par* devoir sinon *par* intérêt propre.

25. L'oiseau pénétra dans la chambre *par* la fenêtre qui était grande ouverte.

26. Es-tu toujours en colère *contre* moi?

27. Je suis prêt à parier dix *contre* un que tu te trompes.

28. Ça se voit que vous n'avez jamais travaillé *dans* une ferme.

29. Ne bois pas *dans* ce verre, il n'a pas été lavé!

30. J'étais *hors de* moi.

31. A trente ans il vit toujours *chez* ses parents.

32. Certains *d'entre* vous se demandent pourquoi cette réunion a été organisée.

D. La modulation de prépositions liées à des verbes

Traduisez les phrases suivantes en faisant une modulation sur les prépositions en italique.

1. Je vous remercie *d'*avoir pensé à moi.

2. *De* quoi parlez-vous?

3. Ayez pitié *de* moi!

4. Etes-vous content *de* votre nouvelle voiture?

5. Cet enfant tient *de* son père, c'est évident.

6. Inscrivez-vous dès maintenant *aux* cours d'été.

7. Le dîner a été superbe: nous avons commencé *par* des huîtres et nous avons fini *par* une mousse glacée aux framboises.

8. Ma fille a été opérée *de* l'appendicite le mois dernier.

9. L'un des devoirs des enfants est de veiller *sur* leurs parents lorsque ceux-ci sont incapacités par l'âge.

10. La décision ne dépend que *du* chef de service.

11. T'intéresses-tu vraiment *à* tes études?

12. Je suis fâché *contre* Jean parce qu'il a ri *de* mes problèmes.

13. Il est temps de remplacer le canapé du salon *par* quelquechose de plus moderne.

14. Nous avons été surpris *de* sa violente réaction.

15. Pour les régimes sans cholestérol il est préférable de substituer des huiles végétales *au* beurre.

16. Les tourelles sombres du manoir se détachaient *sur* un ciel d'orage.

17. Si l'on compare ce tableau de Lancret *à* celui-ci de Watteau, l'influence du maître sur le disciple est nette.

E. La modulations de message

Traduisez les phrases suivantes en faisant une modulation sur les passages en italique. Si possible indiquez de quel changement de catégorie de pensée il s'agit.

1. *Mets le couvert*!
2. *Vous désirez*?
3. *Ce dessin te plaît*?
4. Qu'est-ce qui *ne va pas*?
5. *On m'a dit* que tu me cherchais.
6. *C'est l'heure*! *Rendez* vos devoirs!
7. Ce modèle de chaussure *a beaucoup de succès*.
8. *Vous avez un rire communicatif*!
9. *As-tu encore mal au genou*?
10. Il faut aller au supermarché: on *n'a plus de lait* à la maison.
11. *Avez-vous un emploi* ou *êtes-vous toujours étudiant*?
12. *Ne quittez pas*! Je vous passe le responsable du service.
13. Elle est ravie: *on vient de l'embaucher*.

14. *J'ai appris par* le journal qu'il y avait une grève des chemins de fer.

15. Pourriez-vous m'expliquer ceci *encore une fois? Je ne vous suis plus*!

16. Après une telle mésaventure il serait préférable *que vous ne vous fassiez pas remarquer* pendant quelque temps.

17. Avec l'essor prodigieux de la science et de la technologie des dernières décennies notre conception de l'avenir *se trouve profondément modifiée.*

18. Le candidat à l'élection *ne s'était pas rendu compte* que les priorités des électeurs *avaient changé.*

19. La situation économique *a tendance à s'améliorer. Il n'en reste pas moins* que le chômage stagne à un niveau trop élevé pour être acceptable.

20. Je songerai à changer d'emploi quand *il se présentera une offre qui en vaille la peine.*

Chapter 10 Equivalence

What is equivalence?

An equivalence is a set message modulation. The translator will recognize a need for an equivalence from the context of the message to be translated, that is to say from the situation which has occasioned it.

For instance the meaning of the simple phrase *"C'est à moi"* will be dependent on the situation which has elicited it. *"C'est à moi* de jouer" (*it's my turn*) translates differently from *"C'est à moi* de trouver une solution à ce problème" (*it's up to me* to find a solution to this problem), or even from "Ne touche pas! *C'est à moi!*" (don't touch, *that's mine!*").

An equivalence must replace a global message. It encompasses a translation unit whose elements cannot be translated separately. Failure to realize this would lead to nonsense or mistranslation. The literal translation of a colloquial expression such as "Notre chanson a eu *un succès boeuf*" would undoubtedly bring a puzzled look on the face of an Anglophone until realized that it just means *a tremendous success*. Conversely, trying to see two translation units in the English phrase *a home run*, taken in its figurative sense as in "the new product was a definite *homerun*", would lead to a mistranslation. "Une course à la maison" just won't do, and the solution lies in an equivalent concept, something in the order of *un succès incontestable*.

To come up with an equivalent in the TL, the translator must think of what is commonly said under the same circumstances, and in the same situation. This presupposes a very good knowledge both of the SL and of the TL in all of their idiomatic resources. The result can be stylistically and structurally very different from the SL. Messages requiring the use of an equivalence in translation are an expression of conformity with the standard formulas, idioms and catch phrases of a linguistic group.

We find equivalences in the following categories of situations.

Exclamations and reflex-formulas

These are ready-made words or groups of words used in set situations.
For instance when one is surprised:

	Ça par exemple! Ça alors!: You don't say! Unbelievable!
	Tiens!: Hey!, Look!
or in disbelief:	Voyons!: Come on!
	Allons donc!: Nonsense!
in denial:	Pensez vous!: Come off it!
defiant:	Et alors!: So what!
in pain:	Aïe!: Ouch!
thankful:	Dieu merci!: Thank goodness!
appreciative:	Formidable!: Great! etc.

To this category belong all popular expletives from the meekest (*Flute! nuts! Zut! darn!*) to the strongest.

Prop words

Prop words are words used in conversation to nuance the sense of a message. Very often these are adverbs such as *donc* used to soften any request: "Venez *donc* diner chez nous" *"Why don't you* come and have dinner with us?"*, or to show impatience "Que faites vous *donc?*" "What *on earth* are you doing?"; *bien* used for emphasis: "Tu vas *bien* prendre un petit verre avec moi!" *"Aren't you* going to have a drink with me?"; *alors* used to show impatience: *"Alors,* vous vous dépêchez?" "Are you hurrying *or not?*" Or they can be locutions such as *n'est-ce pas?* used to elicit approval or confirmation: "Vous me préviendrez, *n'est-ce pas?*" "You will let me know, *won't you?*"

Greetings and letter closings

Greetings and forms of address are standard expressions of conformity to social protocol and usage. Their translation must reflect the tonality of the original.

> Bonjour!: Hello! *or* Good morning! Good afternoon!
> Salut!: Hi! *or* So long! depending on whether one is coming or leaving)
> A bientôt! A un de ces jours! A la prochaine!: See you soon! *or* I'll see you!
> Enchanté de faire votre connaissance!: Pleased to meet you!
> Bonnes fêtes de fin d'année!: Happy holidays!

Follow the same rules for epistolary customs, opening and closing formulas such as:

> Je vous prie d'agréer, Monsieur/ Madame/ Mademoiselle, l'expression de mes sentiments distingués: Yours sincerely.
> Dans l'attente de vous lire..: We look forward to hearing from you.
> Veuillez croire, Monsieur, à l'assurance de nos sentiments dévoués: We remain at your service.
> Bien des choses de ma part à...: Please give my best to...
> Grosses bises: hugs and kisses.

Clichés and idioms

We find these hackeneyed phrases under many guises:

in adverbial expressions

après coup: after the fact
dans une certaine mesure: to a certain extent
de toutes ses forces: with all his might
étant donné que: in view of the fact that...

in nominal expressions

une affaire classée: case closed
un cercle vicieux: a catch 22 situation
un délit d'initié: insider trading
le démon de midi: the seven year itch
un feu de paille: a flash in the pan
une fièvre de cheval: a raging fever
une formation préalable: prior training
un gros mot: a four letter word
Monsieur tout le monde: the man in the street
le mot de la fin: the punch line
un moulin à paroles: a chatterbox
une occasion rêvée: a golden opportunity
un panier percé: a spendthrift
une planche de salut: a lifesaver
le premier venu: just anybody
un produit haut de gamme: a top of the line product
un rire communicatif: a contagious laugh
le secret de polichinelle: everybody's secret
une solution de rechange: an alternative solution
une tête de linotte: a scatterbrain
un train d'enfer: a hectic pace
un vieux de la vieille: an old timer
une voie sans issue: a dead end

in verbal expressions
Many of these use food imagery, an essential preoccupation to the French:

avoir du pain sur la planche: to have a lot to do
battre à plate couture: to beat to a frazzle
être dans de beaux draps: to be in hot water
faire bouillir la marmite: to bring home the bacon
mettre les bouchées doubles: to work twice as hard
ne pas se sentir dans son assiette: to feel under the weather
s'occuper de ses oignons: to mind one's own business

tomber dans les pommes: to faint.[1]

Slang and slang expressions

The French "langue verte" or slang is a language by itself and many of its colorful expressions find equivalents in English slang:

C'est pas de blague?: No kidding?
Il a piqué une rogne: He got hot under the collar.
Les flics ont fini par l'épingler: The cops finally nailed him.[2]

Proverbs and axioms

In striking little pronouncements proverbs contain the popular wisdom of nations, essentially the same the world over, and consequently most French proverbs do have equivalents in English. We will just list two here:

Il faut hurler avec les loups. When in Rome do as the Romans do.
Honni soit qui mal y pense! Evil to him who evil thinks!

Official signs and warnings

Signs and warnings constitute ideal material for equivalences, for they sum up a message in a stereotypic situation:

attention à la peinture: wet paint
fermeture pour cause de travaux: closed for renovation
inauguration du magasin: grand opening
priorité à droite: yield to the right
travaux en cours: men at work

and so on.

References to a common socio-cultural heritage

---

[1] For an extended list of such expressions please refer to the appendix under dictionaries of French slang, idioms and colloquialisms, pp.265-6.

[2] See appendix pp.265-6 for dictionaries on French slang.

There is a very vast reservoir consisting of references to socio-cultural facts well known to the linguistic group of the SL, people who share a common education, a common history and culture, and common institutions; but allusions cryptic to the speakers of the TL unless they too are familiar with the culture and civilization of the SL. In any case, the translator, in order to catch their meaning will have to be very well versed in French civilization.

References to *les personnes du troisième âge* (senior citizens), *l'hexagone* (France, whose shape is hexagonal), *l'hémicycle* (the house of representatives shaped in a semi circle), *la Côte d'Azur* (the French Riviera, famous for its azure blue sky and waters), *le débarquement* (the allied landing of D day), *les trente glorieuses* (the economic boom of the 30 years which followed World War II), *Marianne* (the representation of the French Republic as a young woman found in every French town hall -actress Catherine Deneuve sat for the bust-), *la ville lumière* (Paris, the city of lights) to name but a few, along with covert allusions to a literary heritage, such as "C'est un vrai *Harpagon*" or "Nous ne sommes que des *roseaux pensants*" are all meaningful to French denizens but constitute a sort of coded language which needs deciphering for an English speaking public.[3]

> Equivalence as a translation device is often resorted to in the translation of plays (for exclamations, reflex-formulas and colloquialisms) as well as in the translation of ads, newspaper and magazine articles which make frequent references to socio-cultural facts and situations.

---

[3] Neophytes may find some help in the dictionaries on French cultural references listed in the appendix, pp.266-7.

Exercices: L'Equivalence

Exclamations, formules-réflexe, expressions idiomatiques et argotiques, clichés, proverbes, avis officiels, formules de salutation, allusions culturelles figées nécessitent des équivalences dans la LA.
La difficulté pour le traducteur consiste à savoir reconnaître la partie du texte qui nécessite une équivalence comme un message global, comme une unité de traduction dont les éléments sont indissociables les uns des autres, et de ce fait, ne peuvent être traduits séparément.

A. Les diverses catégories d'équivalence

Traduisez les phrases suivantes en donnant une équivalence pour les expressions en italique.

I. Formules-réflexe
1. *Aïe*, je me suis fait mal!
2. *Dites donc*, vous ne pouvez pas faire attention?
3. *Ça par exemple,* il a réussi à son examen!
4. *Allons donc*, tu ne vas tout de même pas me faire croire cette histoire!
5. Ça te dérange, *et alors*?
6. Attendez une minute: *vous voyez bien* que je suis occupé!
7. *Rien à faire*, il refuse absolument de venir.
8. Tu crois pouvoir me battre au tennis? Essaie *un peu*!
9. *Ça suffit*, les enfants, arrêtez de vous chamailler!
10. *Vivement* les vacances pour que je puisse enfin me reposer!

II. Clichés
1. Vos enfants grandissent *à vue d'oeil!*
2. Ecoute, arrête de parler *à tort et à travers*!

3. Ce gosse est insupportable, il réclame des jouets *à tout bout de champ*!

4. Tu te plains sans arrêt, tu ne fais pas ton travail, et *par dessus le marché* tu es exigeant avec tout le monde.

5. *Par les temps qui courent* il ne fait pas bon d'avoir sur soi beaucoup d'argent liquide.

6. La mère et la fille se ressemblent *comme deux gouttes d'eau*.

7. Cet ensemble vous va *comme un gant*.

8. Nous avons acheté ce terrain *pour trois fois rien*.

9. C'est un monsieur *comme il faut*.

10. Ça ne m'ennuie pas *le moins du monde* de vous déposer chez vous.

11. *Chacun à son goût*.

III. Expressions idiomatiques

1. Pose la question à ton patron *pour en avoir le coeur net*!

2. Aujourd'hui, impossible de sortir, *je regrette, je ne suis pas dans mon assiette*.

3. Jacques Dupont? Non, ce nom *ne me dit rien*.

4. C'est difficile, mais *il faut faire contre mauvaise fortune bon coeur*.

5. *Trouvez vous quelquechose à redire à* mon exposé?

6. Georges *a le verbe facile*, mais moi pas.

7. Nous ne nous en sortirons pas, c'est *un cercle vicieux*.

8. J'ai un voyage d'affaires le mois prochain à Paris: c'est *une occasion rêvée* pour aller découvrir les grands restaurants parisiens.

IV. Avis officiels

1. *Défense de fumer*.

2. *Défense de jeter des ordures*.

3. *Ne pas se pencher par la portière*.

4. *Ne pas marcher sur les pelouses*.

5. *Réservé à la clientèle*.

6. *Fermeture annuelle*.

V. Souhaits, salutations, excuses et formules épistolaires

1. *Enchanté*!

2. *Bon voyage!*
3. *A la prochaine!*
4. *Tous mes souhaits pour un prompt rétablissement!*
5. *Je vous prie d'agréer, Monsieur, l'expression de mes sentiments distingués.*
6. *Nous vous présentons toutes nos excuses.* -Mais je vous en prie!
7. *Je t'embrasse affectueusement.*
8. *Veuillez me faire parvenir* un exemplaire de votre brochure sur les croisières en Méditerrannée.
9. *Ayez la gentillesse de me rappeler au bon souvenir de* vos parents.

VI. Argot et expressions argotiques
1. Depuis que son *mec* l'a *planquée* elle ne fait que *chialer*.
2. Les *flics* l'ont *flanqué* en *taule*.
3. Je n'ai *pigé que dalle* à ce *polar*.
4. Ne te *fais pas de bile*, c'est *du gâteau*.
5. Ce *zigoto* a un *sacré culot* pour *faire du grabuge* comme ça en pleine nuit.
6. Tu *déménages!* Ne me *pique* pas mon *bouquin!*

VII. Proverbes et dictons
1. Venez donc à notre soirée samedi! *Plus on est de fous, plus on rit.*
2. Je peux bien me permettre un petit écart, *une fois n'est pas coutume.*
3. Il faut choisir: tu ne *peux pas avoir le beurre et l'argent du beurre.*
4. Ne soyez pas imprudents. *Si vous misez tout sur le même cheval,* vous risquez d'*y laisser votre chemise.*

VIII. Allusions culturelles
1. *La belle époque* en France a été une période d'insouciance et de prospérité pour les classes aisées.
2. Au sortir de la première guerre mondiale, *pendant les années folles,* la mode pour les femmes fut aux cheveux courts et aux robes sans corset.

3. *La pucelle d'Orléans, le vert galant, le roi soleil, l'ogre de la Corse et l'homme du 18 juin* comptent parmi les figures les plus hautes en couleur de toute l'histoire de France.

4. A la veille de la Révolution de 1789 Camille Desmoulins ameuta le peuple de Paris au Palais Royal en lui faisant craindre que le roi préparait *une Saint Barthélémy* des patriotes.

5. En période de conflit social, l'atmosphère au *Palais Bourbon* est fiévreuse.

6. L'essor économique des années soixante et soixante dix a profité à *la génération née après la guerre.*

7. *L'hexagone* arrive en tête des destinations touristiques à l'échelle de la planète.

8. Si vous le voulez bien, *revenons à nos moutons!*

B. Les locutions verbales idiomatiques

Retrouvez les expressions idiomatiques équivalentes en anglais (la signification des expressions idiomatiques françaises est donnée entre parenthèses).

1. arriver comme un cheveu sur la soupe (*arriver à un mauvais moment)*

2. avoir la gueule de bois (*être malade après avoir trop bu*)

3. avoir la langue bien pendue (*parler beaucoup et facilement*)

4. avoir quelquechose pour une bouchée de pain (*pour presque rien*)

5. broyer du noir (*être déprimé*)

6. couper les cheveux en quatre (*chercher des difficultés*)

7. dormir à poings fermés (*dormir d'un profond sommeil*)

8. en avoir plein le dos (*en avoir assez, être fatigué de tout*)

9. être aux anges (*être absolument ravi*)

10. être dans ses petits souliers (*être dans une situation difficile*)

11. être du pareil au même (*être exactement la même chose*)

12. faire l'école buissonnière (*manquer l'école et aller se promener)*

13. faire le grand saut (*passer dans l'autre monde*)

14. faire quelquechose en cinq sec (*faire quelquechose très vite*)

15. manger sur le pouce (*manger quelquechose de simple très vite*)

16. mettre du beurre dans ses épinards (*profiter financièrement d'une situation*)

17. mettre les pieds dans le plat (*intervenir maladroitement*)

18. ne pas savoir sur quel pied danser (*ne pas savoir quoi faire pour arranger la situation*)

19. ne faire ni chaud ni froid à quelqu'un ("ça ne me fait ni chaud ni froid"= *ça m'est égal*)

20. parler à tort et à travers (*dire des choses qui n'ont pas de sens*)

21. passer l'éponge (*pardonner une offense*)

22. perdre les pédales (*devenir fou*)

23. promettre monts et merveilles (*faire des promesses impossibles à tenir*)

24. rendre à quelqu'un la monnaie de sa pièce (*se venger de quelqu'un*)

25. retourner le couteau dans la plaie (*aggraver les choses*)

26. se mettre sur son trente et un (*mettre ses plus beaux habits*)

27. s'occuper de ses oignons (*s'occuper de ses propres affaires*)

28. se porter comme un charme (*être en excellente santé*)

29. tourner autour du pot (*éviter d'aller à l'essentiel*)

30. vendre la mèche (*révéler le secret*)

31. vouloir décrocher la lune (*vouloir l'impossible*)

32. y perdre son latin (*ne rien comprendre*)

C. Les proverbes

1. Retrouvez les équivalents anglais des proverbes français suivants.

Il faut savoir laver son linge sale en famille.
Une hirondelle ne fait pas le printemps.
Ne réveillez pas le chat qui dort.
Un malheur n'arrive jamais seul.
Il faut battre le fer pendant qu'il est chaud.
Mieux vaut tard que jamais.
Il y a loin de la coupe aux lèvres.

2. Parmi les traductions de proverbes précédents relevez-en une qui soit:

- *une traduction littérale*

- *une transposition*

- *une modulation*

- *une équivalence*

D. Les locutions verbales idiomatiques (suite)

Faites correspondre les locutions verbales idiomatiques suivantes avec leur équivalent anglais.

1. jouer avec le feu	_____ to add fuel to the fire
2. vivre au jour le jour	_____ to shout at the top of one's voice
3. remuer ciel et terre	_____ to take something literally
4. prendre quelqu'un en grippe	_____ to sleep late
5. faire d'une pierre deux coups	_____ to bite off more than you can chew
6. passer une nuit blanche	_____ to court danger
7. être né coiffé	_____ to kill two birds with one stone
8. en avoir le coeur net	_____ to live from hand to mouth
9. faire la grasse matinée	_____ to take a dislike to someone
10. dormir à la belle étoile	_____ to spend a sleepless night
11. crier à tue-tête	_____ to catch someone in the act
12. prendre quelquechose au pied de la lettre	_____ to have been born under a lucky star
13. prendre ses jambes à son cou	_____ to move heaven and earth

14. prendre quelqu'un sur le fait　　____ to take to one's heels

15. verser de l'huile sur le feu　　____ to walk out on a job

16. tuer la poule aux oeufs d'or　　____ to get to the bottom of things

17. avoir les yeux plus grands que le ventre ____ to kill the goose with the

　　　golden eggs

18. rendre son tablier　　____ to sleep outdoors

E. Les proverbes (suite)

Faites correspondre les proverbes ou dictons de la colonne de droite avec ceux de la colonne de gauche.

1. Aide-toi le ciel t'aidera　　____ a rolling stone gathers no

　　　moss

2. L'habit ne fait pas le moine　　____ the more, the merrier

3. Comme on fait son lit on se couche　　____ spare the rod and spoil the

　　　child

4. Un tiens vaut mieux que deux tu l'auras　____ when in Rome, do as the

　　　Romans do

5. On ne peut pas avoir le beurre et　　____ don't count your chickens

　　l'argent du beurre　　before they are hatched

6. Tel est pris qui croyait prendre　　____ catchers may find the tables

　　　turned

7. Qui aime bien, châtie bien　　____ when the cat is away, the

　　　mice will play

8. Oeil pour oeil, dent pour dent　　____ dead men tell no tales

9. Paris ne s'est pas fait en un jour　　____ tit for tat

10. Qui se ressemble, s'assemble　　____ you can't have your cake and

　　　eat it too

11. Plus on est de fous, plus on rit   ____ you must not put the cart
before the horse

12. Quand on veut, on peut   ____ the devil you know is better
than the one you don't

13. A quelquechose malheur est bon   ____ once bitten, twice shy

14. A trompeur, trompeur et demi   ____ as you sow, so shall you reap

15. De deux maux il faut savoir choisir
le moindre   ____ a bird in the hand is
worth two in the bush

16. Pierre qui roule n'amasse pas mousse   ____ half a loaf is better than no
bread at all

17. Loin des yeux, loin du coeur   ____ birds of a feather flock
together

18. Il faut hurler avec les loups   ____ where there's a will there's a
way

19. Quand on parle du loup, on en voit
la queue   ____ what goes around comes
around

20. Chat échaudé craint l'eau froide   ____ out of sight, out of mind

21. Quand le chat n'est pas là, les souris
dansent   ____ heaven helps those who help
themselves

22. Il ne faut pas vendre la peau de l'ours
avant de l'avoir tué   ____ you can't tell a book by its
cover

23. Il ne faut pas mettre la charrue devant
les boeufs   ____ talk of the devil and
he's sure to appear

24. Faute de grives on mange des merles   ____ Rome was not built in a day

25. Morte la bête, mort le venin   ____ it's a blessing in disguise

Chapter 11   **Adaptation**

What is adaptation?

| quatre litres | one gallon |

Adaptation is the last device a translator has at his disposal when all else fails. It is therefore the furthest removed from literal translation.

Let us use a simile to better understand the purpose of adaptation. Suppose for a moment that you have undertaken the task of translating an African fable for the benefit of a remote Eskimo tribe. In this fable a silk-cotton tree plays a symbolic key role. Now in all likelihood the Eskimo language will have no equivalent for the tree since its very concept is unknown to its speakers, and it will be up to you to come up with a solution to this semantic problem. The silk cotton tree being only important inasmuch as it is a symbol, any tall bush growing on the tundra and known to your audience will serve the purpose. This, in essence, is what adaptation is all about: carrying a concept over and across the barriers of language and civilization, trying to make sense out of something that is totally foreign to the linguistic group you are translating for.

Differences in geography, customs, conceptions of the world, values, institutions etc., between nations lead to appreciable difficulties when translating from one language to another, and the greater the divergence between the cultures, the greater the difficulty.

Even though English and French have had centuries of a closely interrelated history to prevent a total abyss in mutual understanding, there are still areas of major differences between the two. Common problems in translation arise from the lack of the familiar form of address in English to render the French "*tu*"; from differences in the physical ways of greeting people, in honorific titles, in epistolary customs, in the delineation of time and space, in money and measure units, in meals, shops, occupations, and in institutions, whether educational, social or political.

Linguistic deficiency and compensation

Let us first see how the structural problem created by the lack of a *tu* form in modern English may be compensated for in translation. Even though a verb like *tutoyer, se tutoyer* has no equivalent in the English speaking world, people still make a sharp distinction between those with whom they are on a familiar basis -family and friends- and those with whom they are not -superiors, strangers, mere acquaintances-. Consequently, one way of making the sentence "*Nous nous tutoyons maintenant*" understandable to an English speaking public might be "*We are now on a first name basis*", and one way of translating "*Viens-tu?*" when the speaker has just switched from a previous *vous* to show that the two are now friends, could possibly be "*Bob (or Johnny etc.), are you coming?*"

Adaptation in traditions, usages and institutions

Differences in greeting customs

Greetings often necessitate the use of adaptation in order to prevent lack of understanding or even mistranslation.

For instance, handshaking in Anglo-Saxon and French speaking countries follow different rules of etiquette. In the former you shake someone's hand once only, when first introduced to that person. In France on the other hand, people would consider it very odd, if not downright rude or at least very informal, if you did not shake an acquaintance's hand each time upon meeting or parting. And thus *"Il me serra la main avec effusion"* may be translated as *"He greeted me warmly"* or *"We said an effusive good-bye"* depending on whether the handshake is an expression of greeting or leaving.

The custom of kissing for men of the same family or for long time friends is a Mediterranean one, not shared by Anglo-Saxon nations. Therefore in order not to send the wrong message a translator will have to change a sentence such as *"Les deux hommes se sont embrassés"* into *"The two men gave each other a hug."*

Differences in forms of address and titles

French is far more formal than English in that respect. *"Hello, Mrs. Smith!"* or just plain *"Hello!"* can be considered the equivalent of *"Bonjour Madame!"*, which certainly does not translate as *"Good morning, Lady!"*, the patronizing implication of the English phrase being far off the mark of the very polite form of address in French.

Greeting formulas in letters follow the same pattern: *Dear Sir* to a person you do not know well or do not know at all becomes *Monsieur*. Honorific titles follow rules of their own. Use of the possessive is the norm for army and navy titles: *Mon général, Mon commandant, Mon lieutenant*, while political or administrative titles use the regular civilian title followed by the description of the office held: *Monsieur le président, Madame le juge, Monsieur le maire* etc.

University professors are never addressed as *Professeur X* but simply as *Monsieur* or *Madame*, and certainly never as *Docteur*, a title reserved for physicians, while *le professeur X* designates a teaching physician at a medical university, and *un professeur,* just any teacher at the high school or college level.

Differences in measure units

Measure units may at times necessitate an adaptation. Depending on the public targeted and the context, a translator will have to debate whether or not to give an approximate conversion of French francs into dollars, kilometers into miles, kilos into pounds, or liters into quarts and gallons. The rule is: convert whenever deemed essential to the readers' understanding. Obviously *"Il mesure un mètre quatre-vingt"* has to be rendered as *"He is six feet tall"*, *"Va me chercher un litre de lait"* as *"Go* and *get me a quart of milk"* and *"Le village le plus proche était à trois kms de là"* as *"the nearest village was 2 miles away"*. Sometimes, however, keeping the S.L. measure unit may be preferable, to add local color to the message for instance.

Differences in the division of time and space

This becomes obvious in the way the two languages delineate the periods of the day for greeting purposes or for social use: *"Bonjour!"* can mean *"Good morning"* or *"Good afternoon"* depending on the time of day, and whereas *bonsoir* means *good evening, ce soir* refers to *tonight* and *la nuit dernière* to *last night*. The 24 hour clock is also scrupulously adhered to in public life from the media and entertainment industry to train and plane schedules. References to *"Le journal télévisé de 13 heures"* or *"Le train partira à 21 heures 35"* have to be adapted for English speakers.

Even the delineation of weeks is at odds. The French like to illogically refer to a week's time as eight days and two weeks' time as fifteen days. Taking literally the sentence *"Je vais aller passer huit ou quinze jours à la campagne"* would indeed be a mistranslation. And not just week delineation but ways of counting in cliché expressions are at variance with English usage. "Nous sommes sortis ensemble *deux ou trois fois* le mois dernier" is in fact the equivalent of "We went out *a couple of times* together last month" and "Je ne vais pas te le répéter *trente six fois*" of "I am not going to repeat it to you *a hundred times*".

A French speaker will also use different bearings for space. "Le musée se trouve à deux *rues* d'ici" translates as "The museum is two *blocks* from here" and "Vous trouverez les chaussures pour dames au *premier* étage" as "You will find ladies shoes on the *second* floor" since the first floor in the U.S. corresponds to the British *ground floor* or French *rez de chaussée*.

Differences in shops and stores

They do not always correspond either. A *charcuterie* is not quite a delicatessen, but rather, the shop of a pork butcher who very often doubles as a caterer: there you can find not only pork chops, sausages, ham and cold cuts but also already cooked dishes to take out as well as appetizers and salads. In a *bureau de tabac* newspapers, paperbacks, cigarettes can be purchased as well as lottery tickets, stamps and telecards. And a *grande surface* will combine fish, dairy, meat, deli and bakery-pastry departments along with a liquor aisle, electric appliances, kitchen utensils and sometimes also books, lamps and articles of clothing.

Differences in meals

Let's now compare meals: *le petit déjeuner*, sometimes referred to in this country as *continental breakfast*, and an English type of *breakfast* can hardly be called similar. The difference is even greater between *le déjeuner*, traditionally the main three or four course meal in France, and *lunch*. Dinner, on the other hand is the main meal in Anglo-Saxon countries while *le diner* is very often nothing more than a light supper consisting of a soup, cold cuts and a quick dessert. How is one then to translate a sentence like "*Venez donc déjeuner chez nous dimanche?*" "*Why don't you come have dinner with us Sunday!*" seems the appropriate answer.

Translating the names of dishes in a country famed for its culinary inventiveness and savoir-faire is a very special problem. One way of dealing with it is simply to borrow. *Hors d'oeuvre, foie gras, mousse* and *champagne* have indeed passed into the English language. But unless one is looking for local color, adaptation is sometimes advisable and a *tarte aux pommes* may just have to become an apple pie.

Differences in occupations

Occupations in French and English speaking countries do not necessarily match. A *nanny* for instance is not a must in France, where day care centers for young mothers are both numerous and affordable, and therefore the concept has no real equivalent; although the term *baby sitter*, a recent borrowing, has replaced grand mothers or other relatives who traditionally took care of young children until the politics of economic change split families in all directions. The function of a *concierge*, essentially a woman's job in Parisian apartment buildings, can hardly be construed as similar to the duties of a janitor or custodian. Brokers and *courtiers* do not cover the same realities since investments are a standard service offered by most French banks. *Les cadres*, an often used and vague collective denomination, encompasses technicians and engineers, as well as administrators, teachers, researchers, commercial agents and civil servants. According to the 1946 Parodi-Croizet decree: "are considered as cadres, agents who possess technical, administrative, legal, commercial or financial training and who as proxy of their employer, exert authority over collaborators." In view of this definition, the adaptation which seems to impose itself is the term *middle management*, keeping in mind that a scale exists within this frame and that *cadre débutant* and *cadre supérieur* may be best rendered as *junior* and *senior executive*.

The legal profession is perhaps the best example of discrepancy in the matter. *Avocats*, *notaires* and *avoués* are all lawyers by U.S. definition but specialize in different areas of the law, and respectively correspond to the British terminology of *barristers*, *solicitors* and *attorneys*.

One way of dealing with the problem in translation would be perhaps to borrow the foreign term both for local color and accuracy.

Differences in institutions

State and local institutions may require adaptations in translation for the message to be intelligible to the target audience.

The French educational system with its rigid system of diplomas and different grading system could prove an enigma to English speakers. The baccalauréat which sanctions the end of secondary education is not quite the equivalent of a high school diploma since it also opens the door of admission to college and has in fact been given as the equivalent to two years of a U.S. college education. In a digital grading system which goes from 0 to 20 the passing grade or D is therefore 10. In addition, French teachers are hard graders and a very good grade or 15 out 20 could be construed as the equivalent of an A in the U.S, since a "mention très bien" or 15/20 and above corresponds to a diploma summa cum laude.

Social and political institutions deserve a special mention. *La Sécurité sociale*, a false friend, refers to the French national health and social benefit plan, the same for all the nation. The *allocations familiales* are a more difficult concept to comprehend this side of the Atlantic where this benefit, which refers to family supplemental income given to all parents whether rich, poor or middle class to help them raise their children, simply does not exist. And what of all those acronyms which are part of daily life in France, *S.N.C.F., E.D.F., P.etT.*? and which truly have no U.S. equivalents?

What of the administrative and political institutions? The administrative division of a country equal to only 1/50th of the United States cannot possibly be the same. A *région* just is not a state, nor a *département* a county; a *préfet* though he may have some of the attributes of a governor is not elected but nominated by the government. France, traditionally more centralized than the United States, requires an official *carte d'identité* with photo and particulars to be carried by all its citizens, while a simple driver's license is the standard I.D. needed in America.

Political and institutional references well-known to a French audience doubtless will need to be adapted. The literal translation of a message such as "*L'Elysée a fait pression sur Matignon pour une prompte résolution de l'impasse*" would indeed sound very cryptic to an Anglo-Saxon reader unaware that the Elysée palace is the dwelling place of the French president or the Hôtel Matignon the seat of the prime minister.

Political parties themselves are not divided along the same lines as in American politics but offer a wide range of variations, some nine different tendencies from the communist party to the extreme right or *Front National*, including two parties for environmentalists, although polarization, U.S. style, seems more and more to be the order of the day. Thus *"Etes-vous de gauche ou de droite?"* could be transcoded as *"Are you a liberal or a conservative?"*

Those are just a sample of the difficulties awaiting the translator along the path. Let me give an example of the resourcefulness to which a translator may have to resort, when confronted with the necessity of finding a satisfactory solution in the translation of a concept foreign to the linguistic group targeted. During the 1994 United Nations Cairo Conference on Population Growth, such americanisms as *female empowerment, reproductive health, family leave, reproductive rights*, all relatively new American concepts without any foreign counterparts, created massive problems when the original English drafted document had to be translated into the five other official languages of the U.N., Arabic, Chinese, Russian, Spanish and French. French translators, for instance, had to dig up a word which had been obsolete since the nineteenth century, *santé génésique*, in order to render the concept of *reproductive health*.[1]

Remember that when all else fails and even adaptation proves impossible, a short translator's note explaining the concept or situation is your very last resort. But keep in mind that concision here is the key word, for it is the duty and function of any good translator to appear as invisible as possible.

---

[1] Waldman, Peter. "Lost in Translation: How to Empower Women in Chinese." *Wall Street Journal* Sept. 13 1994.

In summary, it is not sufficient for a translator to know the S.L. thoroughly. The knowledge and understanding of its underlying civilization and culture is also a must. It has to constantly be kept up to date by taking trips to the country, reading its papers, magazines and literature, going to see its movies, watching its TV shows. A language is steeped in the culture which has given birth to it, and you cannot know one while ignoring the other.

Exercices: **L'adaptation**

Dans tous les cas où le concept, la coutume ou l'institution à laquelle se réfère le message à traduire n'existent pas dans la L.A. le traducteur se voit obligé de faire appel à une adaptation, c'est à dire à la recréation d'un concept, d'une coutume, d'une institution équivalente, ou dans les cas extrêmes à une explication succinte qui soit intelligible au groupe linguistique de la L.A.

A. L'adaptation

Faites les adaptations nécessaires à la traduction correcte des messages suivants.

1. *Nous nous tutoyons* depuis toujours.
2. *Je lui ai serré la main* et nous nous sommes séparés.
3. Se retrouvant par hasard après des années les deux hommes *s'embrassèrent* avec effusion.
4. Il est grand et mince: il *mesure un mètre quatre-vingt* et *pèse soixante quinze kilos*.
5. En France la réglementation de la vitesse sur les routes est la suivante: une vitesse maximum de *50 km* à l'heure est permise dans les *agglomérations*, de *90 km* heure en *zone rurale* et de *130 km* heure sur les autoroutes.
6. Va à *l'épicerie du coin* et rapporte-moi *un litre* de lait et *un kilo* de pommes.
7. Le budget de cette *société anonyme* est de l'ordre de *100 millions de francs*.
8. Cet été nous comptons rester *huit ou quinze jours* chez nos amis qui ont *une résidence secondaire* en Normandie.
9. L'an dernier j'ai été tellement occupé que je n'ai eu le temps d'aller au cinéma que *deux ou trois fois*.
10. Il n'y a pas *trente six façons* de s'y prendre. Seule celle-ci est la bonne.

11. Venez donc *déjeuner* chez nous *dimanche en huit*! Ce sera à la fortune du pot!

12. *La Comédie Française* donne une représentation de "L'Avare" *ce soir à 21 heures.*

13. Après demain c'est *ta fête.* Qui veux-tu inviter?

14. Le rayon des produits de beauté se trouve *au rez de chaussée* à gauche de l'escalier roulant.

15. Je vous offre *l'apéritif* à la maison ou au café du coin?

16. Ce bourgogne est délicieux bien que nous l'ayons acheté dans *une grande surface.*

17. Mes plats préférés en hiver? Un bon *pot au feu* avec comme dessert *une tarte Tatin.*

18. Il a voulu nous éblouir en nous emmenant déjeuner dans un restaurant *trois étoiles.*

B. L'adaptation (suite)

Faites les adaptations nécessaires à la traduction correcte des messages suivants.

1. J'ai réussi de justesse à mon examen de maths. Je n'ai eu que *la moyenne.*

2. Tu as fait beaucoup de progrès en anglais ce semestre. *Ta moyenne est passée de 11 à 14.*

3. *Elle vient de passer son baccalauréat et va sans doute préparer un diplôme d'études supérieures.*

4. Son fils a reçu sa maîtrise *avec la mention très bien.*

5. En France *les écoles libres* reçoivent des subsides de l'Etat tout comme *les écoles laïques.*

6. En France *les instituteurs* de l'enseignement primaire et *les professeurs* de l'enseignement secondaire sont *fonctionnaires d'état.*

7. Nous étions en infraction, aussi l'agent de police nous a-t-il réclamé notre *carte d'identité.*

8. Après la victoire de l'équipe régionale au championnat ce fut une atmosphère de fête par toute la ville. On se serait cru *au 14 juillet.*

9. *Le préfet* a envoyé ses nouvelles directives dans tout *le département*.

10. Hier , *au Palais Bourbon, les députés* se sont réunis pour voter *la motion de censure*.

11. *La Sécurité Sociale* fut accordée aux Français sous la quatrième République.

12. Le but des *allocations familiales* mises en place à la Libération fut d'encourager une recrudescence de la natalité.

13. La *S.N.C.F.* consent des tarifs spéciaux aux étudiants, aux personnes du troisième âge ainsi qu'aux *familles nombreuses*.

14. L'un des services des *P. et T.* est celui des chèques postaux.

15. Connaissez-vous les *DOM TOM*?

16. Historiquement *la bourgeoisie* française détient le pouvoir depuis le règne de Louis-Philippe.

17. A quelle tendance politique appartenez-vous, au *P.S.U.* ou au *R.P.R*?

18. Mon gendre est *cadre* chez Renault.

19. *Un notaire* s'occupe des affaires de succession, *un avocat* représente un client lors d'un procès et est chargé de la plaidoirie, tandis qu'*un avoué* doit préparer la procédure du procès.

20. C'est le *professeur* Montagnier qui a le premier découvert le virus du SIDA.

21. *Chère Madame* (formule épistolaire à une connaissance, Mme Dupont).

22. *Monsieur* (formule épistolaire à une personne que vous ne connaissez pas bien).

Chapter 12   Applying Translators' Devices To Literary Translation

The following pages are intended to acquaint the student with literary translation by offering, side by side with their suggested translation, sample sentences taken from masterpieces of French or Francophone literature in various genres and time periods. Each sentence contains a particular translation problem which is dealt with by using one of the four non literal translation devices introduced in previous chapters.

A. Transposition

1. Que l'homme contemple donc la nature entière dans sa haute et pleine majesté, *qu'il éloigne sa vue des* objets bas *qui l'environnent.* (Blaise Pascal, Pensées)

Let man therefore contemplate the whole of nature in its great and full majesty, let him *look away* from the lowly objects *around him.*

2. Je fus hier au Buron, j'en revins le soir. Je pensai pleurer *en voyant* la dégradation de cette terre. (Mme de Sévigné, Lettres)

I went yesterday to Buron and came back at night. I could have wept *at the sight of* the damage done to that land.

3. Tout le reste d'une conversation si désirée ne pouvait *manquer* d'être infiniment tendre. La pauvre Manon me raconta ses aventures, et je lui appris les miennes. (Abbé Prévost, Manon Lescaut)

The remainder of a conversation I had so desired could not *but* be infinitely tender. Poor Manon gave me an account of her adventures and I told her mine.

4. Ami, rire d'un vieillard *désespéré*, cela porte malheur; [mais] si tu dis *vrai*, *à l'action*! (Alfred de Musset, Lorenzaccio)

Friend, making fun of an old man *in despair* brings bad luck; but if you speak *the truth*, then *act on it*!

5. On était *au commencement d'avril* quand les primevères sont *écloses*, un vent tiède se roule sur les plates-bandes labourées, et les jardins, comme des femmes, semblent faire leur toilette pour les fêtes de l'été. (Gustave Flaubert, Madame Bovary)

It was *early April* when primroses are *out*, a warm wind wafts over tilled flower-beds and gardens, like women, seem to be dressing up for the summer parties.

6. *Il pleure* en mon coeur
   Comme *il pleut* sur la ville. (Verlaine, Romances sans paroles)
Tears fall within my heart
As *rain* upon the town.

7. *Aux approches de la guerre*, tous les évènements revêtent un nouveau vernis, qui est *le mensonge*. (Jean Giraudoux, La Guerre de Troie n'aura pas lieu)

As war draws near, every event assumes a new tone, everything *lies*.

8. Florent: Mais tu ne peux pas me reprocher éternellement cet argent. Qu'est-ce que tu veux que j'en fasse?

Thérèse: Oh rien, Florent. Tu *aurais beau* le jeter tout entier au vent, par la fenêtre, en riant, comme l'autre jour, que ma peine ne s'envolerait pas avec lui. (Jean Anouilh, La Sauvage)

Florent: But you can't hold this money against me for ever. What do you want me to do with it?

Thérèse: Oh nothing, Florent. *Even if* you threw it all out the window to the wind with a laugh, as you did the other day, my grief would not fly away with it.

9. Les Français sont *peut-être* des maîtres de la conversation, mais ce sont des enfants lorsqu'il s'agit de parler du temps. C'est là une spécialité dont les Anglais *sont les rois* incontestés. (Pierre Daninos, Les Carnets du major Thompson)

The French *may* be master conversationalists, but they are neophytes when it comes to discussing the weather. That is a domain in which the English *reign* unchallenged.

10. On ne meurt pas d'être né, d'avoir vécu, ni de vieillesse. On meurt de quelquechose [...] un cancer, une embolie, une congestion pulmonaire: c'est aussi brutal et imprévu que *l'arrêt* d'un moteur en plein ciel. (Simone de Beauvoir, Une Mort très douce)

You don't die from being born, from having lived, or from old age. You die from something, cancer, thrombosis, pneumonia: it is as brutal and unforeseen as an engine *coming to a stop* in mid air.

11. "Les épines, à quoi *servent*-elles?" Le petit prince ne renonçait jamais à une question, une fois qu'il l'avait posée. J'étais irrité [...] et je répondis n'importe quoi: "Les épines, ça ne *sert* à rien. C'est de la pure méchanceté de la part des fleurs." (Antoine de Saint Exupéry, Le Petit Prince)

"Thorns, what are they *for*?" The little prince never gave up after he had asked a question. I was annoyed and answered whatever came to mind: "Thorns, they have no *use*. It's pure wickedness on the flowers' part."

12. *Il m'est arrivé* de penser que tout ce travail [...] mon père l'eût aussi bien confié à l'un ou l'autre de ses aides. Ceux-ci ne manquaient pas d'expérience [...]. Quand enfin l'or entrait en fusion [...] je tressaillais en regardant mon père remuer la pâte encore lourde où le charbon de bois *achevait de se consommer*. (Camara Laye, L'Enfant noir)

The thought has *sometimes* crossed my mind that this operation might as well have been entrusted to anyone of my father's aides. They had plenty of experience. When finally the gold metal reached the melting stage, I would shudder, as I watched my father stir the paste, still quite heavy, in which the charcoal *was burning off*.

13. Joyeuse Pitou *entourée de* sa marmaille hurlante et sale, vociféra jusqu'à en perdre le souffle, et, de désespoir et d'épuisement, *finit par* s'effondrer sur le sol. (Jacques Stephen Alexis, Les Arbres musiciens)

Joyeuse Pitou, her dirty and howling brood *around* her, screamed until she was out of breath, and, in despair and exhaustion, *finally* collapsed on the ground.

14. Quand au sortir de la première guerre mondiale on en vint à oublier les griefs que l'on nourrissait à l'encontre des [noirs du] Congo, le jeune homme put louer un petit local sur la Rue-Derrière qui *ne tarda pas* à prospérer, et cela sans l'aide d'aucun maléfice.   (Raphaël Confiant, Eau de café)

When at the end of World War I the grievances which had been nurtured against blacks from the Congo were eventually forgotten, the young man was able to rent in the Rue Derrière a small shop which *soon* prospered, and quite without the help of any evil spell.

B. Modulation

1. Toute *leur vie était employée* non par lois, statuts ou règles mais selon leur vouloir et franc arbitre.   (Rabelais, Gargantua)

Their whole *life was spent* not following laws, statutes or rules but according to their own desires and free will.

2. Ce que nous appelons ordinairement amis et amitiés ne sont qu'*accointances et familiarités nouées* par quelque occasion ou commodité. (Michel de Montaigne, Essais)

What we commonly call friends and friendships are no more than *acquaintances and close associations contracted* by chance or for convenience.

3. Un après-midi j'étais là, regardant beaucoup, parlant peu et écoutant le moins que je pouvais, lorsque je fus abordé par l'un des plus bizarres personnages de ce pays *où Dieu n'en a pas laissé manquer*.   (Denis Diderot, Le Neveu de Rameau)

One afternoon I was there, observing a lot, not saying much and listening as little as possible, when I was accosted by one of the most bizarre characters in this land *where God saw to it that they should not lack*.

4. Ou tu ne penses pas ce que tu dis, ou bien *tu fais mieux* que tu ne penses. (Montesquieu, Les Lettres persanes)

Either you don't believe what you say, or *you are more successful* than you believe.

5. Au loin, par intervalles, *on entendait* les sourds mugissements de la cataracte du Niagara qui dans le calme de la nuit se prolongeaient de désert en désert et expiraient à travers les forêts solitaires. (Alphonse de Chateaubriand, Le Génie du christianisme)

Intermittently, in the distance, the dull roar of Niagara Falls *could be heard*, which in the stillness of the night echoed from wild to wild and died away through the lonely forests.

6. *Je me fis un plaisir* de lui apprendre [...] que Chopin, bien loin d'être démodé, était le musicien préféré de Debussy. "Tiens, c'est amusant" me dit en

souriant finement [Madame de Cambremer-Legrandin]. (Marcel Proust, Sodome et Gomorrhe)

It gave me pleasure to inform her that Chopin, far from being out of fashion, was Debussy's favorite composer. "Well, that's funny." Madame de Cambremer-Legrandin replied with a subtle smile.

7. Tout compte fait, mieux valait que Thérèse disparût, on l'oublierait *plus vite*, les gens *perdraient l'habitude* de parler d'elle. (François Mauriac, Thérèse Desqueyroux)

All things considered, it was better that Thérèse should disappear, she would be forgotten *sooner,* people *would stop* talking about her.

8. On a tout à se dire, mon prince. *L'occasion ne se présentera peut-être pas deux fois.* (Jean Anouilh, Beckett)

We have a lot to talk about, my Lord. *This opportunity might not be found again.*

9. *La brûlure du soleil gagnait* mes joues et j'ai senti des gouttes de sueur s'amasser dans mes sourcils. [...] A cause de cette brûlure que je ne pouvais plus supporter [...] *j'ai fait un pas*, un seul pas en avant. [...] *La mer a charié un souffle épais et ardent.* (Albert Camus, L'Etranger)

The sun was now beginning to scorch my cheeks and I felt beads of sweat gathering in my eyebrows. Because of this sensation which I could no longer bear *I took one step*, one single step forward. *A thick burning gust of wind drifted from the sea.*

10. *Tout est permis aux héros.* (Jean Paul Sartre, Huis clos)
Heroes can do no wrong.

11. Je ne crois pas du tout que j'ai cherché en [l'homme que j'aimerais un jour] un succédané de mon père; *je tenais à mon indépendance*, j'exercerais un métier, j'écrirais, j'aurais une vie personnelle. (Simone de Beauvoir, Les Mémoires d'une jeune fille rangée)

I do not at all believe that I was looking for a father image in the man whom I would love one day; *I valued my independence*, I would hold a job, write, have a life of my own.

12. *Après avoir dépassé le milieu du pont*, [le colonel Nicholson] se pencha au-dessus de la balustrade, comme il le faisait tous les cinq ou six mètres [...].

L'oeil du maître avait aperçu du premier coup le bourrelet d'eau prononcé causé à la surface par une charge.   (Pierre Boulle, Le Pont de la rivière Kwaï)

After he was more than half way across the bridge, Colonel Nicholson leaned over the parapet, as he had done every five or 6 yards.   The master's eye had at once noticed the marked ripple caused on the surface by an underwater load.

13. Mon camarade suit [le requin], l'approche, le prend par la queue, *partagé entre* le désir de tirer fort [...] *et* la crainte qu'il ne se retourne pour mordre. (Jacques Cousteau, Le Monde du silence)

My friend follows the shark, swims up to it, grabs it by the tail, *torn between* the desire to pull hard *and* the fear that it should turn around and bite.

14. Je sentais la sueur dégouliner sur mon front, le long de mon nez, sur mes joues et se former en goutelettes à la pointe de mon menton *tellement m'échauffait la colère.*   (Mongo Beti, Le Pauvre Christ de Bomba)

I could feel sweat trickling down my brow, along my nose, over my cheeks and form droplets at the tip of my chin, *I was burning so with anger.*

C. Equivalence

1. Si je compare tout le reste de *ma vie*, quoiqu'avec la grâce de Dieu *je l'ai passée douce* et sauf la perte d'un tel ami exempte d'affliction [...] si je la compare toute aux quatre années qu'il m'a été donné de jouir de la douce compagnie de ce personnage, ce n'est que fumée, ce n'est qu'une nuit obscure et ennuyeuse. (Michel de Montaigne, Essais)

When I compare all the rest of *my life*, although by the grace of God *it has been kind to me* and save the loss of such a friend free from affliction, when I compare it with the four years during which I was given the opportunity to enjoy the sweet company of this man, it is nothing but smoke, nothing but a dark and tedious night.

2. *Qui ne fait des châteaux en Espagne*?
   Picrochole, Pyrrhus, la laitière, enfin tous,
   Autant les sages que les fous. (Jean de la Fontaine, Perrette et le pot au lait)
   Who has not built castles in the air?
   Picrochole, Pyrrhus, the milkmaid, everyone,
   The wise and the foolish.

3. Elle a des façons de parler qui *me mettent hors de moi*. (Marivaux, Le Jeu de l'amour et du hasard)
   She has a way of speaking which *infuriates* me.

4. On s'ennuie de tout, mon ange, c'est une loi de la nature; *ce n'est pas ma faute*.[...] Si, par exemple, j'ai eu juste autant d'amour que toi de vertu, et c'est sûrement beaucoup dire, il n'est pas étonnant que l'un ait fini en même temps que l'autre. *Ce n'est pas ma faute*. (Pierre Choderlos de Laclos, Les Liaisons dangereuses)

One tires of everything, my angel, it is a law of nature; *I cannot help it*. If, for instance, I had only as much love as you, virtue, and that is probably saying much, it comes as no surprise that they should both end at the same time. *I cannot help it*.

5. Lequel de vous, messieurs, demanda le magistrat [...] s'appelle Andréa Cavalcanti? -Mais quel est *donc* cet Andréa Cavalcanti, demanda Danglars presque égaré. -Un ancien forçat échappé du bagne de Toulon. -Et quel crime a-t-il commis? -Il est prévenu, dit le commissaire de sa voix impassible, d'avoir assassiné le nommé Caderousse, son ancien compagnon de chaîne, au moment

où il sortait de chez le comte de Monte Cristo. (Alexandre Dumas, Le Comte de Monte Cristo)

-Who among you, gentlemen, answers to the name Andrea Cavalcanti? asked the magistrate. -Who *on earth* is Andrea Cavalcanti? asked Danglars almost distraught. -A former convict who ran away from the Toulon forced labor camp. -What's his crime? -He is charged, replied the police superintendent in his calm and collected voice, with having murdered the said Caderousse, his former chain companion, as he was leaving the house of Count Monte Cristo.

6. [Musset] *avait fait des niches* aux *classiques à perruques* de 1830; il aimait les grands classiques de 1660, y compris Racine, *la bête noire* en ce temps-là des *esprits larges*. (Gustave Lanson, Histoire de la littérature française)

Musset *had played pranks* on the *unconditionals of classicism* in 1830; he loved the great classics of 1660, including Racine, who, at the time, was the *pet aversion* of *progressive minds*.

7. "Cette enfant est surchargée de travail, elle se fatigue beaucoup. De plus on lui fait trop sentir, je crains, sa pauvreté. "[...] -"Hélas, me répondit maître Mouche, *il faut bien* la préparer à la vie. On n'est pas sur terre pour s'amuser et pour *faire ses quatre cents volontés.*" (Anatole France, Le Crime de Sylvestre Bonnard)

"The child is overworked, she is tiring herself out. In addition, I fear, she is made to feel too conscious of her poverty." "Unfortunately, replied Schoolmaster Mouche, *we do have to* prepare her for life. You are not here on earth to have fun or *do as you please.*"

8. Le renard était assis au pied de l'acacia. Il regardait le coq perché sur une haute branche et il voulait le manger [...] Le coq ne voulait pas descendre. Il disait qu'il aimait mieux être mangé par ses maîtres que par le renard. "-Je préfère mourir de ma mort naturelle". "-*Qu'il est bête*, mais la mort naturelle, *ce n'est pas ça du tout.*" "-Tu ne sais pas ce que tu dis, renard. Il faut bien que les maîtres nous tuent *un jour ou l'autre.* C'est la loi commune, il n'y a personne qui puisse y échapper. Le dindon lui même, qui *fait tant son rengorgé, y passe* comme les autres. *On le mange aux marrons.*" (Marcel Aymé, Contes du chat perché)

The fox was sitting at the foot of the acacia. He was watching the rooster nested high up on a branch and planned to eat him. The rooster refused to come down. He said that he would rather be eaten by his masters than by the fox. "-I prefer to die a natural death". "-But, *silly, that's not what a natural death is about.*"
"-You don't know what you are saying, fox. Our masters must kill us *sooner or later.* It's our common fate, none of us can escape it. Even the turkey, who *likes to give himself airs, has to face the music. They accomodate him with chestnut stuffing.*"

9. *Pour moi c'était une histoire finie,* et j'étais venu là *sans y penser.* (Albert Camus, L'Etranger)

As far as I was concerned the matter was closed, and I had come here *without giving it another thought.*

10. [Balducci] se leva et se dirigea vers l'Arabe en tirant une cordelette de sa poche. "Qu'est-ce que tu fais?" demanda sèchement Daru. Balducci, interdit, lui montra la corde. "-*Ce n'est pas la peine*". (Albert Camus, L'Exil et le royaume)

Balducci got up and walked toward the Arab taking a small rope from his pocket. "What are you doing?" Daru asked dryly. Balducci, disconcerted, showed him the rope. "-*There's no need.*"

11. Oui, tu connais le prix du mal, et si tu dis que je suis un lâche c'est *en connaissance de cause, hein?* (Jean Paul Sartre, Huis clos)

Yes, you know what evil costs, and when you call me a coward *you know from experience, isn't that so?*

12. Monsieur: je n'ai pas besoin de vos services, Madame.
La concierge: *Ça c'est trop fort!* C'est *pourtant* vous qui m'avez priée, *c'est malheureux,* j'ai pas eu de témoins, *je vous ai cru sur parole, je me suis laissée faire.* Je suis trop bonne. (Eugène Ionesco, Le Nouveau Locataire)

Gentleman: I don't need your services, Madame.

Caretaker: *Well, how do you like that? And* you're the one who begged me! *Pity* I got no witnesses, *I took you at your word,* and *let you take advantage of me.* I'm too kind.

13. *Je prétends* que *le tout* n'est pas *encore* de se marier, mais de rester ensemble *devant le changement des saisons.* (Simone Schwarz Bart, Pluie et vent sur Télumée Miracle)

In my opinion getting married *is one thing* but *what counts* is sticking it out together *when the wind turns.*

14. Le Chinois dit: "Je vais à Sadec cette nuit, je suis obligé, je reviens dans deux jours. Le chauffeur va t'apporter le repas. On te reconduira à la pension avant de partir." Ils se douchent. Elle lui parle de la quarantaine dont elle est l'objet au lycée. Elle rit. "-On ne me parle plus au lycée à cause de toi" "-*C'est une idée que tu te fais.*" "-Non, il y a eu des plaintes de mères d'élèves." Il rit avec elle. Il demande de quoi a peur cette société. (Marguerite Duras, L'Amant de la Chine du nord)

The Chinese says: "I'm going to Sadec tonight, I have to, I'll be back in two days. The chauffeur will bring you your meal. We will drive you to the boarding school before leaving." They take a shower. She tells him of her being ostracized at school. She laughs. "-No one speaks to me at school anymore, because of you." "-*You're imagining things.*" "-No, there were complaints from some students' mothers." He laughs with her. He wants to know what these people are afraid of.

D. Adaptation

1. Maître de philosophie: *La voix A se forme en ouvrant fort la bouche: A.*
M. Jourdain: A, A, oui.
M.P.   *La voix E se forme en rapprochant la mâchoire d'en bas*
                             de celle d'en haut: A, E.
M.J.   A, E, A, E. Ma foi, oui. Ah que cela est beau!
M.P.   *Et la voix I, en rapprochant encore davantage les machoi-*
                             res l'une de l'autre, et écartant les deux coins de la bou-
                             che vers les oreilles. A, E, I.
                                                     (Molière, Le Bourgeois gentilhomme)
English vowels in the alphabet being sounded quite differently
from French vowels, an adaptation of Molière's text to fit English
phonetics seems inevitable.

Philosophy master: *Vowel A is formed by opening your mouth*
slightly with its corners pulled apart.
Mr. Jourdain: A, A, yes.
P.M.   *Vowel E is formed by bringing the lower jaw*
closer to the upper jaw while pulling the corners of your mouth
even further apart: A, E.
M.J.   A, E, A, E,. My word, yes. How beautiful!
P.M.   *And vowel I by dropping the lower jaw, then*
bringing the jaws together with your tongue rising toward your
palate. A, E, I.

2. La façade de la pension donne sur un jardinet [...]. Le long de cette façade,
entre la maison et le jardinet, règne un cailloutis en cuvette large *d'une toise*,
devant lequel est une allée sablée bordée de géraniums.   (Honoré de Balzac, Le
Père Goriot)
The problem is the conversion of measure units used in nineteenth
century France before the acceptance of the metric system. Since
most dictionaries will not list such obsolete words, you will have to
resort to a French monolingual dictionary to figure out the metric
system equivalent before you can do the conversion.

The front of the boarding house overlooks a small garden. Along
the front, between the house and the garden runs a sunken cobbled
space, some *6 feet* wide, and beyond, a sanded path lined with
geraniums.

3. Se dénoncer, grand Dieu! se livrer! [...] A son âge, après avoir été ce qu'il
était! Si encore il était jeune! Mais vieux, *être tutoyé* par le premier venu, être
fouillé par le garde-chiourme, recevoir le coup de bâton de l'argousin, avoir les
pieds nus dans des souliers ferrés! (Victor Hugo, Les Misérables)

*The lack of distinction between "tu" and "vous" in addressing
others in English often creates a problem in translation. Since the
familiar "tu" form can be used as a means of disrespect by a
superior to an inferior, as in this context, compensation in the form
of a verb indicating disparagement may be substituted.*

To confess, good God, to turn himself in! At his age, after what
he had become! If only he were young! But, an old man, *to be
talked down to* by anyone, to be searched by the warder, hit by the
turnkey's club, with bare feet in hobnailed shoes!

4. Madame Alvarez mit une main sur son sein. -En mon âme et conscience,
Gaston, si ça n'était que pour vous et pour moi je vous dirais: "Emmenez
Gilberte où vous voudrez, je vous la confie les yeux fermés". Mais il y a les
autres...Vous êtes connu mondialement. Sortir en tête à tête avec vous, pour
une femme, c'est...
Gaston Lachaille perdit patience. -Bon, bon j'ai compris! Vous voulez me
faire croire que de *goûter* avec moi, voilà Gigi compromise. (Colette, Gigi)

*Meals do not always quite correspond between French and Anglo-
Saxon cultures. Here a "goûter" refers to a late afternoon snack
taken by children after school which usually consists of hot
chocolate, tea or milk and pastries or bread and butter with jam.
English tea, which is a late afternoon light meal for both children
and adults in England seems a close enough equivalent.*

Madame Alvarez placed her hand over her breast. Upon my soul,
Gaston, if we were the only two people concerned I would say to
you: "Bring Gilberte wherever you want, I entrust her to you with
my eyes closed." But there are others... You are known the world
over. For a woman to go out with you alone is...

Gaston Lachaille lost his patience. Oh all right, I see what you
are getting at! You want me to believe that by *having tea* with me
Gigi will be compromised.

5. Les Puybaraud étaient les derniers devant qui [Brigitte] eût consenti volontiers à montrer quelque faiblesse. "Ils vont me prendre pour *une commerçante*" se disait-elle. (François Mauriac, La Pharisienne)
In this context the term "commerçant", "shopkeeper" has a negative social connotation: someone materialistic with intellectual limitations. A simple translation of the word would prove inadequate and an explanatory adaptation is necessary.

The Puybarauds were the last people to whom Brigitte would have wanted to show any weakness. "They will take me for *some petty bourgeois*" she would say to herself.

6. J'entendis un chuchotement qui disait: "-En quelle section es-tu?" D'abord je ne compris pas que c'était mon voisin qui me parlait car il restait parfaitement impassible, le regard fixé sur son emploi du temps. Mais je vis tout à coup le coin de sa bouche remuer imperceptiblement, et il répéta sa question. J'admirai sa technique, et en essayant de l'imiter, je répondis: "-Sixième A2." "-Chic! dit-il. Moi aussi. [...] A cause du latin, je *redouble la sixième.*" Je ne compris pas ce mot, et je crus qu'il voulait dire qu'il avait l'intention de *redoubler d'efforts*. (Marcel Pagnol, Le Temps des secrets)
The adaptation problem here is not the grade conversion since "la sixième" does correspond to "sixth grade", although "septième" and "cinquième" would respectively be fourth and seventh grade, but it is the translation of a play on words: "redoubler une classe" and "redoubler d'efforts", the latter being an idiomatic expression meaning "to try twice as hard." A solution can be found in a similar play on words with "to repeat", the objective for the translator being to convey the idea that the narrator is a naïve and inexperienced young boy.

I heard a whisper saying: "-In what section are you?" At first I did not realize that it was the boy sitting next to me who was speaking, since he remained perfectly impassive and kept his eyes on his study schedule. But all of a sudden I noticed the corner of his mouth moving imperceptibly as he reiterated his question. I admired his technique, and trying to imitate him replied: "-Sixth A2" "-Great! he said, me too! I'm *repeating sixth grade* because of latin." I did not understand that phrase and thought that he meant he wanted *to repeat his lessons*.

7. L'été de mes quinze ans, à la fin de l'année scolaire, j'allai deux ou trois fois canoter *au bois* avec Zaza et d'autres camarades.   (Simone de Beauvoir, Mémoires d'une jeune fille rangée)

To Parisians "le bois" refers to the bois de Boulogne, a large wooded space west of the city. A translation would have to make this explicit to Anglophone readers unfamiliar with this fact.

The summer I turned fifteen, at the end of the school year, I went boating in *the Bois de Boulogne* on a couple of occasions with Zaza and a few other friends.

8. L'asile de vieillards est à Marengo, *à 80 kilomètres* d'Alger.   (Albert Camus, L'Etranger)

Conversion of distances are essential for an American public to understand.

The old people's home is in Marengo, *some 50 miles* from Algiers.

Exercices Généraux:
Les Procédés de Traduction non Littéraux

A. Lisez les extraits littéraires suivants ainsi que leurs traductions. Déterminez si, pour les passages en italique traduits, vous avez affaire à une transposition, une modulation, une équivalence ou une adaptation.

1. Pathelin: Je m'en veux aller à la foire [...]
   Guillemette: Mais *vous n'avez ni sou ni maille.* Qu'y ferez-vous?
   Pathelin: C'est mon secret. Si je n'apporte assez de drap pour vous et moi, alors traitez moi de menteur. Quelle couleur préférez-vous? [...]
   Guillemette: Apportez ce que vous pouvez. *Un emprunteur ne choisit pas.*
   (La Farce de Maître Pathelin)
   Pathelin: I intend to go to the fair.
   Guillemette: But *you don't have a penny.* What will you do there?
   Pathelin: The secret's mine. If I don't bring back enough cloth for you and me, then call me a liar. What color do you prefer?
   Guillemette: Bring what you can. *Beggars can't be choosers.*

2.   Le meunier repartit:
   "Je suis âne, il est vrai, j'en conviens, je l'avoue.
   Mais que dorénavant on me blâme, on me loue,
   Qu'on dise quelquechose, ou qu'on ne dise rien
   J'en veux faire à ma tête."
   (Jean de La Fontaine, Le Meunier, son fils et l'âne)
               And the miller replied:
   "I'm an ass, it is true, I admit, I confess,
    But whether hereafter they give me blame or praise
    Speak their mind, hold their peace
    I shall do as I please."

3. Le génie et les grands talents manquent souvent; quelquefois aussi les *seules* occasions: tels peuvent être loués de ce qu'ils ont fait, et tels de ce qu'ils auraient fait. (La Bruyère, Les Caractères**)**

There is often a lack of genius and great talent; sometimes, too, of opportunity *only*: some may be praised for what they have achieved, others for what they might have achieved.

4. *Il se fit* alors un grand silence; *on cessa de danser* et les violons *ne jouèrent plus, tant on était attentif à contempler* les grandes beautés de cette inconnue. *On n'entendait qu'un bruit confus*: "Ah, qu' *elle est belle!*" Le roi même, *tout* vieux qu'il était, *ne laissait pas* de la regarder, et de dire tout bas à la reine qu'il y avait longtemps qu'il n'avait vu une si belle et si aimable personne. (Charles Perrault, Cendrillon)

Then a great silence *fell upon the assembly; all dancing stopped* and the violins *came to a halt, so intense was the attention bestowed upon* the great charms of this stranger. *Only a confused rumor could be heard*: "Oh, what *a beauty!*" Even the king, old *though* he was, *could not help* looking at her, whispering to the queen that it was a long time since he had seen such a beautiful and lovable person.

5. *Il me faut* des torrents, des rochers, des sapins, des bois noirs, des montagnes, des chemins raboteux à monter et descendre." (Jean Jacques Rousseau, Confessions)

I need torrents, rocks, fir-trees, dark woods, mountains, bumpy paths to follow up and down.

6. Le lendemain à neuf heures [...] Julien descendit de sa prison pour aller dans la grande salle du *palais de justice*. *[Il] avait bien dormi*, il était fort calme, et *n'*éprouvait d'*autre* sentiment *qu'*une pitié philosophique pour cette foule d'envieux qui, sans cruauté, *allait* applaudir à son arrêt de mort. [...] *On eût dit* ce jour là *qu'il n'avait pas vingt ans*. (Stendhal, Le Rouge et le noir)

The following day at nine, Julien came from his prison cell down to the main hall of the *Law Court*. *He had had a good night's sleep*, was quite composed, and felt *nothing beyond* philosophical pity toward the envious crowd *about to* applaud, without cruelty, his death sentence. On that day *he barely looked twenty*.

7. *Si* la crise industrielle tirait à sa fin, si les usines rouvraient une à une, l'état de guerre *n'en restait pas moins déclaré, sans que* la paix fut désormais possible. (Emile Zola, Germinal)

Even though the industrial crisis was drawing to an end, and the factories reopening one by one, the state of war *was still on*, and peace no longer possible.

8. Deux hommes restaient encore, les mains dans les poches [...], le bonnet de laine *enfoncé* jusqu'aux yeux.   (Guy de Maupassant, Contes du jour et de la nuit)

Two men stayed on, hands in their pockets, their woolen cap *down* to their eyes.

9. Chère imagination, ce que j'aime *surtout* en toi, c'est que tu *ne pardonnes pas*. (André Breton, Manifeste du surréalisme)

Dear imagination, what I like *best* about you is that you *leave no room for error*.

10. A quoi faire servir cette force que je sens *en moi*? Comment *tirer le meilleur parti* de moi-même? Est-ce en me dirigeant vers un but? Mais ce but, comment le choisir? Comment le connaître, aussi longtemps qu'il n'est pas atteint? (André Gide, Les Faux monnayeurs)

How am I to use the strength I feel *inside*? How *make the best* of myself? By heading for a goal? How am I to select that goal, know what it is, as long as it has not been reached?

11. En été deux fois par semaine, Adrienne allait au jardin cueillir des fleurs *sous les yeux attentifs* de son père [...]. Le reste du temps, sa tâche *se réduisait à* parcourir la maison [...] et à s'assurer que tout était en ordre. (Julien Green, Adrienne Mesurat)

In the summer twice a week, Adrienne would go and pick flowers in the garden carefully watched by her father. The rest of the time her *only* duty was to go through the house and see to it that everything was tidy.

12. *Ce qui me plaît surtout en lui* c'est qu'il *possède* et cultive une voix agréable, grave et mélodieuse. (Jean Giono, Naissance de l'Odyssée)

What I most like about him is this pleasant, deep and melodious voice *of his* which he cultivates.

13. Estragon: Qu'est-ce que nous avons fait hier?
    Vladimir: Ce que nous avons fait hier?
    Estragon: Oui.
    Vladimir: *Ma foi...* (se fâchant) Pour jeter le doute, *à toi le pompon. Pour moi, nous étions* ici. (Samuel Beckett, En attendant Godot)

Estragon: What did we do yesterday?
Vladimir: Yesterday? What did we do?
Estragon: Yes.
Vladimir: *Well...* (getting angry)   When it comes to raising doubts, *you take the cake. We must have been* here.

14. Je passai des vers à la prose.[...] A peine eus-je commencé d'écrire, je posai ma plume *pour jubiler.* Rien ne me troublait plus que de voir mes *pattes de mouche* échanger peu à peu leur luisance de feux follets *contre* la terne consistance de la matière: *c'était la réalisation de l'imaginaire.* (Jean Paul Sartre, Les Mots)

I went from verse to prose. No sooner did I start writing when I put down my pen *in exultation.* Nothing moved me more than to watch my *chicken scratch* exchange, little by little, its will o'the wisp gleam *for* the dull consistency of matter: *fantasy had come into being.*

B. Select sentences from a French literary text or magazine and in your translation give:
- *one transposition*
- *one modulation*
- *one equivalence*
- *one adaptation*

Chapter 13   **Translating Titles**

General advice

A title is very important to a translation. It is unfortunately all too tempting for the novice translator to start an assignment by translating the title right away, usually dismissing it with a word for word translation, and then move on to the rest of the text as being alone worthy of any effort.

Titles serve a double purpose. Their first function is that of an abstract, insofar as they must reflect the theme of the excerpt, book or article, in order to prepare the reader for what is to follow. At the same time they must be tantalizing and try to make an impact on the potential reader. Authors and publishers alike are very aware of this fact: the title of any written material along with the book cover serve as an ad to catch the readers' eye and entice to further reading. Therefore it is ultimately the title which will promote the book, and very special care should be devoted to it.

Here are a few hints on determining what is to be done about titles in translation.

- **Titles should be translated last**, only after you have reached a thorough understanding of the text. You should be able to summarize the main lines of the text before you even attempt to decide on its title. After all, a title serves as the key that opens the door to a story.
- **You can afford to take more liberty with the title** than with the text itself. At your disposal you also have the same tools:

literal translation, when there are no structural or cultural obstacles; transposition, if a more idiomatic touch is needed; modulation, to give the title an interesting twist and focus both for stylistic and semantic reasons; equivalence to render idioms; or even adaptation, for all cases in which the original title is untranslatable due to metalinguistic obstacles.

- **Be aware that English and French favor different approaches when it comes to titles**.
  French has a marked preference for brief titles, usually nouns:
  ex. *Les Essais* (Montaigne), *Les Méditations* (A. de Lamartine), *Les Misérables* (V. Hugo), *L'Education sentimentale* (G. Flaubert), *Le Rouge et le noir* (Stendhal); *L'Assommoir* (Zola), *Une Vie* (G. de Maupassant), *Le Rire* (H. Bergson), *Colline* (J. Giono), *Les Mandarins* (S. de Beauvoir), *La Nausée* (J.P. Sartre), *La Peste* (A. Camus), *L'Espoir* (A. Malraux), *Le Petit Prince* (A. de Saint Exupéry), *L'Oeuvre au noir* (M. Yourcenar), *L'Amant* (M. Duras), *Le Procès verbal* (J. M. Le Clézio), *Le Rivage des Syrtes* (J. Gracq), *Belle du Seigneur* (A. Cohen), etc.
  Whereas English loves verbs and does not mind entire sentences:
  ex. *She Stoops to Conquer* (Goldsmith), *The Importance of Being Earnest* (Oscar Wilde), *Where Angels Fear to Tread* (E.M. Forster), *For Whom the Bell Tolls* (E. Hemingway), *Brideshead Revisited* (E. Waugh), *The Lady's not for Burning* (Christopher Frye), *The Iceman Cometh* (E. O'Neil), *The Mirror Cracked* (A.Christie), *Rosencrantz and Guildenstern are Dead* (Tom Stoppard), etc.
  This noun versus verb preference should be kept in mind for a transposition whenever possible, that is to say whenever a noun in the French title has a corresponding verb. "Choosing a Husband" and "Educating the Masses" to translate "Le Choix d'un mari" and "L'Education des masses" sounds better and more dynamic in English than "The Choice of a Husband" or "The Education of the Masses".

Translation devices applied to the translation of titles

The following list of titles in translation contains some interesting ideas for the would be translator.

1. **Remembrance of Things Past**: with its title borrowed from Shakespeare, the landmark English translation of Marcel Proust's *A la Recherche du temps perdu* by C.K. Scott Moncrieff is nothing short of an adaptation, albeit one with a real catch and a poetic ring. *A Search for Lost Time* a more recent translation by James Grieve has tried to remain more literal and faithful to the original, without being as fetching.

2. **She Came to Stay**: which translates Simone de Beauvoir's first novel *L'Invitée* is one of those rare examples in which a translation can actually improve on the original. It does so by cleverly anticipating on the plot with the use of a sentence-title in the English way, while the French title remains non-committal and more cryptic.

3. **No Exit**: the English rendering of Jean Paul Sartre's famous play *Huis clos* in which, after their death, three villainous protagonists find themselves locked in a room symbolizing hell with no hope of escape and no future except tormenting one another, is also an adaptation derived from the plot, since *huis clos*, a legal term meaning *trial behind closed doors*, is not a concept altogether well known in Anglo-Saxon countries.

4. **Lucifer and the Lord**: for Sartre's *Le Diable et le bon Dieu*, has the merit of retaining both the original's alliteration and antithetical rythm.

5. **Around the World in Eighty Days**: is an adept transposition of Jules Verne's *Le Tour du monde en 80 jours* which manages to remain both close to the French title and idiomatic.

6. **The Would be Gentleman**: an interesting modulation-adaptation of Molière's challenging title *Le Bourgeois gentilhomme*. In this version, the translator, Morris Bishop, does away with the concept of bourgeois and middle class to concentrate instead on the English calque for gentilhomme and tabulate on the main character's chief fault, his vain and unreasonable desire to be socially better than he is.

Many **adaptations** are in fact nothing but recreations of titles. Here poetic license can take over, especially when the translator is himself a celebrated writer, as in the case of Christopher Fry, whose *Tiger at the Gates* for Giraudoux's *La Guerre de Troie n'aura pas lieu* or *Rings Around the Moon* for Anouilh's *L'Invitation au château* stray very far from the original.

So do titles which, by breaking away from either too bland or abstract French counterparts, are more explanatory in translation than in the SL, a gimmick deemed necessary to entice an Anglo-American readership, titles such as *The Lost Domain* for Alain Fournier's *Le Grand Meaulnes*, or *Wind, Sand and Stars* for Saint Exupéry's *Terre des hommes*, *Red gloves* for Sartre's *Les Mains sales*, or *A Change of Heart* for Michel Butor's *La Modification*, and *The Order of Things* for Michel Foucault's *Les Mots et les choses*.

Sometimes all that is needed is a **word modulation**, be it a preposition, adjective or noun modulation, as evidenced by the following renditions.

> The School *for* Wives: L'Ecole *des* femmes (Molière)
> The Roads *to* Freedom: Les Chemins *de* la liberté (Sartre)
> A Very *Easy* Death: Une Mort très *douce* (Beauvoir)
> *Masters'* of the Dew: Les *Gouverneurs* de la rosée (Jacques Roumain)
> Death of a *Nobody*: Mort de *quelqu'un* (Jules Romains)
> Four*some*: S*cène* à quatre (Ionesco)

A modulation may help keep the translation close to the original phonetically if not semantically.

> The Vipers' *Nest*: Le *Noeud* de vipères (Mauriac)
> The Satin *Slipper* : Le *Soulier* de satin (Paul Claudel)

The following modulation is double, abstract to concrete and plural to singular.

> The S*eed* and the Fr*uit*: Les S*emailles* et les *moissons* (Henri Troyat)

A modulation may be able to save a pun.

> L'Importance d'être *constant*: The Importance of Being E*arnest* (Oscar Wilde).

Here the word modulation is crucial since the title is a play on the words earnest and Ernest, name of the main character, but the French translator has saved the day with his trove of a corresponding first name and adjective in the target language. More often than not, however, a play on words just cannot be saved, as in the case of Patrick Modiano's *La Place de l'Etoile* which refers both to the famous Parisian square where the Arch of Triumph stands, and to the place where Jews had to display the yellow star of David on a coat over their heart, during the occupation of France by Nazi Germany. The English title simply reads *A Jewish Story*.

A transposition-modulation, might solve a translation problem.
> as in Malraux's *Man's Fate* for *La Condition humaine*.
> *Fruits of the Earth* for André Gide's *Les Nourritures terrestres*.

An equivalence will work for idioms.
> *Death on the Installment Plan* for Céline's *Mort à crédit*.

Or cliché-titles.
> *The Prime of Life*: *La Force de l'âge* , and *The Force of Circumstance*: *La Force des choses* (Beauvoir).

And sometimes, quite simply, a **literal translation** is just about the best thing.
> *The Flowers of Evil*: Baudelaire's *Les Fleurs du mal*; *Heartbreak*: Louis Aragon's *Le Crève-coeur*; *The Bald Soprano*: Ionesco's *La Cantatrice chauve*; *Being and Nothingness*: Sartre's *L'Etre et le néant*; *The Stranger*: Camus' *L'Etranger*; *Waiting for Godot*: Beckett's *En attendant Godot*.

But one must beware of literal translation when the phrase to be translated is in fact an idiom, as happened in the case of François Truffaut's classical film *Les 400 Coups*, inacurately rendered as *The 400 Blows* in the English version. The French title should have been replaced within its proper context, the idiomatic expression *faire les 400 coups* which, in English, is the equivalent of *to sow one's wild oats* or *to run wild*. A more fitting title would have been perhaps *Wild Oats*.

And occasionally a translation may even be superior to the original, proving the old adage "traduttore, traditore" false, as in the French version of the American movie title *The Truth about Cats and Dogs*, *Comme un chien dans un jeu de filles* which cleverly plays on words around the expression *"comme un chien dans un jeu de quilles"*.

Exercices: Les Titres

Traduire le titre d'un article ou d'un livre n'est pas quelquechose de secondaire: n'oubliez pas que c'est le titre qui va accrocher ou rebuter votre lecteur potentiel. En général les titres se traduisent en dernier, après que le traducteur connaisse son texte à fond. C'est seulement à ce moment-là qu'il sera en mesure de décider s'il faut garder le titre original en faisant une traduction littérale, faire une transposition qui sonne de façon plus idiomatique dans la L.A., risquer une modulation qui soit stylistiquement et sémantiquement plus intéressante, ou même s'il faut carrément se lancer dans une adaptation au cas où le titre de la L.D. serait intraduisible.

A. Le jeu des titres

Essayez de traduire les titres des oeuvres françaises et francophones suivantes.

1. La Ballade des dames du temps jadis (François Villon)
2. Mignonne allons voir si la rose... (Pierre de Ronsard)
3. Le Malade imaginaire (Molière)
4. L'Esprit des Lois (Charles de Montesquieu)
5. Les Mémoires d'outre-tombe (François-René de Chateaubriand)
6. Les Misérables (Victor Hugo)
7. On ne badine pas avec l'amour (Alfred de Musset)
8. Les Fleurs du mal (Charles Baudelaire)
9. Le Petit Chose (Alphonse Daudet) (*chose* est le mot qu'on emploie quand on ne peut pas se rappeler du vrai nom d'une personne)
10. Les Enfants terribles (Jean Cocteau)
11. L'Etre et le néant (Jean Paul Sartre)
12. L'Homme révolté (Albert Camus)

13. Oh! les beaux jours (Samuel Beckett)
14. Tueur sans gages (Eugene Ionesco)
15. Les Bonnes (Jean Genêt)
16. L'Emploi du temps (Michel Butor)
17. Les Bouts de bois de Dieu (Ousmane Sembène)
18. Pieux Souvenirs (Marguerite Yourcenar)
19. Antan d'enfance (Patrick Chamoiseau)
20. Moi, Tituba, sorcière noire de Salem (Maryse Condé)

B. Classiques français et leurs traductions anglaises

Faites correspondre les titres originaux avec leurs traductions.

1. Le Bourgeois gentilhomme (Molière)	___ Endgame
2. Notre Dame de Paris (V. Hugo)	___ Exit the King
3. Le Tour du monde en 80 jours (J. Verne)	___ Man's Fate
4. A la recherche du temps perdu (M. Proust)	___ Strait is the Gate
5. Le Blé en herbe (Colette)	___ No Exit
6. La Porte étroite (A. Gide)	___ The Would be Gentleman
7. Partage de midi (P. Claudel)	___ The Ripening Seed
8. L'Alouette (J. Anouilh)	___ The Sea Wall
9. Les Mémoires d'une jeune fille rangée (S. de Beauvoir)	___ Around the World in Eighty Days
10. Huis clos (J. P. Sartre)	___ Remembrance of Things Past
11. La Condition humaine (A. Malraux)	___ The Hunchback of Notre Dame
12. Fin de partie (S. Beckett)	___ Memoirs of a Dutiful Daughter
13. Le Roi se meurt (E. Ionesco)	___ Noontide
14. L'Ere du soupçon (N. Sarraute)	___ The Lark
15. Un Barrage contre le Pacifique (M. Duras)	___ The Age of Suspicion

C. Titres français de classiques anglo-américains

Essayez de retrouver les titres originaux des traductions françaises suivantes.

1. Beaucoup de bruit pour rien

2. La Mégère apprivoisée
3. Le Songe d'une nuit d'été
4. Peines d'amour perdues
5. L'Ecole de la médisance
6. Les Hauts de Hurlevent
7. Les Grandes espérances
8. La Foire aux vanités
9. Alice au pays des merveilles
10. L'Importance d'être constant
11. Gens de Dublin
12. Pour qui sonne le glas
13. La Case de l'oncle Tom.
14. Un Tram nommé désir
15. Les Raisins de la colère
16. L'Attrappe-coeur

D. Titres de films

Retrouvez les titres originaux des films suivants.

1. La Ruée vers l'or
2. Autant en emporte le vent
3. L'Homme qui en savait trop
4. Psychose
5. Bons Baisers de Russie
6. Blanche neige et les sept nains
7. La Belle et le clochard
8. La Panthère rose s'en mêle
9. Les Dents de la mer
10. S.O.S. fantômes
11. L'Empire contre attaque
12. Les Incorruptibles
13. Retour vers le futur
14. Les Aventuriers de l'arche perdue
15. Le Cercle des poètes disparus
16. La Famille Pierrafeu

17. L'Arme fatale

Chapter 14
Guidelines
For the Translation of Literary Prose

Sticking to the text vs. demonstrating originality

One of the first questions a beginning translator will probably ask is: how much leeway do I have with the translation of a text? The answer is easy to formulate but more difficult to adhere to: try to strike a happy balance between not keeping enough distance and keeping too much distance from the source text. There are dangers in being extreme. Remaining too close to the source text and to its wording might blind the translator to its ideas and spirit and lead to paraphrasing; the result being a version which could sound too much like a translation. On the other hand, straying too far from the source text by attempting to be overly creative and idiomatic might lead to losing sight of the original message with all its nuances and result in an adaptation more than a translation.

What are the basic guidelines to follow for a successful literary translation?

1. Difference between literary and non-literary translation
Literary translation essentially differs from non-literary translation in that accuracy alone will not be enough: of equal importance with the message is the spirit of the text. That, too, must be rendered.
2. Adapt to tone of text

Determine the tone of the text: is it prosaic, poetic, philosophical, didactic, classical, romantic, modern, old fashioned, confidential etc.? and adapt your translation to it.

3. Adapt to language level

Determine the language level from the social context: are we dealing with a highly refined language register, one that betrays education, erudition and sophistication; or with a simple colloquial approach, one characteristic of everyday conversation; or still with a specific lingo, such as adolescent speech, or proletarian speech, slang, or the language of the various ethnic groups within the Francophone community?

4. Adapt to author's style

Determine the style of the author and remember that a translator must not have a style of his own, but, like the chameleon, must be versatile. If an author has a convoluted style (such as Proust), writing quirks (such as the synonymous word pairs in Rabelais and Montaigne), makes ironical quips (such as Voltaire) resist the impulse to change anything in an effort to "improve" on the original. These are distinctive characteristics which are the trademark of well known authors, and makes them instantly recognizable. You, as a translator, have the duty to remain humble and resist any temptation to edit, modify, add or delete words or groups of words, in short, act as a co-author. Your task is not to make an adaptation, but rather to faithfully render a message, style, tone, and atmosphere.

5. Necessary and unnecessary changes

Watch out for words or phrases which are placed in emphatic positions. Do not alter sentence structure, word order, or punctuation unless these run counter to English usage. In case such a modification becomes absolutely necessary in order to yield an idiomatic translation, or for unequivocal understanding, you may take liberties with the grammatical categories and structures as required by the various translation devices, but not with tenses.

Keep the tense the author intended for his story, except for those cases which are covered in chapter seven on *Literal Translation.*[1]

6. Adapt to time period

Adapt your vocabulary to the period of the text translated. In the translation of an old text you will obviously not be required to create a pastiche, but the carefully metered use of period vocabulary will add a touch of obsolescence and replace the piece in its historical context. After all, an eighteenth century novel or short story should not sound like a twentieth century one. Here, recourse to comparative literature between authors of the same century can be of invaluable help in establishing affinities between styles and genres, and in gleaning ideas to recreate an atmosphere through the use of similar words and syntax.

Working method

1. Getting acquainted phase: read the text to be translated right through once to get its overall message and tone. Do a quick textual and discourse analysis reviewing all the elements mentioned earlier. Is it a narration? And if so, is the narration in the first or third person? Is the narrator an omniscient one, a specific character, or the author himself? Is it a description, a dramatic scene, an essay etc.? Is the tenor of the text psychological, social, philosophical? What kind of style is used, what sort of language? When was the text written? Be aware of all the implications. You may even have to read between the lines if the text is cryptic.

2. Deciphering phase: read the text a second time for a close semantic and structural analysis. Delineate translation units, underline all words and expressions that remain obscure or present a problem and resort to a monolingual dictionary in the S.L. to determine their meaning. Study words in their context. If the text is stylistically very complex, watch out for separators such as colons, semi-colons, and commas. Also watch out for verbs and verb endings and determine their tenses.

---

[1] See pp.66-8, special problems with tenses.

3. Transcoding phase: this is the most important and difficult part of the translating process, the passage from the S.L. to the T.L. in thoughts and words. For a correct semantic transfer watch out for the proper lexical register, for false cognates, abstract meanings, words in context, and idioms. Apply the various translation devices as needed for an accurate and idiomatic rendition. For a correct syntactic transfer watch out for proper word order, necessary ellipses and structural changes brought about by the use of translation devices. In your search for the right word or expression, use a thesaurus, a good bilingual dictionary, and a monolingual dictionary in the T.L. as necessary.[2]

4. Finishing phase: the rough product or first draft of phase three must be worked into a satisfactory and harmonious translation, one that reads as smoothly as the original. A subtle balance must now be struck between remaining as literal and close to the S.L. text as possible, and departing from it as required by idiomatic usage in the T.L., so as not to give readers the feeling that they are dealing with a translation. In case several solutions are possible in the translation of a particular phrase or sentence, retain the one which will best fit in the context. This phase is the icing on the cake and the overall success of the project depends upon it.

5.Checking phase: this entails a final proofreading of the translation in comparison with the original text to correct mistakes and oversights.

1	2	3	4	5
getting acquainted with text	deciphering: structural and semantic analysis	transcoding SL-TL	finishing touch stylistic corrections	proofreading comparison with original

---

[2] See appendix pp.262-4 for a list of mono and bilingual dictionaries.

We shall now apply these guidelines to a sample of literary texts by classical French authors from different time periods and offer a suggested translation as an example of the finished product aimed at. A comparison of the source text with its translation should give the student some idea about the degree of freedom allowed in such translations.

Prose Text 1   **Il faut cultiver notre jardin**

The following excerpt is the conclusion to Voltaire's philosophical tale, Candide. The hero, a young man, has been influenced by the teaching of his master Pangloss, a philosopher who professes that "everything is for the best in the world". He has scoured the world in pursuit of happiness and of his beloved Cunégonde, yet has found instead nothing but evil, man made disasters as well as metaphysical ones, in the guise of intolerance, cruelty, cheating, exploitation, wars, storms, illness and earthquakes. What then is the purpose of life? And what practical attitude is one to adopt?

Il y avait dans le voisinage un derviche[1] très fameux, qui passait pour le meilleur philosophe de [2] la Turquie; [Candide, Pangloss et Martin] allèrent le consulter; Pangloss porta la parole[3] et lui dit: "Maître, nous venons vous prier de nous dire pourquoi un aussi étrange animal que l'homme a été formé." "-De quoi te mêles-tu? dit le derviche, est-ce là ton affaire?"[4] "-Mais, mon révérend père,[5] dit Candide, il y a horriblement de mal sur la terre.[6] "-Qu'importe, dit le derviche, qu'il y ait du mal ou du bien?[7] Quand sa Hautesse[8] envoie un vaisseau en Egypte, s'embarrasse-t-Elle[9] si les souris qui sont dans le vaisseau sont à leur aise ou non?" "-Que faut-il donc faire? dit Pangloss." "-Te taire" dit le derviche. "-Je me flattais,[10] dit Pangloss, de raisonner un peu avec vous des effets et des causes, du meilleur des mondes possibles, de l'origine du mal, de la nature de l'âme et de l'harmonie préétablie."[11] Le derviche, à ces mots, leur ferma la porte au nez.[12]

Pendant cette conversation, la nouvelle s'était répandue qu'on venait d'étrangler à Constantinople deux vizirs du banc et le mufti,[13] et qu'on avait empalé plusieurs de leurs amis.[14] Cette catastrophe faisait partout un grand bruit[15] pendant quelques heures. Pangloss, Candide et Martin, en retournant[16] à la petite métairie,[17] rencontrèrent un bon vieillard qui prenait le frais[18] à sa porte sous un berceau d'orangers. Pangloss, qui était aussi curieux que raisonneur,[19] lui demanda comment se nommait le mufti qu'on venait d'étrangler. "-Je n'en sais rien,[20] répondit le bonhomme, et je n'ai jamais su le nom d'aucun mufti ni d'aucun vizir. J'ignore[21] absolument l'aventure dont vous me parlez; je présume qu'en général, ceux qui se mêlent des affaires publiques périssent quelquefois misérablement, et qu'ils le méritent; mais je ne m'informe[22] jamais de ce qu'on fait[23] à Constantinople; je me contente d'y envoyer[24] vendre les fruits du jardin que je cultive." Ayant dit ces mots, il fit entrer les étrangers dans sa maison; ses deux filles et ses deux fils leur présentèrent plusieurs sortes de sorbets qu'ils faisaient eux-mêmes, du kaïmak[25] piqué d'écorces de cédrat confit, des oranges, des citrons, des limons, des ananas, des dattes, des pistaches, du café de Moka [...]. Après quoi les deux filles de ce bon musulman parfumèrent les barbes de Candide, de Pangloss et de Martin.

"Vous devez avoir, dit Candide au Turc, une vaste et magnifique terre?" "-Je n'ai que vingt arpents,[26] répondit le Turc, je les cultive avec mes enfants; le travail éloigne de nous trois grands maux, l'ennui, le vice et le besoin.[27]"

Candide, en retournant dans sa métairie, fit de profondes réflexions[28] sur le discours du Turc. Il dit à Pangloss et à Martin: "Ce bon vieillard me paraît s'être fait[29] un sort bien préférable à celui des six rois avec qui nous avons eu l'honneur de souper." "Les grandeurs, dit Pangloss, sont fort dangereuses, selon le rapport de tous les philosophes; car enfin [   ] vous savez comment périrent [...] Richard II d'Angleterre, Edouard II, Henri VI, Richard III, Marie Stuart,[30] Charles Ier, les trois Henri de France, l'empereur Henri IV? Vous savez..." "-Je sais aussi, dit Candide, qu'il faut cultiver notre jardin." "-Vous avez raison, dit Pangloss; car, quand l'homme fut mis dans le jardin d'Eden, il y fut mis [...] pour qu'il travaillât, ce qui prouve que l'homme n'est pas né pour le repos" "-Travaillons sans raisonner, dit Martin, c'est le seul moyen de rendre la vie supportable.[31]"

Toute la petite société entra dans ce louable dessein,[32] chacun se mit à exercer ses talents. La petite terre rapporta beaucoup. Cunégonde était à la vérité bien laide; mais elle devint une excellente pâtissière; [...] et Pangloss disait[33] quelquefois à Candide: "-Tous les évènement sont enchaînés dans le meilleur des mondes possibles; car enfin, si vous n'aviez pas été chassé d'un beau château à grands coups de pied dans le derrière[34] pour l'amour de Mademoiselle Cunégonde, si vous n'aviez pas été mis à l'Inquisition, si vous n'aviez pas couru l'Amérique à pied, si vous n'aviez pas donné un bon coup d'épée[35] au baron, si vous n'aviez pas perdu tous vos moutons du bon pays d'Eldorado, vous ne mangeriez pas ici des cédrats confits et des pistaches." "-Cela est bien dit, répondit Candide, mais il faut cultiver notre jardin."

(Voltaire, Candide)

Guiding Notes

The above text is a narrative which includes some drama in the form of dialogue inserts. The style is distinctive of its author, classical and concise; the tone, full of irony and satire. The rythm is lively and swift and tends to the quick demonstration of Voltaire's philosophical tenets. In order to be faithful, the translation must respect these characteristics, render the irony while keeping to the rythm by taking particular care not to cumber the sentence with heavy grammatical structures or unnecessary padding. It is also advisable to maintain the eighteenth century flavor whenever possible by giving preference to words of that period, i.e. words of latin derivation, over newer terms.

---

[1] **Derviche**:   keep this Turkish borrowing to add a touch of exoticism as Voltaire intended.

[2] **Le meilleur philosophe de la Turquie**:   avoid a barbarism by keeping in mind that the use of a superlative in English entails a preposition modulation when followed by the name of a place.

[3] **Porta la parole**:   an eighteenth century turn of phrase meaning "fut le porte parole."

[4] **De quoi te mêles-tu?   Est-ce là ton affaire?**:   keep the tone of informal conversation;   use an equivalence.

[5] **Mon révérend père**:   customs in titles differ between English and French;   no possessive adjective in English is used when the person is addressed directly.

[6] **Il y a horriblement de mal sur la terre**:   a literal translation is simply impossible here;   "horriblement" implies both degree in horror and amount: try a transposition with an adjective and a noun instead.

[7]   **Qu'importe...que...ou**:   keep the parallel construction with the proper conjunction to introduce alternative possibilities.

[8] **Sa Hautesse...Elle**:   again involves usage in titles;   certain titles are always feminine in French regardless of the sex of their holder when refering to the third person, i.e. Sa Hautesse le sultan..., Sa Majesté le roi..., Sa Sainteté le pape....   This involves use of the feminine personal pronoun.   Watch for the appropriate gender in English.

[9] **S'embarrasse-t-elle?**:   se soucie-t-elle?

[10] **Je me flattais**:   eighteenth century phrase meaning "j'espérais."

[11]   **De raisonner un peu...harmonie préétablie**:   this is an ironical and condensed summary of Leibnitz's philosophical theories which Voltaire has tried to prove wrong throughout his tale.   Keep to a literal translation.

[12] **Leur ferma la porte au nez**:   a word modulation will be necessary for this idiomatic expression.

[13] **Vizir...mufti**:   see note 1.

[14] **On venait...on avait... amis**:   a message modulation using the passive voice will avoid the awkward use of the indefinite English pronoun "one".

[15] **Faisait un grand bruit**:   use a verb and a noun modulation for this idiom.

[16] **En retournant**: several translations are possible here; "while" followed by the gerund as in the text or a noun transposition.

[17] **Métairie**: check the meaning of this term in a French monolingual dictionary before deciding on a translation since this is not a concept prevalent in America.

[18] **Qui prenait le frais**: qui prenait l'air frais.

[19] **Raisonneur, raisonner**: in this text, used as false cognates in the sense of argumentative, to argue.

[20] **Je n'en sais rien**: give an equivalence.

[21] **J'ignore**: false cognate meaning "je ne sais pas".

[22] **Je ne m'informe jamais**: je ne demande jamais de renseignements.

[23] **Ce qu'on fait**: ce qui se passe.

[24] **Je me contente d'y envoyer**: do not translate literally as "I am content to send there...", this would fail to understand the nuances of the verb "se contenter de" which are closer to "to be satisfied". Try an adverb transposition instead: "J'y envoie simplement".

[25] **Kaïmak**: see note 1.

[26] **Arpent**: an old French measure now obsolete, roughly the equivalent of one acre.

[27] **L'ennui, le vice et le besoin**: remember that general terms take the definite article in French but not in English.

[28] **Faire une réflexion**: one TU meaning "réfléchir".

Fit de profondes réflexions: make an adverb transposition on the adjective "profondes".

[29] **S'être fait**: do not overlook the reflexive aspect of this verb and keep it in mind for your translation.

[30] **Marie Stuart**: English speakers do not refer to this queen of Scotland by the same name.

[31] **Supportable**: false cognate.

[32] **Entra dans ce dessein**: eighteenth century phrase meaning "se rallia à ce projet."

[33] **Pangloss disait à Candide**: the iterative aspect of the imparfait must not be overlooked, Voltaire does not say "Pangloss dit à Candide."

[34] **Chassé à grands coups de pied dans le derrière**: "chassé à coups de pied" would be simple to render as a cross transposition: "kicked out". But the difficulty here lies in translating the manner in which Candide was kicked out and which Voltaire intended as being both comical and shameful: with hard kicks in the backside. An English translation fails to be as fluid as the French expression and a loss is incurred.

---

[35] **Donner un coup d'épée**: one TU; donner un *bon* coup d'épée: introduces a connotation of finality with a comical note, the sword thrust that did the baron in.

Let's Tend Our Garden

There lived in the vicinity a very famous dervish, reputed to be the best philosopher in Turkey. Candide, Pangloss and Martin went to consult him. Pangloss acted as spokesman and said: "Master, we have come to beg of you to tell us why such a strange animal as man was created." "-Why stick your nose into this? replied the dervish, what business is it of yours?" "-But, Reverend Father, said Candide, there is a horrible amount of evil on earth." "-What does it matter, the dervish said, whether there is good or evil? When His Highness sends a vessel to Egypt, does He worry that the mice on board are comfortable or not?" "-What are we to do then?" said Pangloss. "-Hold your tongue" replied the dervish. "-I was hoping, said Pangloss, to be able to argue with you for a while about effects and causes, the best of possible worlds, the origin of evil, the nature of the soul, and preestablished harmony." The dervish, upon this, slammed the door in their face.

During this conversation, the news had spread that two viziers of the sultan's council and the mufti had just been strangled in Constantinople, and that several of their friends had been impaled. This catastrophe was creating a big stir everywhere for a few hours. Pangloss, Candide and Martin, on their way back to the small farm they sharecropped, came upon a good old man who was taking the fresh air on his doorstep under an arbor of orange trees. Pangloss, who was as curious as he was argumentative, inquired after the name of the mufti who had just been strangled. "-I have no idea, replied the old man, and I have never known the name of any mufti or vizier. I know absolutely nothing of the event to which you are referring; I presume that generally people who meddle in public affairs sometimes come to a miserable end, and that they deserve to, but I never enquire about what goes on in Constantinople; it's enough for me to send the fruit of the garden I farm to be sold there." Having said this, he ushered the strangers into his house; his two daughters and his two sons offered them several sorts of home made sherbets, some Kaïmak flavored with candied citron peel, oranges, lemons, limes, pineapples, dates, pistachios and Moka coffee. After which, the two daughters of this good moslem perfumed the beards of Candide, Pangloss and Martin.

"-You must, Candide said to the Turk, be the owner of a vast and magnificent estate?" "-I only have twenty acres, the Turk replied; I farm them with my children; work keeps at bay three great evils, boredom, vice and want." Candide, on his way back to his farm, reflected deeply upon the Turk's remarks. He said to Pangloss and Martin: "-This good old man seems to me to have made for himself a life far preferable to that of the three kings with whom we had the honor of having supper." "-Greatness, said Pangloss, is a very dangerous thing, in the recorded opinion of all philosophers; for, after all, you do know how Richard II of England, Edward III, Henri VI, Richard III, Mary Queen of Scots, Charles Ist, the three Henri of France, the emperor Henry IV perished? You do know..." "-I also know, said Candide, that we must tend our garden." "-You're right, said Pangloss: for when man was put in the garden of Eden, he was put there to work; which proves that man was not born to be idle." "-Let's work without arguing, said Martin, that's the only way to make life bearable."

The entire company joined in this praiseworthy venture, each started exerting his talents. The small landholding yielded plenty. Cunegonde was indeed quite ugly; but she became an excellent pastry cook; and Pangloss would sometimes say to Candide: "-All events are linked together in the best of possible worlds; for, after all, had you not been driven away from a beautiful castle by hard kicks in your backside for the love of Mademoiselle Cunegonde, had you not suffered at the hands of the Inquisition, had you not scoured America on foot, had you not run the baron through with your sword, had you not lost all your sheep in the good land of Eldorado, you would not be here eating candied citron and pistachios." "-Quite so, Candide replied, but let's tend our garden."

Prose Text 2   La Vieille servante

The passage below is an example of Flaubert's esthaetics of realism, the portrait of a woman who has given her whole life to service and hard work. It is incidental in the unfolding of the novel, Madame Bovary, from which it is taken, but stands in sharp contrast to the life and aspirations of the heroine, Emma, a romantic who finds no place in a petty and materialistic world. It is meant as a social comment on the life of the working poor during the July Monarchy in contrast to the increasing prosperity of the bourgeois class.

"Catherine Nicaise Elizabeth Leroux, de[1] Sassetot-la-Guerrière, pour cinquante-quatre ans de service dans[2] la même ferme, une médaille d'argent - du prix de vingt-cinq francs![3] "

"-Où est-elle, Catherine Leroux?[4] " répéta le conseiller.[5] Elle ne se présentait pas,[6] et l'on entendait des voix qui chuchotaient:[7]

-Vas-y![8]

-Non.

-A gauche!

-N'aie pas peur!

-Ah! qu'elle est bête![9]

-Enfin[10] y est-elle? s'écria Tuvache.

-Oui, la voilà!

-Qu'elle approche donc![11] "

Alors on vit s'avancer sur l'estrade une petite vieille femme[12] de maintien craintif, et qui paraissait se ratatiner dans ses pauvres[13] vêtements. Elle avait aux pieds[14] de grosses galoches[15] de bois, et, le long des hanches,[16] un grand tablier bleu. Son visage maigre, entouré d'un béguin[17] sans bordure, était plus plissé de rides[18] qu'une pomme de reinette[19] flétrie, et des manches[20] de sa camisole rouge[21] dépassaient[22] deux longues mains, à articulations noueuses. La poussière des granges, la potasse des lessives et le suint des laines les avaient si bien encroûtées, éraillées, durcies,[23] qu'elles semblaient sales quoiqu'elles fussent rincées d'eau claire,[24] et, à force d'avoir servi,[25] elles restaient entrouvertes, comme pour présenter d'elles-mêmes l'humble témoignage[26] de tant de souffrances subies. Quelquechose d'une rigidité monacale relevait[27] l'expression de sa figure. Rien de triste ou d'attendri n'amollissait ce regard pâle. Dans la fréquentation des animaux,[28] elle avait pris[29] leur mutisme et leur placidité. C'était la première fois qu'elle se voyait au milieu d'une compagnie si nombreuse; et, intérieurement effarouchée par les drapeaux, par les tambours, par les messieurs en habit[30] noir et par la croix d'honneur[31] du conseiller, elle demeurait tout immobile, ne sachant s'il fallait s'avancer ou s'enfuir,[32] ni pourquoi la foule la poussait et pourquoi les examinateurs[33] lui souriaient. Ainsi se tenait, devant ces bourgeois épanouis, un demi-siècle de servitude.[34]

"Approchez, vénérable Catherine Nicaise Elizabeth Leroux!" dit M. le conseiller,[35] qui avait pris des mains du président la liste des lauréats.[36] Et tour à tour examinant la feuille de papier, puis la vieille femme, il répétait[37] d'un ton paternel:

"Approchez, approchez!"

"-Etes-vous sourde?[38] " dit Tuvache, en bondissant sur son fauteuil. Et il se mit à lui crier dans l'oreille: "Cinquante-quatre ans de service! Une médaille d'argent! Vingt-cinq francs! C'est pour vous."

Puis, quand elle eut sa médaille, elle la considéra. Alors un sourire de béatitude[39] se répandit sur sa figure[40] et on l'entendait qui marmottait[41] en s'en allant:[42] "-Je la donnerai au curé[43] de chez nous, pour qu'il me dise des messes."

"-Quel fanatisme!" s'exclama le pharmacien, en se penchant vers le notaire.[44]

La séance était finie;[45] la foule se dispersa,[46] et, maintenant que les discours étaient lus, chacun reprenait son rang et tout rentrait dans la coutume:[47] les maîtres rudoyaient[48] les domestiques, et ceux-ci frappaient les animaux, triomphateurs indolents qui retournaient à l'étable, une couronne verte entre les cornes.[49]

(Gustave Flaubert, Madame Bovary)

Guiding Notes

This nineteenth century excerpt makes use of three different writing techniques: narration, description and dialogue. The tone between these sections varies greatly and proper care must be taken to adopt a familiar register for dialogues and a literary one for the detailed descriptions. An essential element of Flaubert's style is the proper selection of the "mot juste", the right word. This also has to be kept in mind in the translation, particularly where descriptions are concerned, and use of a thesaurus is strongly recommended.

---

[1] **De Sassetot la Guerrière**: choose a preposition indicating origin.
[2] **Dans une ferme**: a preposition modulation is needed here.

[3] **Du prix de vingt-cinq francs**: various translations are possible, one of which involves a transposition with an adjective. In a literary context do not convert francs into dollars, it is best to keep the French currency for local color in order to situate the story in its geographical and historical context.

[4] **Où est-elle, Catherine Leroux?**: the use of the name along with the personal pronoun is a gallicism with which English usage is at variance.

[5] **Le conseiller**: i.e. "conseiller de préfecture", a member of the "conseil du préfet" or council of the highest executive official in the region.

[6] **Elle ne se présentait pas**: avoid an unidiomatic reflexive verb in English; find a message modulation instead.

[7] **On entendait des voix qui chuchotaient**: use the passive voice to render the construction with the indefinite pronoun "on".

[8] **Vas-y**: use a speech equivalent.

[9] **Qu'elle est bête**: use a speech equivalent.

[10] **Enfin, y est-elle?**: the adverb "enfin" is used here in a conversational context and does not carry the same meaning as in a demonstrative context. It denotes impatience on the part of the speaker. Find an equivalence.

[11] **Qu'elle approche donc!**: a subjunctive used as an imperative for the third person; "donc" here is a prop word used in familiar conversation and does not have its usual meaning of "therefore". Find a speech equivalent.

[12] **Alors on vit s'avancer...**: use a passive construction.

[13] **Ses pauvres vêtements**: is the adjective taken in a concrete or abstract sense? Choose your translation accordingly.

[14] **Elle avait aux pieds**: use a preposition modulation.

[15] **De grosses galoches**: look up meaning in a French monolingual dictionary to help you figure out the English equivalent.

[16] **Le long des hanches**: use a preposition modulation.

[17] **Un béguin**: a bonnet.

[18] **Etait plus plissé de rides**: is it possible to economize words in the translation?

[19] **Une pomme de reinette**: a russet apple.

[20] **Des manches...**: use a preposition denoting origin.

[21] **De sa camisole rouge**: look up "camisole" in a monolingual dictionary to determine the proper equivalent.

[22] **Dépassaient**: visualize the image in order to find the right message modulation in English.

[23] **Les avaient si bien encroûtées, éraillées, durcies**: look up unknown words in a bilingual dictionary, then go to a thesaurus for the right words in this context.

[24] **Quoiqu'elles fussent rincées d'eau claire**: use of the subjunctive imperfect is dictated by conjunction "quoique"; a pluperfect seems appropriate in English to express anteriority of the action in relation to the previous clause.

[25] **A force d'avoir servi**: most dictionaries give "by dint of" as an equivalent to "à force de". The main difference is that "by dint of" is now obsolete, unlike "à force de" which is still very much in use and connotes the constant repetition of an action; find a solution in a message modulation, a transposition or a different preposition.

[26] **Comme pour présenter d'elles mêmes**.... find a non literal translation.

[27] **Relevait**: abstract meaning.

[28] **Dans la fréquentation des animaux**: a literal translation is not possible; the phrase means "du fait qu'elle avait tant vécu au milieu des animaux"; a transposition or a modulation can be resorted to.

[29] **Elle avait pris**: the verb is used in an abstract sense.

[30] **En habit noir**: false cognate.

[31] **La croix d'honneur**: the cross of the Legion of Honor created by Napoleon the First to reward those having provided exceptional services to the State.

[32] **Ne sachant s'il fallait s'avancer ou s'enfuir**: use a personal construction instead of this impersonal one.

[33] **Les examinateurs**: false cognate; here we are not dealing with an exam but with a contest, and with the award of prizes by judges.

[34] **Ainsi se tenait, devant ces bourgeois épanouis, un demi-siècle de servitude**: try and find the proper words to render this concise and striking formula.

[35] **M. le conseiller**: i.e. Monsieur le conseiller; this very formal address cannot be rendered in English.

[36] **Lauréats**: false cognate; think of the situation: who are these lauréats? what do they stand to win?

[37] **Il répétait**: do not overlook the iterative aspect of this past tense.

[38] **Etes-vous sourde?**: a modulation using a negative expression would probably be the best idiomatic way of translating this question.

[39] **Un sourire de béatitude**: use a transposition with an adjective.

[40] **Se répandit sur sa figure**: use a message modulation; think of the concept.

[41] **Qui marmottait**: the relative pronoun can be economized in the English translation without incurring any loss when the imparfait is rendered as a gerund.

[42] **En s'en allant**: use a noun transposition.

[43] **Au curé**: false cognate; the French word may be borrowed for local color.

[44] **Le notaire**: false cognate; a "notaire" takes care of wills and estates.

[45] **La séance était finie**: use an adverbial transposition for the verb.

[46] **La foule se dispersa**: avoid a reflexive verb in English.

[47] **Tout rentrait dans la coutume**: find an equivalent.

[48] **Les maîtres rudoyaient**...: the following list of imparfaits must be rendered as past progressives.

[49] **Entre les cornes**: English usage requires the use of the possessive adjective before parts of the body.

The Old Servant

"To Catherine Nicaise Elizabeth Leroux from Sassetot-la-Guerrière, for fifty four years of service on the same farm, a silver medal, worth twenty five francs!"

"Where is Catherine Leroux?" repeated the councillor.

There was no sign of her, and voices could be heard whispering:

-Go ahead!

-No

-To the left!

-Don't be afraid!

-What a fool!

-Is she here or isn't she? cried Tuvache.

-Yes, there she is!

-Let her step forward then!

At that moment a little old woman of frightened appearance who seemed to have shrivelled up inside her shabby garments, was seen coming onto the platform. She had clumsy wooden clogs on her feet and a big blue apron around her hips. Her skinny face, framed in an edgeless peasant's coif, was more wrinkled than a withered russet apple, and from the sleeves of her red jacket hung her long gnarled hands. The dust of barns, the lye of washings and the grease of raw wool had left them so scabby, chafed and hardened that they looked dirty, even though they had been rinsed out in clear water; and from years of service they remained half open, as if to bring their own humble testimony to the many hardships endured. A touch of monastic austerity enhanced her countenance. Nothing sad or tender softened her pale eyes. Living as she did among the animals, she had assumed their muteness and placidity. It was the first time she found herself in the midst of such a large crowd, and inwardly scared by the flags, the drums, the gentlemen in black coats and the councillor's decoration, she stood transfixed, not knowing whether she should proceed or turn around and flee, or why the crowd was pushing her on and the judges smiling at her. Thus stood, before those beaming bourgeois, half a century of bondage.

"-Step forward, venerable Catherine Nicaise Elizabeth Leroux!" said the councillor who had taken the list of award recipients from the chairman's hands. And now looking at the sheet of paper, now at the old woman, he kept repeating in a fatherly tone: "Step forward!"

"-Can't you hear?" said Tuvache springing from his chair. And he began to shout in her ear:

"-Fifty four years of service! A silver medal! Twenty five francs! It's for you."

After she got her medal, she examined it. Then her face broke into a blissful smile and she could be heard mumbling on her way out: "I'll give it to the priest back home, to say masses for me."

"-Such fanaticism!" exclaimed the pharmacist leaning toward the lawyer.

The show was over. The crowd dispersed; and now that the speeches had been read, everyone resumed his own rank, everything reverted to normal: masters were bullying their servants, and servants beating the animals, who, placid in their triumph, were returning to their barn with green wreaths between their horns.

Prose Text 3   Un Univers dans une tasse de thé

This is the central passage of Proust's Remembrance of Things Past.   It recounts the magical moment when Marcel, the narrator, unexpectedly finds a way to recapture his past, the nostalgic days of his boyhood.

Il y avait déjà bien des années[1] que, de Combray, tout ce qui n'était pas le théâtre et le drame[2] de mon coucher n'existait plus pour moi, quand un jour d'hiver, comme je rentrais à la maison, ma mère, voyant que j'avais froid, me proposa de me faire prendre,[3] contre mon habitude,[4] un peu de[5] thé. Je refusai d'abord et, je ne sais pourquoi, me ravisai.[6] Elle envoya chercher[7] un de ces gâteaux courts et dodus appelés petites madeleines[8] qui semblent avoir été moulés dans la valve rainurée d'une coquille de Saint-Jacques.[9] Et bientôt, machinalement,[10] accablé par la morne journée et la perspective d'un triste lendemain, je portai à mes lèvres une cuillerée du thé où j'avais laissé[11] s'amollir un morceau de madeleine. Mais à l'instant même où[12] la gorgée[13] mêlée des miettes du gâteau toucha mon palais,[14] je tressaillis, attentif à ce qui se passait d'extraordinaire en moi.[15] Un plaisir délicieux[16] m'avait envahi, isolé, sans la notion de sa cause. Il m'avait aussitôt rendu les vicissitudes de la vie indifférentes, ses désastres inoffensifs, sa brièveté illusoire [...]. J'avais cessé de me sentir médiocre, contingent,[17] mortel. D'où avait pu me venir cette puissante joie?[18] Je sentais[19] qu'elle était liée au goût du thé et du gâteau, mais qu'elle le dépassait infiniment, ne devait pas être de même nature. D'où venait-elle?[20] Que signifiait-elle ? Où l'appréhender?[21] Je bois une seconde gorgée où je ne trouve[22] rien de plus que dans la première, une troisième qui m'apporte un peu moins que la seconde. Il est temps que je m'arrête, la vertu du breuvage[23] semble diminuer.[24] Il est clair que la vérité que je cherche n'est pas en lui,[25] mais en moi [...]. Je pose la tasse et me tourne vers mon esprit.[26][...]

Et tout d'un coup le souvenir m'est apparu. Ce goût, c'était celui[27] du petit morceau de madeleine que le dimanche matin à Combray [...] quand j'allais lui dire bonjour dans sa chambre, ma tante Léonie m'offrait[28] après l'avoir trempé[29] dans son infusion de thé ou de tilleul.[30] La vue de la petite madeleine ne m'avait rien rappelé avant que je n'y eusse goûté,[31] peut-être parce que, en ayant souvent aperçu depuis, sans en manger,[32] sur les tablettes des pâtissiers, leur image avait quitté ces jours de Combray pour se lier à d'autres plus récents; peut-être parce que, de ces souvenirs[33] abandonnés si longtemps hors de la mémoire, rien ne survivait, tout s'était désagrégé [...]. Mais, quand d'un passé ancien[34] rien ne subsiste, après la mort des êtres, après la destruction des choses,[35] seules, plus frêles mais plus vivaces, plus immatérielles, plus persistantes, plus fidèles, l'odeur et la saveur restent encore longtemps, comme les âmes, à se rappeler, à attendre, à espérer, sur la ruine de tout le reste, à porter[36] sans fléchir, sur leur gouttelette presque impalpable, l'édifice immense du souvenir.[37]

Et dès que j'eus reconnu le goût du morceau de madeleine trempé dans le tilleul que me donnait[38] ma tante [...] aussitôt la vieille maison grise sur la rue, où était sa chambre, vint comme un décor de théâtre s'appliquer au petit pavillon donnant sur[39] le jardin, qu'on avait construit[40] pour mes parents [...] et avec la maison, la ville [...], la Place[41] où on m'envoyait avant déjeuner, les rues où j'allais faire des courses, les chemins qu'on prenait[42] si le temps était beau. Et comme dans ce jeu où les Japonais s'amusent à tremper dans un bol de porcelaine rempli d'eau, de petits morceaux de papier jusque-là indistincts qui, à peine y sont-ils plongés,[43] s'étirent, se contournent, se colorent, se différencient,[44] deviennent des fleurs, des maisons, des personnages consistants et reconnaissables, de même[45] maintenant toutes les fleurs de notre jardin [...], et les nymphéas de la Vivonne, et les bonnes gens du village et leurs petits logis et l'église et tout Combray et ses environs, tout cela[46] [...] est sorti, ville et jardins, de ma tasse de thé.[47]

(Marcel Proust, Du côté de chez Swann)

Guiding Notes

The passage is an introspective narration written in the first person and delving into things psychological: the author has been searching into his memory to find the key to an unexpected and powerful feeling of joy which occurred as he was eating a French cookie and drinking some tea.

Translation difficulties here arise mostly from the choice of vocabulary and from the grammatical and syntactical structure. The language is refined and literary and Proustian style is famous for its long winded and balanced sentences which can unfurl into an entire paragraph. Any attempt on the translator's part to cut them for the sake of clarity would interfere with a stylistic effect, for Proust's long sentences show the progress of thoughts as they arise and develop in the mind of the narrator. Let yourself be guided by their structure. Word order is also important since certain groups of words are placed in positions of emphasis in order to catch the reader's attention. Particular care should be taken to keep them in the limelight, at the beginning or at the end of the sentence.

[1] **Il y avait déjà bien des années**: there is no need to keep the impersonal construction in the translation.

[2] **Le théâtre et le drame**: these terms are to be taken in the abstract; Proust refers to the scenes that used to accompany his going to bed when he was a child at Combray.

[3] **Proposa de me faire prendre**: the function of verb "faire" here is causative.

[4] **Contre mon habitude**: go beyond a literal translation to remain idiomatic.

[5] **Un peu de thé**: this direct object is separated from its verb by the phrase "contre mon habitude" as permitted by French syntax; can a verb be similarly separated from a direct object in English?

[6] **Je me ravisai**: je changeai d'avis.

[7] **Elle envoya chercher**: use a preposition transposition in place of the second verb.

[8] **Appelés petites madeleines**: borrow the French word since there is no English equivalent: Proust has made them famous even outside of France.

[9] **Une coquille de Saint Jacques**: the shell of a scallop; the French term is named after St James because pilgrims on their way to the shrine of St. James of Compostella have been wearing it as a badge since the Middle Ages.

[10] **Machinalement**: go beyond a literal translation; think of the idea beyond the words.

[11] **Où j'avais laissé**: dans laquelle j'avais laissé; English needs to explicit "où" as a relative pronoun.

[12] **A l'instant même où…**: constitutes one T.U.; "où" here serves the function of a relative pronoun refering to its antecedent "instant"; "où" as a relative pronoun in French can be indiscriminately linked to expressions of place or time; where expressions of time are concerned in English a modulation becomes necessary: "où" has to change to "when".

[13] **La gorgée**: implies the intake of liquid food contrary to solid food as with "bouchée".

[14] **Mon palais**: polysemous word; select the proper meaning given the context.

[15] **A ce qui se passait d'extraordinaire en moi**: aux choses extraordinaires qui se passaient en moi.

[16] **Délicieux**: a false friend in this context; "delicious" in English only refers to food.

[17] **Contingent**: look up the meaning of this word in a French monolingual dictionary before deciding on a translation.

[18] **D'où avait pu me venir cette puissante joie?**: does English follow the French preposition order here?

[19] **Je sentais…**: one T.U. which can be padded in translation.

[20] **D'où venait-elle?**: see note 18.

[21] **Appréhender**: a partial false cognate here since this particular meaning of the verb "to apprehend" is now obsolete in English; a synonym in French would be "saisir", "capturer".

[22] **Où je ne trouve…**: notice the change of tense with this verb and the following; what is the author's purpose? Can the same stylistic effect be achieved in English? For a translation of "où" see note 11.

[23] **Breuvage**: false cognate; does not refer to "beverage" whose French equivalent is "boisson non alcoolisée".

[24] **Diminuer**: whereas the French language likes abstract words, English prefers concrete ones; find a more expressive way of translating this concept.

[25] **En lui**: what preceding noun does this pronoun refer to? Watch for the proper gender in English.

[26] **Je me tourne vers mon esprit**: a literary turn of phrase; go to the idea beyond the words to find a translation.

[27] **Ce goût, c'était celui…**: gallicism; emphatic construction to place the word "goût" in the limelight; a literal translation being impossible, find another way of emphasizing this particular word in English.

[28] **Quand j'allais…m'offrait…**: what is the value of these imparfaits? How should you render them?

[29] **Après l'avoir trempé**: conjunction "après" is always followed by the past infinitive in French: is English usage the same?

[30] **Son infusion de thé ou de tilleul**: "thé" refering to "tea" and "tilleul" to a kind of herbal tea called "linden tea", the problem here arises from the repetition of the word "tea" within a short interval. an awkward effect; find a circumlocution.

[31] **Avant que je n'y eusse goûté**: conjunction "avant que" necessitates use of the pluperfect subjunctive; can English simplify the translation here? What does pronoun "y" refer to?

[32] **Sans en manger**: do not overlook the translation of indefinite pronoun "en"; what word does it refer to?

[33] **Ces souvenirs**: false cognate.

[34] **Un passé ancien**: "ancien" is not the equivalent of "ancient' here; give a word modulation.

[35] **Après la mort des êtres, après la destruction des choses**: use verb transpositions instead of nouns.

[36] **A se rappeler, à attendre, à espérer…à porter**: in a parallel construction prepositions are repeated in front of each word in French; does English follow the same syntactical rule?

[37] **L'édifice immense du souvenir**: key expression placed in an emphatic position at the end of the sentence; keep it there in your translation and try to find an equally striking formula.

[38] **Donnait**: iterative or progressive aspect?

[39] **Donnant sur**: one word in English.

[40] **Qu'on avait construit**: use a passive construction.

[41] **La Place**: false cognate.

[42] **Les chemins qu'on prenait**: can a passive construction be used here? Who does this "on" stand for, someone indefinite or someone more specific?

[43] **A peine y sont-ils plongés**: why is there a word inversion here?

[44] **S'étirent, se contournent...**: is it necessary for these verbs to remain reflexive in the translation?

[45] **De même**: de la même manière.

[46] **Tout cela**: padding is needed in English.

[47] **Tasse de thé**: be aware of the semantic difference between "tasse de thé" and "tasse à thé"; which one refers to contents and what is the proper translation here?

A Whole World in a Cup of Tea

Many years had elapsed during which nothing of Combray beyond the stage and tribulations of my bedtime existed for me any longer, when, coming home one winter day, my mother, who saw that I was cold, offered to have me take some tea, something I didn't usually do. I declined at first, and then, for no particular reason, changed my mind. She sent for one of those short and plump little cakes called "madeleines" which look as though they have been molded from the grooved shell of a sea scallop. And soon, without thinking, disheartened by that dreary day and the prospect of another bleak day to come, I took to my lips a spoonful of tea in which I had let a piece of madeleine soften. But just as the sip of liquid with the cake crumbs touched my palate, I shuddered, fascinated by the extraordinary changes taking place within me. A delightful feeling had come over me, disconnected, with no notion of what had brought it about. At once it had made the vicissitudes of life indifferent to me, its disasters, harmless, its brevity, an illusion. I had ceased to feel ordinary, unessential, mortal. Where could this powerful feeling of joy have come from? I had a feeling that it had something to do with the taste of tea and cake, but that it went infinitely beyond, that it had to be of a different nature. Where was it coming from? What was its significance? Where was I to capture it? I take a second sip in which I find nothing more than in the first, a third which brings even less. It is time for me to stop, the magic of the potion seems to be wearing out. It is clear that what I am looking for does not rest in it but in me. I put down the cup and begin to concentrate.

And all at once the memory resurfaced. This was the taste of the little piece of madeleine which, on Sunday mornings at Combray when I went to her room to say hello, my aunt Leonie used to offer me after she had dipped it in her tea or linden infusion. The sight of the little madeleine had recalled nothing before tasting it; perhaps because, having often seen such cakes since, without eating any, on the shelves of pastry shops, their image had left those Combray days to fix itself to more recent ones; perhaps because, of all those memories so long foregone and put out of mind, nothing survived, everything had desintegrated. But when of a distant past nothing remains, after people are dead, after things are destroyed, alone, more frail yet more enduring, more immaterial, persistent and faithful, smell and taste stay on like souls to remember, wait, hope when all else lies in ruin, and to carry unflinchingly, in their almost impalpable droplet, the gigantic monument of recollection.

And as soon as I had recognized the taste of the piece of madeleine dipped in tea which my aunt used to give me, at once the old grey house on the street where her bedroom was, came like a stage backdrop right next to the little pavilion overlooking the garden which had been built for my parents; and with the house, the town, the square where they used to send me before lunch, the streets where I ran errands, the country lanes where we walked in fair weather. And just as in that Japanese game in which you dip small indistinguishable pieces of paper into a porcelain bowl filled with water, and no sooner are they in the water than they stretch, assume shapes, color, characteristics, become flowers, houses, substantial and recognizable people, in the same way at that very moment all the flowers of our garden, the water lilies on the Vivonne, the good folk of the village, their little dwellings, the church, and Combray with its surroundings, all of that, town and garden, came out of my cup of tea.

Chapter 15
Guidelines
For the Translation of Dialogues and Plays

The translation of plays as well as the translation of dialogues which are to be found in novels and short stories is of a specific kind. It calls for an approach slightly different from the one generally applying to literary prose.

An oral text is essentially different from a written one in that a different sort of language is used: no one speaks as one writes. Therefore, for this act of communication to sound true, the translation of a dialogue will have to try and reproduce the direct speech of conversation.

Problems specific to the translation of dialogues and plays

There are particular difficulties and problems involved in the process. Here, as in prose translation, a preliminary textual analysis of the passage is a must:

- What is the dramatic context? What are the circumstances, the time, place and atmosphere?
- Setting the background is important in order to select the level of language that is most suitable for the translation. One crucial prerequisite will be to determine the language register of the character or characters speaking, so as to adapt to it in the TL: Who is speaking? What is his or her quality in life? To whom

is the message addressed? Is the speaker using informal, popular language? slang? or highly refined speech? Is it contemporary French or is it the tongue of Molière, Marivaux or Musset's time?

- Sometimes various levels of language will have to be used in the same play to reflect the different social status of the characters. As as example, the valets and maids in Molière's plays do not express themselves as do their masters and mistresses. And among the masters and mistresses themselves the range is wide from simple and uneducated bourgeois such as M. Jourdain to the literary circles of the précieuses and the noble courtiers of the Sun King. All the characters' social rank must be mirrored in the way they speak. For samples of appropriate cues and repartees in period plays one can turn to comparable English plays of the same era, i.e. Restoration drama in the case of Molière's plays, or Oscar Wilde and G.B. Shaw in the case of Paul Claudel, Jean Giraudoux etc. For samples of the various registers in contemporary speech in the TL, one can turn to television, the radio, the movies, or other plays.

Equivalence as the preferred translating device for dialogues

The translation of dialogues, more than any other translation, demands that one goes beyond words, grammar and syntax to the meaning of the original message. Conversation is "par excellence" the domain of interjections, colloquial expressions, idioms, set phrases, clichés and reflex formulas, all impossible to translate literally. Moreover, since the text to be translated is also intended to be acted out on the stage, a certain rythm, a certain fluency must be maintained in accordance with the rythm of the SL. Reading the text aloud will help to get a feel both for intonation and rythm. And sometimes, what is not said, but rather implied can be as important as what is actually verbalized. Consequently, equivalence, a device which goes to the spirit rather than the letter of a message, will be the preferred strategy for the translator of plays. And the goal to keep in mind will be to produce the same effects as the original.

Use of a specific vocabulary

In dialogue, language reflexes play a prominent role, particularly the use of prop words which help the speaker along a sentence. Answer-words like *bon, mais oui,* or reinforcing words such as *bien, donc, alors, mais, surtout,* as well as words that reiterate a question at the end of a sentence such as *hein* and *n'est-ce pas* are typical of an oral text.[1] Just remember that in a conversational context these adverbs will have a meaning different from the one they would assume in a prose context, and that whereas "Je me sens *bien*" may mean "I feel *well*", "Vous viendrez *bien* nous voir!" is the equivalent of "You will come and see us, *won't you?*". Likewise, *donc* in "Je pense, *donc* je suis" (I think *therefore* I am), does not have the same function as the *donc* in "Tu ne vois *donc* pas que je suis occupé?" *(Can't* you see that I am busy?) or even the *donc* in "Repasse *donc* demain!" whose purpose is to soften a request (*Why don't you* come back to morrow?). *Surtout* in the following context "*Surtout* n'allez pas croire qu'il s'agit d'une critique" no longer means *above all* but is closer to *please*: (*Please* do not construe it as a criticism), while *mais* cannot be translated as *but* in "*Mais* je le ferai avec plaisir!" (*Of course,* I'll gladly do it!)

The neophyte translator who intends to become serious about dialogue translation will also have to develop glossaries of common reflex formulas and clichés in conversation, many of which are not recorded in standard dictionaries and presuppose a good spoken mastery of the SL. Expressions such as "*Vous voulez rire!*" (*You must be joking!*), "*mon vieux*" (*old buddy*), "*Ne te dérange* pas" (*Don't bother*) etc. And never forget that the context or situation is of prime importance in determining the final significance of one such phrase or sentence. For example, an insignificant little *dites donc!* may mean *Listen* as in "Dites donc, n'oubliez pas de me

---

[1] See chapter on equivalence: exclamations and reflex formulas, prop words.

téléphoner"; *go ahead*! as in "Dites donc, ne vous gênez pas!"; or even *and how!* as in "Votre fils a grandi, dites donc!". Specialized dictionaries, dictionaries of colloquialisms in particular, will prove of great help in that respect.[2]

---

[2] For a list of such dictionaries see appendix p.266.

Play Excerpt 1   **Les Martin**[1]

Mr. and Mrs. Martin have been invited to dinner by the Smiths. They arrive early and make conversation while waiting for their hosts. This passage is typical of Ionesco's manner: characters are no better than puppets and the absurdity of the situation is reinforced by the platitudes and clichés which are their only means of communication. Laughter is mainly induced by a comic of repetition.

M. Martin: Mes excuses,[2] Madame,[3] mais il me semble si je ne me trompe,[4] que je vous ai déjà[5] rencontrée quelque part.

Mme Martin: A moi aussi, Monsieur, il me semble que je vous ai déjà rencontré quelque part.

M. Martin: Ne vous aurais-je pas déjà aperçue,[6] Madame, à[7] Manchester, par hasard ?[8]

Mme Martin: C'est très possible. Moi, je[9] suis originaire de[10] la ville de Manchester. Mais je ne me souviens pas très bien, Monsieur, je ne pourrais pas dire si je vous y ai aperçu ou non!

M. Martin: Mon Dieu,[11] comme c'est curieux! Moi aussi je suis originaire de la ville de Manchester, Madame!

Mme Martin: Comme c'est curieux!

M. Martin: Comme c'est curieux!... Seulement, moi, Madame, j'ai quitté la ville de Manchester, il y a cinq semaines environ.

Mme Martin: Comme c'est curieux! Quelle bizarre coïncidence! Moi aussi, Monsieur, j'ai quitté la ville de Manchester, il y a cinq semaines environ.

M. Martin: J'ai pris le train d'une demie après huit le matin, qui arrive à Londres à un quart avant cinq, Madame.[12]

Mme Martin: Comme c'est curieux! comme c'est bizarre! et quelle coïncidence! J'ai pris le même train, Monsieur, moi aussi![13]

M. Martin: Mon Dieu comme c'est curieux! Peut être bien alors, Madame, que[14] je vous ai vue dans le train?[15]

Mme Martin: C'est bien[16] possible, ce n'est pas exclu, c'est plausible et après tout, pourquoi pas!...Mais je n'en ai aucun souvenir,[17] Monsieur!

M. Martin: Je voyageais en[18] deuxième classe, Madame. Il n'y a pas de deuxième classe en Angleterre, mais je voyage quand même[19] en deuxième classe.

Mme Martin: Comme c'est bizarre, que c'est curieux et quelle coïncidence!
moi aussi, Monsieur, je voyageais en deuxième classe!

M. Martin: Comme c'est curieux! Nous nous sommes peut être bien[20]
rencontrés en deuxième classe, chère Madame!

Mme Martin: La chose est bien possible et ce n'est pas du tout exclu. Mais
je ne m'en souviens pas très bien, cher Monsieur!

M. Martin: Ma place[21] était dans le wagon[22] numéro 8, sixième
compartiment, Madame!

Mme Martin: Comme c'est curieux! Ma place aussi était dans le wagon
numéro 8, sixième compartiment, cher Monsieur!

M. Martin: Comme c'est curieux et quelle coïncidence bizarre! Peut-être
nous sommes nous rencontrés dans le sixième compartiment, chère Madame?

Mme Martin: C'est bien possible, après tout! Mais je ne m'en souviens pas,
cher Monsieur!

M. Martin: A vrai dire,[23] chère Madame, moi non plus je ne m'en
souviens pas,[24] mais il est possible que[25] nous nous soyons aperçus là, et si j'y
pense bien, la chose me semble même très possible![26]

Mme Martin: Oh vraiment, bien sûr, vraiment,[27] Monsieur!

M. Martin: Comme c'est curieux!...J'avais la place numéro 3 près de[28] la
fenêtre, chère Madame.

Mme Martin: Oh mon Dieu comme c'est curieux et comme c'est bizarre,
j'avais la place numéro 6 près de la fenêtre, en face de vous,[29] cher Monsieur.

M. Martin: Oh mon Dieu, comme c'est curieux et quelle coïncidence!...Nous étions donc[30] en vis-à-vis, chère Madame! C'est là que[31] nous
avons dû[32] nous voir!

Mme Martin: Comme c'est curieux! C'est possible mais je ne m'en
souviens pas, Monsieur! [...]

M. Martin: Depuis que je suis arrivé à Londres[33] j'habite rue Bromfield[34]
chère Madame.

Mme Martin: Comme c'est curieux, comme c'est bizarre! Moi aussi,
depuis mon arrivée à Londres, j'habite rue Bromfield, cher Monsieur.

M. Martin: Comme c'est curieux, mais alors, mais alors, nous nous
sommes peut-être rencontrés rue Bromfield, chère Madame.

Mme Martin: Comme c'est curieux, comme c'est bizarre! C'est bien
possible après tout! Mais je ne m'en souviens pas, cher Monsieur.

M. Martin: Je demeure au numéro 19, chère madame.

Mme Martin: Comme c'est curieux, moi aussi j'habite au numéro 19, cher
Monsieur.

M. Martin: Mais alors, mais alors, mais alors, mais alors, mais alors,
nous nous sommes peut-être vus dans cette maison, chère Madame?

Mme Martin: C'est bien possible, mais je ne m'en souviens pas, cher
Monsieur.

M. Martin: Mon appartement[35] est au cinquième étage, c'est le numéro 8, chère Madame.

Mme Martin: Comme c'est curieux, mon Dieu, comme c'est bizarre! et quelle coïncidence! Moi aussi j'habite au cinquième étage, dans l'appartement huit, cher Monsieur.

M. Martin (songeur):   [...]Vous savez, dans ma chambre à coucher j'ai un lit. Mon lit est couvert d'[36] un édredon vert. Cette chambre avec ce lit et son édredon vert, se trouve[37] au fond du corridor, entre les waters[38] et la bibliothèque,[39] chère Madame!

Mme Martin: Quelle coïncidence, ah mon Dieu, quelle coïncidence! Ma chambre à coucher a, elle aussi, un lit avec un édredon vert et se trouve au fond du corridor, entre les waters, cher Monsieur, et la bibliothèque!

M. Martin: Comme c'est bizarre, curieux, étrange! Alors, madame, nous habitons dans la même chambre et nous dormons dans le même lit, chère Madame. C'est peut-être là que nous nous sommes rencontrés!

Eugène Ionesco, La Cantatrice chauve, Editions Gallimard

Guiding Notes

The tone of the above dialogue, between two educated people who do not seem to know each other even though they share the same name, is one of formal conversation and conformity to social etiquette. The characteristics of the exchange are the pervading use of commonplace expressions and clichés. There is nothing natural or spontaneous about the way they talk to each other, no original thought or feeling. The language remains superficial and devoid of meaning, and communication only a mechanical exchange which the author turns into a joke. The only comical element comes from the repetition of certain trivial phrases which recur as a leit motiv throughout the excerpt and it is therefore stylistically essential that these be kept the same in translation. The passage does not present any specific difficulty beyond the fact that one should remember to translate French idioms and clichés not literally but with English equivalents.

---

[1] **Les Martin**: French family names remain invariable in the plural. Is it the case in English?

[2] **Mes excuses**: use a verbal equivalent.

[3] **Madame, Monsieur**: selection of the proper form of address in translation must be made in conformity with the local usage and it is therefore dependent upon where the play takes place.

[4] **Si je ne me trompe**: find an equivalent phrase.

[5] **déjà**: the idea of anteriority does not necessarily have to be rendered as "already".

[6] **Ne vous aurais-je pas aperçue**: the conditional indicates the idea of possibility which can be conveyed in English with an adverb or a modal verb.

[7] **A Manchester**: a preposition modulation is needed for large cities.

[8] **Par hasard**: false friend; the English phrase may be padded.

[9] **Moi, je**: gallicism emphasizing the personal pronoun; no literal translation is possible; how does an English speaker usually emphasize a word in speech?

[10] **Suis originaire de**: several solutions are possible here, one of them involving a transposition with an adverb or a preposition indicating origin.

[11] **Mon Dieu**: this French interjection is not as strong as its English literal counterpart; find an equivalent.

[12] **J'ai pris le train d'une demie après huit le matin**...: the comical effect here comes from copying a typically English syntactical structure which does not exist in the S.L., making obvious to a French audience that these are English characters. Unfortunately the speech oddity disappears in translation and there would be no point in copying a French structure to make them speak like French people. This is a classic case of loss in translation.

[13] **Moi aussi**: avoid a "Me too"; this is a conversation between people who speak grammatically correctly.

[14] **Peut-être bien alors... que**: il est possible alors; remember that "peut-être" can be rendered by a modal auxiliary verb connoting possibility; "bien": here this adverb does not have the same value as in a prose text and serves to reinforce "peut-être".

[15] **Dans le train**: modulate on the preposition.

[16] **Bien**: the adverb here modifies "possible" and is synonymous with "tout à fait"

[17] **Je n'en ai aucun souvenir**: do not forget to translate "en"; "souvenir" is a false friend.

[18] **En deuxième classe**: is the preposition necessary in English?

[19] **Quand même**: one T.U.; may be translated as a group of words or just one word.

[20] **Peut-être bien**: see note 14.

[21] **Ma place**: false friend.

[22] **Le wagon**: this is a borrowing from English which has changed meaning in the transfer; select the proper word within the context keeping in mind that the scene takes place in England and that the characters are English.

[23] **A vrai dire**: one T.U. which can be rendered as one word in English.

[24] **Moi non plus je ne m'en souviens pas**: how can this answer be simplified in English?

[25] **Il est possible que**: see note 14.

[26] **Si j'y pense bien la chose me semble même très possible**: give an equivalence.

[27] **Oh vraiment, bien sûr, vraiment**: the piling up of exclamations is just as nonsensical in the S.L. as in translation; the author's purpose is to point out the lack of original thought.

[28] **Près de**: find a preposition different from a literal translation.

[29] **En face de**: see note 28.

[30] **Donc**: here synonymous with "alors".

[31] **C'est là que**: gallicism and emphatic construction.

[32] **Nous avons dû**: does "devoir" here convey obligation or probability? what modal auxiliary verb and what tense could translate this meaning?

[33] **Depuis que je suis arrivé à Londres j'habite**: for a situation which started in the past and is still going on, the present tense in the main clause and "depuis" plus an indication of time are used in French; what tense is needed in English to convey the same?

[34] **Rue Bromfield**: preposition padding is necessary.

[35] **Mon appartement**: keep in mind that the scene takes place in England and involves English characters.

[36] **Couvert de**: preposition modulation.

[37] **Se trouve**: use a passive construction.

[38] **Les waters**: a common way of referring to the bathroom in everyday speech; use a British expression.

[39] **La bibliothèque**: a polysemous word; may refer to a piece of furniture or to the room in which this piece of furniture stands; choose in function of the context.

The Martins

Mr. Martin: Excuse me, Madam, but it seems to me, unless I am mistaken, that I have met you somewhere before.

Mrs. Martin: To me too, Sir, it seems that I have met you somewhere before.

Mr. Martin: Could I have caught sight of you in Manchester by any chance?

Mrs. Martin: That's quite possible. I am from the city of Manchester! But I can't remember for sure, Sir, I could not say if I saw you there or not!

Mr. Martin: Good Lord, how odd! I too am from the city of Manchester, Madam!

Mrs. Martin: How odd!

Mr. Martin: How odd!...Only I, Madam, left the city of Manchester about five weeks ago.

Mrs. Martin: How odd! What a strange coïncidence! I, too, Sir, left the city of Manchester about five weeks ago.

Mr. Martin: I took the 8:30 morning train which gets into London at 4:45, Madam.

Mrs. Martin: How odd! how strange! and what a coïncidence! I also took that same train, Sir.

Mr. Martin   Good Lord, how odd! Could it be then, Madam, that I saw you on the train?

Mrs. Martin: It's quite possible, it's not unlikely, it's conceivable, and after all, why not!...But I have no recollection of it, Sir.

Mr. Martin: I was travelling second class, Madam. There is no second class in England, but I travel second class all the same.

Mrs. Martin: How strange, how odd, and what a coïncidence! I, too, Sir, was travelling second class!

Mr. Martin: How odd! We may well have met in second class, dear Lady!

Mrs. Martin: That's certainly a possibility, and it's not at all unlikely. But I do not remember for sure, dear Sir!

Mr. Martin: My seat was in coach number 8, sixth compartment, Madam!

Mrs. Martin: How odd! My seat was also in coach number 8, sixth compartment, dear Sir!

Mr. Martin: How odd and what a strange coïncidence! Could we possibly have met in the sixth compartment, dear Lady?

Mrs. Martin: That's quite possible, after all! But I do not recall it, dear Sir!

Mr. Martin: Honestly, dear Lady, neither do I, but we may have seen each other there, and, the more I think about it, the more likely it seems.

Mrs. Martin: Oh! indeed, of course, indeed, Sir!

Mr. Martin: How odd!.. I had seat number 3 by the window, dear Lady.

Mrs. Martin: Oh good Lord, how odd and how strange, I had seat number 6, by the window, across from you, dear Sir.

Mr. Martin: Oh good Lord, how odd and what a coïncidence!...We were then facing each other, dear Lady! That's where we must have seen each other!

Mrs. Martin: How odd! That's possible but I do not recall it, Sir.

Mr. Martin: Honestly, dear Lady, neither do I. However, it's quite possible that we saw each other on that occasion.

Mrs. Martin: That's true, but I am not at all sure that we did, Sir.

Mr. Martin: Since coming to London I have been living on Bromfield Street, dear Lady.

Mrs. Martin: How odd, how strange! I, too, since coming to London have been living on Bromfield Street, dear Sir.

Mr. Martin: How odd, well then, well then, we may have met on Bromfield Street, dear Lady.

Mrs. Martin: How odd, how strange! That's quite possible, after all! But I do not recall it, dear Sir.

Mr. Martin: I live at number 19, dear Lady.

Mrs. Martin: How odd, I, too, live at number 19, dear Sir.

Mr. Martin: Well then, well then, well then, well then, well then, could we possibly have seen each other in that house, dear Lady?

Mrs. Martin: That's quite possible, but I do not recall it, dear Sir.

Mr. Martin: My flat is on the fifth floor, it's number 8, dear Lady.

Mrs. Martin: How odd, good Lord, how strange! and what a coïncidence! I, too, live on the fifth floor, in flat number 8, dear Sir!

Mr. Martin (musing): How odd, how odd, how odd, and what a coïncidence! You know, in my bedroom I have a bed. My bed is covered with a green eiderdown. That room, with that bed and its green eiderdown, is located at the end of the hallway, between the water closet and the bookcase, dear Lady!

Mrs .Martin: What a coïncidence, ah good Lord, what a coïncidence! my bedroom too has a bed with a green eiderdown and is located at the end of the hallway, between the water closet, dear Sir, and the bookcase!

Mr. Martin: How strange, odd, bizarre! Then, Madam, we live in the same room and sleep in the same bed, dear Lady. May be that's where we met!

Play Excerpt 2   L'Education d'un parvenu[1]

Mr. Jourdain is a rich but uneducated bourgeois with rather coarse manners who has decided to emulate the sophisticated ways of noblemen of his time. To this end he has secured the services of various masters who will be teaching him music, dancing, fencing and philosophy. Here is part of the "philosophy" lesson.

M. Jourdain: Il faut que je vous fasse une confidence.[2] Je suis amoureux d'[3] une personne de grande qualité,[4] et je souhaiterais que vous m'aidassiez[5] à lui écrire quelque chose dans un petit billet que je veux laisser tomber[6] à ses pieds.

Le maître de philosophie: Fort bien.[7]

M. Jourdain: Cela sera galant, oui.[8]

Le maître: Sans doute. Sont-ce des vers[9] que vous voulez écrire?

M. Jourdain: Non, non; point de vers.

Le Maître: Vous ne voulez que de la prose?

M. Jourdain: Non, je ne veux ni prose ni vers.

Le maître: Il faut bien que[10] ce soit l'un ou l'autre.

M. Jourdain: Pourquoi?

Le maître: Par la raison, monsieur, qu'il n'y a pour s'exprimer que la prose ou les vers.[11]

M. Jourdain: Il n'y a que la prose ou les vers?

Le maître: Oui, monsieur. Tout ce qui n'est point prose est vers, et tout ce qui n'est point vers est prose.

M. Jourdain: Et comme l'on parle, qu'est-ce que c'est donc[12] que cela?

Le maître: De la prose.[13]

M. Jourdain: Quoi? quand je dis, "Nicole, apportez-moi mes pantoufles et me donnez mon bonnet de nuit", c'est de la prose?

Le maître: Oui, monsieur.

M. Jourdain: Par ma foi,[14] il y a plus de quarante ans que je dis de la prose[15] sans que j'en susse[16] rien, et je vous suis le plus obligé du monde[17] de[18] m'avoir appris cela. Je voudrais donc lui mettre dans un billet: Belle marquise,[19] vos beaux yeux me font mourir d'amour; mais je voudrais que cela fût mis d'une manière galante,[20] que cela fût tourné gentiment.

Le maître: Mettre que les feux de ses yeux réduisent votre coeur en[21] cendres, que vous souffrez nuit et jour pour elle les violences d'un...

M. Jourdain: Non, non, non; je ne veux point tout cela. Je ne veux que ce que je vous ai dit: Belle marquise, vos beaux yeux me font mourir d'amour.

Le maître: Il faut bien étendre[22] la chose.

M. Jourdain: Non, vous dis-je; je ne veux que ces seules paroles-là[23] dans le billet, mais tournées à la mode, bien arrangées comme il faut.[24] Je vous prie de me dire un peu, pour voir,[25] les diverses manières dont on les peut mettre.

Le maître: On les peut mettre, premièrement, comme vous avez dit: Belle marquise, vos beaux yeux me font mourir d'amour. Ou bien: D'amour mourir me font, belle marquise, vos beaux yeux. Ou bien: Mourir vos beaux yeux, belle marquise, d'amour me font. Ou bien: Me font vos beaux yeux mourir, belle marquise, d'amour.[26]

M. Jourdain: Mais, de toutes ces façons-là, laquelle est la meilleure?

Le maître: Celle que vous avez dite: Belle marquise, vos beaux yeux me font mourir d'amour.

M. Jourdain: Cependant[27] je n'ai point étudié,[28] et j'ai fait cela tout du premier coup. Je vous remercie de tout mon coeur, et vous prie[29] de venir demain de bonne heure.[30]

Le maître: Je n'y manquerai pas.[31]

                    (Molière, Le Bourgeois gentilhomme)

Guiding Notes

The greatest difficulty here lies in the choice of proper vocabulary and grammar to convey the atmosphere of a seventeenth century conversation between a philosophy master who knows how to turn a phrase and his pupil, a rich bourgeois who has had very little education and tries to mimic the genteel ways of the nobility. The discrepancy in the manner of their speech should be felt in the translation.

---

[1] **L'Education d'un parvenu**: the title needs some special attention. Education: the gerund would be preferable to a noun. Parvenu: refers to a person who has reached an important social position in life without having had time to acquire the proper manners that should go along with it. Find a French borrowing which means just that.

[2] **Faire une confidence**: dire un secret.

[3] **Je suis amoureux de**: a preposition modulation is needed.

[4] **De grande qualité**: a seventeenth century way of saying "de haute noblesse".

[5] **Je souhaiterais que vous m'aidassiez**: the tense sequence is very complex here. According to classical rules of grammar, the use of a conditional in the

main clause brings about an imperfect subjunctive in the subordinate clause. This is no longer the case in modern French, in which a simpler present subjunctive has replaced the imperfect subjunctive of the age of Molière. However the message is that Monsieur Jourdain, whose French is not always the best, is trying to mimic the speech of the high society he is now rubbing elbows with. Due to the lack of subjunctive in English (let alone a subjunctive imperfect) the English translator will have to try and duplicate the effect of a very fancy phraseology through some other means.

[6] **Laisser tomber**: one T.U.

[7] **Fort bien**: elegant seventeenth century way of agreeing with someone; find an equivalent.

[8] **Cela sera galant, oui**: find a less literal way of reiterating the first part of the sentence than "yes".

[9] **Sont-ce des vers?**: a very refined way of saying "Est-ce que ce sont des vers...?"; des vers: de la poésie.

[10] **Il faut *bien* que**: the adverb here emphasizes the idea of necessity; find an equivalent.

[11] **Il n'y a pour s'exprimer que la prose ou les vers**: impersonal construction which would be better personalized in English: try a modulation by reversing the order and making the direct object the subject of the sentence.

[12] **Donc**: alors.

[13] **De la prose**: can the partitive article be rendered in translation?

[14] **Par ma foi**: a seventeenth century exclamation; find an equivalent which also has an obsolete flavor.

[15] **Il y a plus de quarante ans que je dis de la prose**: when a situation or action has been going on for a specific amount of time and is still going on as we speak, the tense of the main verb is the present in French; what is it in English?

[16] **Sans que j'en susse rien**: imperfect subjunctive of verb "savoir".

[17] **Je vous suis le plus obligé du monde**: refined expression of politeness; find an equivalent.

[18] **De m'avoir appris cela**: a preposition modulation is needed.

[19] **Marquise**: a French title of nobility for a lady; it is best to borrow the term since "marchioness" would place the dialogue in an English context.

[20] **D'une manière galante**: one T.U.; one adverb in English.

[21] **En cendres**: use a preposition modulation.

[22] **Etendre**: used in its figurative meaning, "élaborer".

[23] **Je ne veux que ces seules paroles-là**: Mr. Jourdain's phraseology is redundant; "ne...que" and "seules" serve exactly the same purpose. This lack of grammatical correctness should be felt in the translation.

[24] **Comme il faut**: one T.U.

[25] **Pour voir**: find a speech equivalent.

[26] **On les peut mettre...d'amour**: faced with his pupil's intransigence the philosophy master takes the request to the letter and switches the order of the various components of the sentence; each new version must progressively offer a more bizarre syntax in order to end with the most outlandish suggestion.

[27] **Cependant**: pourtant.

[28] **Je n'ai point étudié**: je ne suis jamais allé à l'école.

[29] **Je vous prie**: polite formula; find an equivalent.

[30] **De bonne heure**: one T.U., "tôt".

[31] **Je n'y manquerai pas**: give an equivalent.

Educating a Nouveau Riche

Mr. Jourdain: I must tell you something in confidence. I am in love with a lady of the best quality, and I should like you to help me write her a note which I want to drop at her feet.

Philosophy master: Very well.

Mr. Jourdain: It will be gallant, won't it?

Master: Certainly. Is it verse you wish to write her?

Mr. Jourdain: No, no; no verse.

Master: You only want prose?

Mr. Jourdain: No, I want neither prose nor verse.

Master: It must be one or the other.

Mr. Jourdain: Why?

Master: For the reason, Sir, that prose or verse are the only means of expression we have.

Mr. Jourdain: Only prose or verse?

Master: Yes, Sir. All which is not prose is verse and all which is not verse is prose.

Mr. Jourdain: And the way we speak, what's that then?

Master: Prose.

Mr. Jourdain: What? when I say "Nicole, bring me my slippers and give me my nightcap", that's prose?

Master: Yes, Sir.

Mr. Jourdain: Upon my word, I have been talking prose for over forty years and did not even know; and I am most obliged to you for telling me. So, I would like to put in a note: Beautiful Marquise, your pretty eyes make me die of love", but I would like it to be gallantly put, nicely turned.

Master: You want to put down that the fire in her eyes reduces your heart to ashes, that for her, night and day you suffer the torments of...

Mr. Jourdain: No, no, no, I don't want all that. I only want what I've told you: Beautiful marquise, your pretty eyes make me die of love.

Master: We should elaborate on the matter somewhat.

Mr. Jourdain: No, I tell you; I want nothing but those words by themselves in the note, fashionably turned though, properly arranged. Why don't you please tell me, just to get an idea, the various ways in which it can be done.

Master: First of all, we can write, as you said: Beautiful Marquise, your pretty eyes make me die of love. Or else: Of love, beautiful Marquise, your pretty eyes make me die. Or else: Die your pretty eyes, beautiful

Marquise, of love make me. Or else: Die make your pretty eyes me, beautiful Marquise, of love.

Mr. Jourdain: But of all those ways, which is the best?

Master: The one you chose: Beautiful Marquise, your pretty eyes make me die of love.

Mr. Jourdain: Yet I have never studied, and I did it on my very first try. I thank you with all my heart, and pray come again to morrow early.

Master: I shall, without fail.

Play Excerpt 3   **L'Enfer c'est les autres**[1]

The play "No Exit" is a vulgarization of Sartre's philosophy of existentialism. It illustrates two themes central to his ideas: first, choice as a determinating factor towards building one's own essence, personality and worth; and second, the eye or judgment of the Other as a limitation to one's own freedom and as influence over one's choices. If man lets the judgment of the Other interfere with his choices and actions, there is no freedom and the resulting situation is hell. Thus can the famous formula "L'enfer, c'est les autres" be interpreted.

The three characters in the play, two women: Inès, Estelle and one man, Garcin, have died and gone to hell for their sins. They are locked in a room and while away the time by mentally torturing each other.

Garcin: Tu sais ce que c'est qu'un lâche, toi.[2]
Inès: Oui, je le sais.[3]
Garcin: Tu sais ce que c'est que le mal, la honte, la peur [...] Oui, tu connais le prix du mal.[4] Et si tu dis que je suis un lâche, c'est en connaissance de cause,[5] hein?[6]
Inès: Oui.[7]
Garcin: C'est toi que je dois convaincre:[8] tu es de ma race.[9] [...]
Inès: Tu veux vraiment me convaincre?
Garcin: Je ne veux plus rien d'autre. [Ces voix de mes compagnons vivants, ces voix qui me traitaient de[10] lâche] je ne les entends plus, tu sais. C'est sans doute qu'ils en ont fini[11] avec moi. Fini: l'affaire est classée,[12] je ne suis plus rien sur terre, même plus un lâche. Inès, nous voilà seuls: il n'y a plus que vous deux pour penser à moi. [Estelle] ne compte pas. Mais toi, toi qui me hais, si tu me crois, tu me sauves.
Inès: Ce ne sera pas facile! Regarde-moi: j'ai la tête dure.
Garcin: J'y mettrai le temps qu'il faudra.[13]
Inès: Oh! Tu as tout le temps. *Tout* le temps.[14]
Garcin (*la prenant aux épaules*[15]) Ecoute, chacun a son but, n'est-ce pas?[16] Moi, je[17] me foutais de[18] l'argent, de l'amour. Je voulais être un homme. Un dur. J'ai tout misé sur le même cheval.[19] Est-ce que c'est possible qu'on soit[20] un lâche quand on a choisi les chemins les plus dangereux? Peut-on juger une vie sur un seul acte?[21]
Inès: Pourquoi pas? Tu as rêvé trente ans[22] que tu avais du coeur;[23] et tu te passais mille petites faiblesses[24] parce que tout est permis aux héros.[25]

Comme c'était commode! Et puis, à l'heure du danger, on t'a mis au pied du mur[26] et... tu as pris le train pour Mexico.

Garcin: Je n'ai pas rêvé cet héroïsme.[27] Je l'ai choisi. On est ce qu'on veut.[28]

Inès: Prouve-le. Prouve que ce n'était pas un rêve. Seuls les actes décident de ce qu'on a voulu.[29]

Garcin: Je suis mort[30] trop tôt. On ne m'a pas laissé le temps de faire *mes* actes.

Inès: On meurt toujours trop tôt - ou trop tard. Et cependant la vie est là, terminée; le trait est tiré, il faut faire la somme.[31] Tu n'es rien d'autre que ta vie.[32] [...] Tu es un lâche, Garcin, un lâche parce que je le veux! Et pourtant, vois comme je suis faible, un souffle; je ne suis rien que le regard qui te voit, que cette pensée incolore qui te pense.[33] *(Il marche sur elle les mains ouvertes).*{...} Mais qu'espères-tu? On n'attrape pas[34] les pensées avec les mains. Allons,[35] tu n'as pas le choix: il faut me convaincre. Je te tiens.[36]

Estelle: Garcin, venge-toi.

Garcin: Comment?

Estelle: Embrasse-moi, tu l'entendras chanter.[37]

Garcin: C'est pourtant vrai, Inès. Tu me tiens, mais je te tiens aussi.

[...]

Inès: Que vas-tu chercher sur ses lèvres?[38] L'oubli? Mais je ne t'oublierai pas, moi. C'est moi qu'il faut convaincre. Moi.[39] Viens, viens! Je t'attends. Tu vois, Estelle, il desserre son étreinte, il est docile comme un chien. Tu ne l'auras pas.

Garcin: Il ne fera donc jamais nuit?

Inès: Jamais.

Garcin: Tu me verras toujours?

Inès: Toujours.

(Garcin abandonne Estelle et fait quelques pas[40] *dans la pièce.)*

Garcin: [...] *(il rit)* Alors c'est ça l'enfer. Je n'aurais jamais cru... Vous vous rappelez: le soufre, le bûcher, le gril[41] ... Ah! quelle plaisanterie. Pas besoin de gril, l'enfer, c'est les autres.

(Jean Paul Sartre, Huis clos, Editions Gallimard)

Guiding Notes

The language register in this three party exchange is contemporary familiar speech which at times even lapses into vulgarity. The main comprehension and translation challenges stem from the use of colloquialisms, clichés and common sayings which abound and cannot be rendered literally. The translation must give the feeling of modern speech and give preference to the familiar phrases of everyday conversation over more literary ways of expression. The rythm is quick, sentences are short and Sartre's love of striking formulas summing up his philosophical ideas permeates the passage.

---

[1] **L'Enfer, c'est les autres**: is the emphasis on the word "les autres" to be kept? How?

[2] **Tu sais ce que c'est qu'un lâche, toi**: find a specifically English way of emphasizing the personal pronoun; ce que c'est que: ce que cela signifie; give a modulation.

[3] **Oui, je le sais**: simplify this answer in your translation; this is where English is more elliptic than French.

[4] **Le prix du mal**: give a verb transposition for "prix".

[5] **C'est en connaissance de cause**: idiom, "c'est parce que tu en as fait l'expérience"; find an equivalent.

[6] **Hein?**: interjection asking for an answer; here it is asking for a positive answer; give an equivalent.

[7] **Oui**: there are other ways of agreeing beside saying "yes".

[8] **C'est toi que je dois convaincre**: how can the personal pronoun be emphasized here?

[9] **Tu es de ma race**: to be taken in the abstract; give a modulation.

[10] **Qui me traitaient de**: qui m'appelaient.

[11] **Ils en ont fini avec moi**: find a familiar expression to express this idea.

[12] **L'affaire est classée**: a set expression meaning "c'est fini, on met cette affaire de côté"; find an equivalent.

[13] **J'y mettrai le temps qu'il faudra**: find a modulation.

[14] **Tout le temps**: pad this phrase in your translation.

[15] **Aux épaules**: use a preposition modulation.

[16] **Ecoute, chacun a son but, n'est-ce pas?**: you can modulate on "écoute" as well as on "chacun".

[17] **Moi, je**: use an adverb to emphasize the personal pronoun here.

[18] **Je me foutais de**: a vulgar way of saying "cela m'était égal"; give an equivalent in the same language register.

[19] **J'ai tout misé sur le même cheval**: a popular saying; can this image be kept in the translation? Are there other ways of saying the same thing in English? Select the best one in view of the context.

[20] **Qu'on soit...on a choisi**: is a passive voice possible here to translate the indefinite pronoun "on"? What are some of the other solutions?

[21] **Peut-on juger une vie sur un seul acte?**: use a passive voice.

[22] **Trente ans**: English needs to pad this expression of time with a preposition.

[23] **Tu avais du coeur**: "coeur" is used here in a figurative way meaning "courage".

[24] **Tu te passais mille petites faiblesses**: tu fermais les yeux sur mille petites faiblesses; is the actual number significant, or is it a figure of speech? How can it be translated?

[25] **Tout est permis aux héros**: find a modulation.

[26] **On t'a mis au pied du mur**: a picturesque way of saying "on t'a demandé de prouver ton courage"; find an equivalent.

[27] **Cet héroïsme**: remember that stylistically English prefers verbs over nouns.

[28] **On est ce qu'on veut**: see note 20.

[29] **Seuls les actes décident de ce qu'on a voulu**: find a striking and concise formula like this one.

[30] **Je suis mort**: is this a present or a passé composé? what English tense is right here in view of the context?

[31] **Le trait est tiré, il faut faire la somme**: refers metaphorically to the line drawn under a set of numbers before adding up; keep the image.

[32] **Tu n'es rien d'autre que ta vie**: see note 29.

[33] **Qui te pense**: qui te juge.

[34] **On n'attrape pas**: pad with a modal auxiliary verb.

[35] **Allons**: give an equivalent prop word.

[36] **Je te tiens**: the verb is to be taken figuratively, "je te tiens en mon pouvoir".

[37] **Tu l'entendras chanter**: not to be taken literally; given the context this expression means "tu vas l'entendre rouspéter".

[38] **Que vas-tu chercher sur ses lèvres?**: modulate.

[39] **C'est moi qu'il faut convaincre. Moi**: emphasize the personal pronoun in a different way.

[40] **Fait quelques pas**: give a verb modulation.

[41] **Le soufre, le bûcher, le gril**: these are the traditional images the French have of hell; English imagery is different; use word modulations.

Other People, That's What Hell Is

Garcin: Yes, *you* know what it means to be a coward.
Inès: Yes, I know.
Garcin: You know all about evil, and shame and fear. Yea, you know
what evil costs. And when you call me a coward, it's from experience, right?
Inès: Right.
Garcin: You're the one I have to convince: we're of the same kind.
Inès: You really want to convince me?
Garcin: I want nothing more now. The voices of my companions on
earth, those voices calling me a coward, I no longer hear them, you know.
Probably because they're through with me. It's all over, case closed. I'm
nothing on earth any more, not even a coward. Estelle does not count. But you,
you who hate me, if you believe me, I'm saved.
Inès: That won't be easy! Take a good look at me: I'm stubborn.
Garcin: I'll give it all the time that's needed.
Inès: Oh! you have plenty of time. All the time in the world.
Garcin (*grabbing her by the shoulders*): Look, we all have our goal in life,
don't we? Personally, I didn't give a damn about money or love. I wanted to
be a man. A tough man. I bet everything I had on one horse. Can you possibly
be a coward when you make the riskiest choices? Can your life be judged by a
single action?
Inès: Why not? For thirty years you imagined that you were brave;
and you closed your eyes to quite a few little lapses because heroes can do no
wrong. How convenient that was! And then in the hour of danger, you were
put to the test and...hopped onto the next train for Mexico.
Garcin: No, I didn't imagine I was a hero. It was a deliberate choice.
You are who you want to be.
Inès: Prove it. Prove that it was no dream. Actions speak louder
than intentions.
Garcin: I died too soon. I was not given enough time to do *my* deeds.
Inès: People always die too soon - or too late. Anyway, there's
your life, it's come to an end. The line has been drawn, it's time to add up.
You are your life and nothing more. You are a coward, Garcin, a coward
because that's the way I want it! And yet see how weak I am, just a puff of
wind; nothing but the eyes that see you and the invisible thought that judges
you. (*he walks towards her with his hands open*). What do you think you are

doing? You can't catch thoughts with your hands. You see, you have no choice: I must be convinced. You're in my power.

Estelle: Garcin, get even with her.

Garcin: How?

Estelle: Kiss me, you'll see her squirm.

Garcin: She's right, Inès. I'm in your power, but you too are in mine.

Inès: What do you hope to get by kissing her? To forget? But *I* won't forget you. I'm the one you have to convince. The only one. Come now, come! I'm waiting. See, Estelle, how he's letting go of you, he's as tame as a dog... He'll never be yours!

Garcin: Won't the night ever come?

Inès: Never.

Garcin: You'll always see me?

Inès: Always.

(*Garcin leaves Estelle and takes a few steps across the room.*)

Garcin (*He laughs*): So, this is hell. I never would have thought... Do you remember: fire and brimstone, flames and hot coals. Ah! what a joke. There's no need for hot coals, other people, that's what hell is.

Chapter 16
Guidelines for the Translation of Poetry

Poetry translation: a difficult but creative enterprise

The translation of poetry is the most difficult of all translations. Why? Because in this process, contrary to prose, rendition of the meaning behind the words is no longer the one and only important consideration. In the configuration of a poem other factors come into play: form, rythm, sounds, harmony, tone, which contribute in no small part to the overall impact on the reader.

But poetry translation is also the most creative of all translations, for, very often, translating a poem is nothing short of re-creating the poem. There will be losses, additions, alterations to the original in order to keep some of its vital elements. Between freedom and submission the translator must strive to find a happy medium, to respect the spirit while avoiding to remain a slave to the letter.

Is poetry translation the reserved domain of poets?

Many poets have translated other poets. Several of Ronsard's and Du Bellay's most famous pieces are recreations of poems by Horace or Petrarch. Baudelaire set out to translate Edgar Allan Poe, and we also have, among others, Paul Valéry's translations of Thomas Hardy, Saint-John Perse's translations of T.S. Eliot and vice versa, Marianne Moore's translations of the fables of La Fontaine and Yves Bonnefoy's translations of Shakespeare and Yeats. Should we say then that it takes a poet to translate another poet? It probably does, for not only do you have to be aware of the music and pattern of the sounds, the rythm and flow of the poem, the power of suggestion of the words, the images, metaphors and symbols, but you also have to try and reproduce the same effects in the TL. However, even if you are not a poet, poetry translation can yield much fun as an exercise in style, provided you are armed with patience and willing to let your ideas simmer a while, for several days if necessary, until a solution finally surfaces. You can be aided in your attempts by the various books on prosody and the rhyming dictionaries on the market. Of course not all poetry is equally difficult to translate, and a descriptive or narrative poem in blank verse will be easier than, say, a sonnet with its rhyme constraints, or a surrealistic poem with its disruption of conventional syntax, thought patterns, words and image associations which aim at recreating a language.

The different levels of poetry translation

There are four great categories of poetry translation depending on the degree of faithfulness to the original.

1. **A literal translation** will remain faithful to the meaning of the poem in the SL while maintaining its complete poetic integrity. Needless to say, this is rarely possible, due to differences in word sounds, especially vowel sounds which are essential to the music of a poem, and due to differences in syntax between English and French. To illustrate the difficulty let's take the case of nasal sounds, which do not exist in English: how is one then to translate a poem like Verlaine's *Chanson d'automne* in which nasals play a prime part in conveying a melancholy mood?

2. **An approximation**, while trying to remain faithful and keeping some of the source elements such as sense, structure, rhyme scheme etc., will take more liberties, due to the difficulties mentioned above and other considerations like rhyme constraints.

3. **An adaptation** will be more remote from the source both in sense and structure.
4. **An imitation** will be a re-creation of the poem: other than borrowing the theme, the mood and may be some of the symbols and metaphors from the source of inspiration, the new poem will have a life and originality of its own.

In short, do not expect to be able to render the poem in its entirety. Depending on the degree of difficulty, the yield may vary from three quarters to half or even less, although every rule has its exceptions, and in the history of literature there have been documented cases in which the translation or imitation has proved superior to the original. Which allows us to maintain, despite Robert Frost's affirmation to the contrary, that poetry is not "what gets lost in translation".

How to proceed with the translation of a poem

1. An indispensable preliminary step will be a semantic, visual and phonetic analysis of the poem
- For meaning (theme, message, obvious and hidden ideas, metaphors and symbols). Look up all words you are not familiar with.
- For form (type of poem: i.e. sonnet, ode, ballad etc., meter, rhyme scheme, stanzas, rhetorical figures, time period).
- For rythm and structure (run on lines, repetitions and parallel constructions, pauses, words placed in emphatic positions).
- For poetic effect of sounds (alliterations, rhymes and internal rhymes, music and harmony of sounds: are they sharp or deep? Are they important? Do they convey a cheerful or a pensive and melancholy mood? Are there special correspondences and modulations between them ?)
- And finally don't forget that a poem is meant to be read or recited out loud in order to fully appreciate its rythm, music and harmony.

2. Make a first draft concentrating just on the translation of ideas and images and keeping to the structure of the model as a framework without concern for artistry.

3. Put the translation into verse

- Determine what meter is best to convey the atmosphere and rythm of the poem. Here, a major difficulty lies in the fact that romance languages have a syllabic count whereas Anglo-Saxon languages, with very few exceptions, have a stress count. Keep in mind that alexandrine verse (twelve syllables in the line) is best rendered by pentameters (five stress counts), but also sometimes by tetrameters (four stress counts), which are generally used respectively for decasyllabic (ten syllable) and octosyllabic (eight syllable) verse. And on occasion, octosyllables have been successfully translated as trimeter when padded with extra unstressed words (which may even be foreign to the original text).
- Determine what sounds to keep for the rhymes and stick to the original rhyme scheme. Many rhyming dictionaries are available to make the task less daunting,[1] but you will have to do some juggling around to keep to the limits imposed by the rhymes.
- Select words on the basis of both meaning and music and try to rescue the internal rhymes, alliterations and other poetic effects. Use language that is appropriate to the period of the poem. Do not use twentieth century language for an ancient poem if it can be avoided so as not to betray the original atmosphere. And do not forget to pay particular attention to the last line of a short poem, especially in the case of a sonnet, for the last line is usually the most crucial and the most artistic, the one which gives the poem its tone and often its central idea.

---

[1] The rhyming dictionaries found in the appendix p.267 should be especially helpful.
Also useful: *Roget's Thesaurus* when looking for the right word, or for a specific sound in a word (as for alliterations).

French rules of prosody

A prerequisite to poetry translation is, of course, a basic knowledge of the rules of French and English prosody,[2] that is to say of the science and art of versification, an understanding of the various forms and structures of poems, meters, rhymes and rhyming patterns, types of stanzas, etc. There are also a certain number of conventions in French versification of which one must be aware before tackling the process of textual analysis.

The first of these conventions is that all compulsory as well as optional liaisons must be made when reciting the poem to better emphasize the sounds, for greater musicality, and also to help in delineating the syllable count. Thus the following line from José Maria de Hérédia's poem *"Le Conquérant"*:

> Et les vents alizés inclinaient leurs antennes

must be pronounced:

> Et les vents zalizés zinclinaient leurs zantennes

whereas in standard French only the last of these liaisons would be a compulsory one.[3]

Another convention affects the sounding of unaccented vowel *e*, which can be pronounced or mute depending on its position in the line and on the word that follows. When found inside the line before a consonant or aspirate *h*, *e* is pronounced and counts as a syllable (unlike standard French). When placed before a vowel or mute *h*, it is mute and does not count as a syllable (as in standard French). When found at the end of the line, it may or may not be pronounced, but does not count as a syllable.

---

[2] For more on the English and French rules of prosody refer to the books listed in the appendix p.267.

[3] Compulsory liaisons are made between words with a close syntactic connection, such as between article and noun, possessive or demonstrative adjective and noun, or pronoun and verb. Optional liaisons are all of the others, except for the very rare cases in which a liaison is forbidden, such as after the conjunction "et".

Finally, the delineation of a line into syllables to determine the type of verse will take a little practice.

A syllable is a basic phonetic unit formed according to the following pattern:

> 1. sounded consonant + sounded vowel (or nasal vowel: an, on, in, un)
> 2. or sounded consonant + sounded vowel + sounded consonant (under condition that the next consonant in the word or following word is different)

Let's take an example from one of Ronsard's *Sonnets à Marie*:

Comme on voit sur la branche au mois de mai la rose

Co	mon	voi	sur	la	bran	chau	moi	de	mai	la	roz
1	2	3	4	5	6	7	8	9	10	11	12

The first two *m*'s count only as one consonant since they are the same sound. Nasal vowels *an* and *on* count as regular vowels. Unsounded final consonants *t* and *s* in *voit* and *mois* do not count. The syllabic pattern is therefore mostly of the consonant + vowel type, except for syllables 4 and 12 which end in sounded consonants. Vowel *e* in *comme* and *branche* disappears before vowels *on* and *au*, whereas in *de* the sound is maintained because followed by a word starting in a consonant, *mai*. In the last word *rose* the *e* is mute since it is in the final position, and consequently only gives a single syllable: *roz*. This yields a twelve syllable count, the so-called alexandrine verse, named after a mediaeval poem on Alexander the Great, which for the first time used the twelve syllable line.

The alexandrine is the longest verse. There are eleven other lengths from the monosyllabic (1) to the hendeca syllabic verse (11). All are not equally popular with poets and, generally speaking, the alexandrine, decasyllabic, octosyllabic and tetrasyllabic are the most widely used.

Poem 1   Ode à Cassandre

Mignonne, allons voir si la rose
Qui ce matin avait déclose
Sa robe de pourpre au soleil,
N'a point perdu cette vesprée
Les plis de sa robe pourprée,
Et son teint au vôtre pareil

Las! voyez comme en peu d'espace,
Mignonne, elle a dessus la place,
Las! las! ses beautés laissé choir!
O vraiment marâtre nature
Puisqu'une telle fleur ne dure
Que du matin jusques au soir!

Donc, si vous m'en croyez, mignonne,
Tandis que votre âge fleuronne
En sa plus verte nouveauté,
Cueillez, cueillez votre jeunesse:
Comme à cette fleur la vieillesse
Fera ternir votre beauté.

(Pierre de Ronsard)

Guided translation:

Step one: translation in prose:

My little beauty, let's go see if the rose
Which this morning had displayed

Its crimson dress in the sun
Has by these vespers lost none
Of the folds of its crimson gown,
And of its complexion so much like yours.

Ode to Cassandra

Step two: translation in verse:

See if the rose, my pretty maid,
Which to morning's sun had dis-
-played
The gorgeous crimson of its dress
Has kept the beauty of its prime
Or lost that tint by vesper time
Which could rival your loveliness.

Alas! see how in so short a space,
Pretty one, it has upon the spot,
Alas! alas! let its beauties drop!

O Nature, you truly wicked stepmother,
Since such a flower only lasts

From morning till evening!

So, if you believe me, pretty one
As long as your tender age is in bloom
In its freshest novelty
Gather, gather the blossom of your youth,
For old age, as it did this flower,
Shall tarnish your beauty too.

Alas! see how in so short a space
Petals dropped all over the place.
Their transient beauty makes us
grieve!
Nature, o cruellest stepmother,
Your child's bloom so soon to
smother
That it can't last from morn to eve!

My pretty girl, believe this truth:
Make the most of your lovely youth
Think of the rose's crimson bloom.
Time flies! so always remember:
May gives way to bleak December.
Age one day shall your beauty
doom.

Notes

We owe the translation of this XVIth century odelette, Ronsard's most famous, to Walter Schaap who has converted the octosyllabic verse to an iambic tetrameter. Perhaps the most extraordinary feature of this poem is the osmosis which the poet has effected between the flower and the young girl by dressing one with the normal attributes of the other and vice versa. The tone is light and gallant, and music plays a role through sound harmony, internal rhymes and alliterations.

A closer examination of the differences between the original and its translation reveals some loss, namely in the obsolete flavor which permeates Ronsard's piece, due to words such as *choir*, *fleuronne*, and particularly *marâtre*, a word which is evocative of fairy tales. Yet, the translation, while more modern in tone and taking liberties with the text, particularly in the last stanza, maintains Ronsard's a-a-b-c-c-b rhyme scheme, and keeps the theme of "seize the day while you may" characteristic of Ronsard's poetry.

Poem 2   Rondeau

Le temps a laissé son manteau
De vent, de froidure et de pluie,
Et s'est vêtu de broderie,
De soleil luisant, clair et beau.

Il n'y a bête ni oiseau,
Qu'en son jargon ne chante ou crie:
Le temps a laissé son manteau
De vent, de froidure et de pluie.

Rivière, fontaine et ruisseau
Portent en livrée jolie
Gouttes d'argent, d'orfèvrerie;
Chacun s'habille de nouveau
Le temps a laissé son manteau.

(Charles d'Orléans)

Roundel 1

The weather's cast his cloak away
Of nasty wind and chill and rain,

To don princely raiments again,

Of shining sun radiant and gay.

Furry beast and feathered bluejay
Proclaim all round in happy strain:
The weather's cast his cloak away
Of nasty wind, and chill and rain.

Fountains, brooks, rivers on this day
Are wearing in their pretty train

Roundel 2

Cast off is Nature's winter gear
Her cloak of cold, of wind and
rain,

She's donned her springtime
clothes again,
Her bright sunlight, so fine and
clear.

To every beast and bird give ear.
They all rejoice in sweet refrain:
Cast off is Nature's winter gear
Her cloak of cold, of wind and
rain.

Each brook, river and placid mere
Splashes like silvery, golden rain

Beads of silver and golden chain;

Everyone's clothed in new array

The weather's cast his cloak away.

In jeweled gown and glittering
                            train;

How dazzling does the world
                            appear!

Cast off is Nature's winter gear.

(Walter Schaap)

Notes

The rondeau, a fixed lyrical form of French origin used in the Middle Ages, runs on two rhymes and usually consists of thirteen lines, a refrain or burden taken from the first line, and a set rhyme scheme: abba, abab, abbaa.

The spelling of the original XVth century poem has been modernized for easier reading. This is a simple piece, with a merry tone, in tribute to the coming of Spring after a long and nasty winter. Music here plays an essential role and accordingly, sounds in the translation must be carefully selected in order to render this cheerfulness and vivacity, this feeling of coming back to life after a hibernating pause, and of celebrating the renascence of nature after the dreary winter months.

Two translations are offered as an exercise in stylistics to show the various effects which can be achieved with contrasting figures of style, and a variety of rhymes. Their chief disparity lies in the choice of a different personification as a central figure for the poem. Both manage to remain pretty close to the original in spite of the constraints of the rhyme scheme which has led to some divergences (*radiant and gay* for *clair et beau*; *on this day* for *fontaine*; *train* for *livrée*; *golden chain* for *orfèvrerie*), and to some necessary padding in order to maintain the meter (*bête ni oiseau* is expanded into: *furry beast and feathered bluejay* in the first version, and *fontaine* into *placid mere*, *portent en livrée jolie* into *their jeweled gown and glittering train* in the second). The second English version is somewhat less literal due to the choice of a different metaphor and departs slightly from the original poem in the last stanza.

Poem Three   Demain dès l'aube

Demain dès l'aube, à l'heure où blanchit la campagne
Je partirai. Vois-tu, je sais que tu m'attends.
J'irai par la forêt, j'irai par la montagne,
Je ne puis demeurer loin de toi plus longtemps.

Je marcherai les yeux fixés sur mes pensées
Sans rien voir au dehors, sans entendre aucun bruit,
Seul, inconnu, le dos courbé, les mains croisées,
Triste, et le jour pour moi sera comme la nuit.

Je ne regarderai ni l'or du soir qui tombe
Ni les voiles au loin descendant vers Harfleur
Et quand j'arriverai je mettrai sur ta tombe
Un bouquet de houx vert et de bruyère en fleur.

(Victor Hugo, Les Contemplations)

Guided translation

Step one: our first task is to decipher the poem, to make a close translation without regard for meter, music or rhyme, just to get familiar with the structure, themes, images, symbols and general mood. This is a lyrical poem, typical of the romantic manner, which uses simple, direct language and closely associates emotions with images of nature. It evokes the annual pilgrimage made by the poet to the grave of his daughter, a young bride of several weeks who tragically drowned while taking a boat ride on the Seine river with her husband.

To morrow, at dawn, when the countryside turns white
I shall set out. You see, I know thou art awaiting me
I shall go through forest and mountain
I cannot stay away from thee any longer.

I shall walk with my eyes fixed upon my thoughts
Without seeing anything outside, without hearing any sound

Alone, a stranger, shoulders bent, hands folded
Sad, and the day to me shall be like the night.

I will not look at the gold of the sunset
Nor at the sails in the distance heading towards Harfleur
And when I arrive, I shall place on thy tomb
A bouquet of green holly and heather in bloom.

Step two: this step involves recreating the poem in translation by working with meters, alliterations, rhymes, rhyme scheme, rythm, parallel constructions, enjambements and the music of sounds.

The fixed form here is the sonnet. The original alexandrine verse (twelve syllable count) is best rendered as an iambic pentameter. The rhyme scheme: abab, cdcd, efef has to be maintained. The enjambements of the first-second and eleventh-twelfth lines also have to be kept, as well as the parallel construction of the sixth line. However, the symbolic image of the green holy and blooming heather probably has to be sacrificed to rhyme constraint and Harfleur, a port in Normandy, which would evoke nothing to an Anglo-Saxon reader can be done away with. One major divergence (and betrayal) with the source poem in the following translation is the special emphasis given to the last word through its position: whereas Hugo chose to end his poem on an image of life and beauty (*en fleur*), the translation insists on an image of death (*grave*) although it manages to maintain until the very end the unexpected shock, to the reader, of the death of the loved girl.

To morrow as the dawn grows bright over the land
I will set out. Thy sweet call's come to me.
Mountains and woods I shall withstand
No longer can I be separated from thee.

This journey will take me wrapped in a pensive state,
Deaf to the sounds of life, blind to a world of light,
Walking lone, a stranger, hands folded and prostrate,
Sad, and the day shall seem just as the night.

With the golden sunset and the sails in the bay
The beauty of the earth now must my senses waive
And before I reach thee, I'll pick along the way
The bouquet I shall place quietly on thy grave.

Chapter 17
Guidelines
For the Translation of Non Literary Texts

Content vs. style

Non literary texts constitute a vast and multifaceted category. From highly specialized reviews and magazines on law, science, economics, business, and technology, from works of vulgarization, company catalogs and publications, marketing documentation on export oriented products, down to newspaper and magazine articles on current events and to ads, non literary texts offer an increasingly large source of material for translation and have given rise to the development of an important translation industry.

The main difference in the treatment of literary and non-literary translation can be summed up in a few words: whereas in literary translation a translator's responsibility is towards the author (i.e. faithfulness to original meaning, form and spirit), in non-literary translation it is towards the reader (i.e. keeping the integrity of the message and making it clear). Non literary translation is basically an act of communication in which stylistics does not play a great role. Of paramount importance is accuracy, not artistry. Information, data, facts and concepts are what counts, not style, structure, poetics or atmosphere.

The translator of non literary material can therefore, with an easy conscience, indulge in taking liberties with the form and structure of the text, if the exactitude of the message being passed along stands to benefit by such a measure, and if a check is run to verify that none of the ideas and nuances of the source text have been overlooked.

Non Literary and Specialty Languages

The language used in non literary texts is a language different both from the one used in literature and in conversation. It is a structured and dense language packed with information. For technical and scientific material, a highly specialized vocabulary is used, often understandable only to experts in the field. Even specialized dictionaries will sometimes fail to provide a TL equivalent. Since new concepts are constantly emerging due to discoveries in every domain, new words must also be coined, and when one realizes that it takes years to put a dictionary together, it is easy to understand why dictionaries cannot keep up with neologisms. Translators in a specific field of expertise must compile their own data, make their own glossary of specialized terms. This can be done by going to other experts for advice and making a habit of reading specialized reviews in both the SL and the TL in order to figure out equivalents. Relatively recent inventions such as fax machines, word processors, VCR's and cellular phones still have not found their way into standard bilingual dictionaries but their French equivalents can easily be determined in light of the proper context.

The language used in non-literary texts is a strong indicator of all the changes which are occurring in the tongue of a linguistic group both semantically and morphologically on account of sociological and technical factors. Newspapers, magazines and reviews will show all the "in" phrases and buzz words of the moment, many of which are newly coined and therefore present special difficulties for the translator.

What is especially important in the translation of a non literary text is knowing what kind of audience is being targeted in order to adopt the appropriate tone and vocabulary: is the text destined for a scholarly readership or is it a work of vulgarization intended for the general public? Is the purpose to inform, as with technical material and journalism, or to proffer an opinion as with editorials, or even to persuade as with marketing documentation and ads?

Taking liberties with sentence structure

In the development of a logical thought French and English tend to adopt opposite approaches: while French goes from the circumstancial to the essential, English favors the reverse sequence. [1]

Let us give one example:

> Avec le fulgurant essor des techniques spatiales et electroniques - les premières ont permis d'explorer les mondes proches; grâce aux secondes, les observatoires terrestres sont devenus des dizaines de fois plus performants -, notre image du cosmos s'est trouvée, en quelques décennies, profondément modifiée. (*France-Amérique*, Terre-Lune: un couple de 4,5 milliards d'années, 31/8/91)

We suggest the following as a translation closer to the reasoning pattern of the English language. The cause-effect sequence of the French sentence is turned around into an effect-cause statement with a break down of the sentence for more clarity:

> Our vision of the cosmos has undergone deep changes within a few decades due to the prodigious advance in space and electronic technologies. The first have allowed man to explore near planets and the second doubled or tripled the performance ability of earth laboratories.

Thus, in French, sentences aiming at the demonstration or illustration of an idea will very often start with a delineation of the circumstances in the form of a participial clause introducing a relationship of relativity, time, cause or concession and will end with the essential point, the main clause. When rendered literally into English with the same clause order, the result sounds very awkward and very much like a translation. A more satisfactory solution is to reshuffle the clause sequence in the sentence and explicit the participial clause by means of a relative pronoun or a

---

[1] Vinay, J.P. and J. Darbelnet. *La Stylistique comparée du français et de l'anglais*. Paris: Didier, 1958, pp.202-3.

conjunction of time, cause or concession followed by a conjugated verb.

For instance:

> Les femmes formant aujourd'hui 44% de la population active, la France paraît se diriger vers le modèle scandinave. (*Bilan Economique et Social*, Les femmes au premier plan, 1991)

The present participle *formant* introduces a relationship of cause and effect between the subordinate and the main clause which reads better if explicited in English with an appropriate phrase:

> France seems to be headed towards a Scandinavian type of society given the fact/ if you consider that women today account for 44% of the workforce.

A second example with a past participle benefits by being developed into a full relative clause in English and by starting with the main nominal group:

> Voulu par Georges Pompidou peu avant sa mort en 1974, maintenu par Valéry Giscard d'Estaing qui ne l'aimait guère, le TGV fut inauguré par François Mitterrand quelques mois après son premier septennat, le 22 septembre 1981. (*Bilan Economique et Social*, 1991)
> The French high speed train, which had been commissioned by President Georges Pompidou just before he died in 1974, and maintained by his successor Valery Giscard d'Estaing who was not much in favor of it, was finally inaugurated by François Mitterrand on September 22, 1981, at the beginning of his first term.

Improving on the original

Improving on the original text would be anathema in any literary translation. However, non literary material and especially newspaper and magazine articles can be shoddily written because put together with deadlines in mind. Reporters cannot afford to agonize like Flaubert over *le mot juste* or the right word. Often sentence construction leaves much to be desired. Whenever confusion is possible in the mind of the intended reader do not hesitate to clarify the text by expliciting the idea and even by rewriting the sentence. Instead of sticking to the structure, follow the ideas behind the words.

French journalists have a particular idiosyncrasy: the use of ellipses. Often the main verb will be missing from a sentence. For a better comprehension and a more flowing style it is advisable to reestablish it in English along with the proper tense.
An example:

> Troisième volet de l'avance nipponne que les occidentaux comprennent aujourd'hui: la conception rapide des nouveaux modèles. (*Bilan Economique et Social*, Une Course mondiale derrière les Japonais, 1991)

Suggested translation:

> The third facet in the Japanese lead which western countries are now beginning to take into account is their ability to quickly develop new models.

Remember the translation of a non-literary text must strive to make the reading as easy as possible, especially if the text is destined for the average reader. Always adapt your style to the intended audience.

Conventions in newspapers and magazines

A. Conventions in headlines and titles

When it comes to headlines and the titles of articles, customs are different between English and French. English headlines recap the gist of the story, telegram style, in a whole sentence without definite or indefinite articles.
One illustration:

> Rights to Life: Some Fear U.S. Efforts to Patent Genes May Inhibit broader Research . (*Wall Street Journal*, 4/17/1992)

Not so in French. A similar article in *Le Monde* (12/7/1991) reads:
Le commerce du génome humain condamné par le Comité d'éthique.
Or compare two other related articles, the first taken from the *Wall Street Journal* (10/1/ 1992), the second from *Le Bilan Economique et Social,* 1991:

> Importing Solutions: Car Makers Fight Japanese by Copying Them.
> Une course mondiale derrière les Japonais.

French titles tend to be more succinct. And although the story-recap in imitation of the English trend is seen more frequently, a nominal group still is often the preferred form. A random selection of headlines from *Le Monde* has yielded the following:

> Le rêve d'Albertville
> L'Occident gorbimaniaque
> Les trois Europes
> La Saga du chocolat

for which possible translations might be:

> Albertville has a dream
> West suffers from Gorbimania
> Are there three Europes?
> How to make chocolate.

B. Conventions in the use of tenses

French journalistic style sometimes makes a special use of the present, future perfect and conditional tenses.

1. The historical present: a stylistic device designed to bring more reality and life into the narration. The historical present is not nearly as prevalent in English as in French. In a context clearly marked as belonging to the past it is best to revert to the past tense in your translation.

> En 1884 le colonel Sandherr, chef des Renseignements militaires, *reçoit* de l'un de ses agents alsaciens une lettre dénonçant le capitaine [Dreyfus] comme un espion allemand. (*L'Express*, 3/17/1994)
> In 1884 Colonel Sandherr, chief of military Intelligence *received* from one of his Alsatian agents a letter denouncing Captain Dreyfus as a German spy.

2. The future perfect (futur antérieur): the grammatical function of the future perfect is to anticipate on the actual occurrence of a future action or situation in relation to a time marker connoting the future. After a conjunction of time (quand, lorsque etc.) the futur antérieur in French also serves to indicate that a future action or situation will take place prior to another future action or situation, although, in this case English uses a present perfect.

> Demain, à cette heure *je serai arrivé* à Paris. Tomorrow, at this time *I will have arrived* in Paris.
> Quand *tu auras terminé* tes devoirs, nous dinerons. When *you have finished* your homework, we will have dinner.

In journalism, an additional use is made of the futur antérieur: it is often applied to past actions or situations in a sort of retrospective over a rather exceptional course of events, for instance when taking stock of someone's achievements by examining the situation from a vantage point of view, such as at that person's death. In such a context only a past tense can be used in English.

> Le président Mitterrand *aura dirigé* son pays pendant deux septennats.
> (*Journal de Genève-Gazette de Lausanne*, 9 janvier 1996)
> President Mitterrand *led* his country for two consecutive terms.

3. The present conditional: often used to make unverified statements. By using the conditional present the journalist wishes to convey that there is no proof as yet that the reported fact is accurate and declines responsibility should the statement prove to be false. Since there is no such use of the English present conditional, the translator will have to circumvent the problem with a short indication:

> Selon Oliver Stone le président Kennedy *aurait été* victime d'un complot organisé par le complexe militaro-industriel américain inquiet de l'intention prêtée au président de rappeler les troupes engagées au Vietnam (*Le Monde*, 12/21/1991)
> Oliver Stone's *theory* is that President Kennedy *was* the victim of a plot engineered by the American military industrial complex worried about the president's alleged intention of recalling the troops from Vietnam.
> La vie sur notre planète *serait* née grâce à une molécule arrivée d'au-delà du système solaire. (*L'Express*, 16-22 mai 1996)
> *It appears that* life on Earth was born of a molecule originated from beyond the solar system.

Cultural references in newspapers and magazines

Newspapers and magazines target a linguistic group with a specific culture and civilization in common. Consequently they make constant references to particular facts, events, or people, which their readers are able to recognize instantly. Translating such articles presupposes an adequate knowledge of the cultural heritage of the S.L. on the part of the translator, first to recognize them and second to make them intelligible to the readers of the T.L. In America for instance everyone knows what *the big apple* stands for, but would it be the same in France? Conversely in France a reference to *l'homme du 18 juin* immediately conjures up General de Gaulle and his June 18th 1940 BBC broadcast calling for the rally of Free France against the Nazi invaders, but in order to make it clear to an English speaking readership a translator would have to substitute the General's name for the epithet.

Many of these references are not only historical, political, sociological, they are also literary. Allusions from a repertory of the great French classics, Montaigne, Corneille, Racine, Molière, La Fontaine, Voltaire etc. or from a repertory of the world's great classics, will pop up even in a non-literary context.

We shall quote as an example an article from *Le Monde* (12/26/1991) on the enthusiastic welcome by Mrs. Thatcher, then prime minister of England, of Michael Gorbachev, then leader of the USSR just prior to the end of the cold war:

> Chaque fois que [Mrs. Thatcher] reçut [Mr. Gorbachev] à Londres, elle avait pour lui les yeux de Chimène.

clearly an allusion to Corneille's seventeenth century play *Le Cid*:

> Tout le monde pour Rodrigue a les yeux de Chimène.

But it is one thing to recognize the allusion, and quite another to translate it. Since Corneille's heroine and her dilemma of love fighting against honor will most likely mean nothing to an American public, the translator will have a choice: either find an equivalence in the Anglo-American literary repertory, or make the author's intention explicit in a more prosaic way, for instance by showing that Mrs Thatcher's is torn between her "honor", her allegiance to her western allies, and her "instinct", her confidence in this Russian leader with a new style. This will necessitate a circumlocution which will have to be kept as short as possible.

Another article in *France-Amérique*, entitled *En attendant les Russes*, is an obvious allusion to Samuel Beckett's play *En attendant Godot*. The translator here is luckier, for *Waiting for Godot* is also well known this side of the Atlantic. No explanation will therefore be necessary and it is up to the reader to catch the implication.

The phrase *Dallas au pays des merveilles* found in a review of Oliver Stone's film *JFK* in *Le Monde* is clearly an allusion to Lewis

Carroll's *Alice in Wonderland* and examples of cultural hints in a non-literary context are many.

As a general rule, when the allusion or the figure of style is not essential to the understanding of the text, it is perhaps best left alone or at least simplified.

Article 1
Mitterrand: la fin d'un combat honorable mené contre soi-même[1]
Mitterrand: un homme libre qui avait trop souvent tutoyé la mort pour la craindre[2]

François Mitterrand est mort,[3] selon l'annonce officielle, lundi 8 à 8h.30 au siège de son bureau[4] avenue Le Play près du Champ-de-Mars[5] à Paris.[...] Mitterrand, quatrième président de la Ve République créée par le général de Gaulle, aura dirigé[6] son pays pendant quatorze ans, soit deux septennats,[7] longevité présidentielle sans précédent.[8] L'ancien[9] chef de l'Etat était atteint depuis 1992 -une intervention chirurgicale[10] l'avait alors rendu public- d'un cancer de la prostate.[11] Il avait réussi à poursuivre son mandat[12] jusqu'au bout malgré des épisodes de souffrance aiguë. Les Français, classe politique comprise,[13] lui étaient reconnaissants de la bonne grâce avec laquelle il avait supporté sa maladie.

Le respect d'Helmut Kohl
En cette matinée[14] d'hiver [...] les Français auront été cueillis à froid[15] par la nouvelle. [...] Mitterrand, qui s'était sportivement[16] retranché de la vie publique depuis sa retraite,[17] avait été aperçu il y a quelques jours en Egypte où il aimait passer les fêtes de fin d'année[18] sous le soleil du Nil.[19] Dans la rue, avec ce mélange de pudeur affective et de volonté de paraître qui les caractérise,[20] les Parisiens exprimaient de la surprise et des commentaires convenus devant un évènement qui avait été peut-être un peu trop préparé pour laisser de la place à la spontanéité. Tous manifestaient cependant peine et estime.[21]

A l'étranger comme dans les rédactions de presse se mettait en place un énorme flux d'hommages dont celui du chancelier Kohl fut probablement le plus senti.[22] Le chancelier avait déjà eu l'occasion[23] d'écrire, au moment de la retraite du président, son respect pour cet improbable mais fidèle compagnon de route d'une décennie.[...]

Au siège du bureau présidentiel, familiers et notables se pressaient immédiatement pour rendre un dernier hommage[24] au président, en présence de la famille. Au début de l'après-midi,[25] les proches[26] annonçaient que, conformément au voeu de l'ancien président, ses obsèques n'auraient pas lieu à

Paris mais à Jarnac (Charente-Maritime) [où étaient ses racines familiales] et dans l'intimité.[27] [...]

"C'est une oeuvre"

A la télévision, c'est sur un ton très personnel que le président Jacques Chirac[28] a rendu hommage hier soir à son prédécesseur: "François Mitterrand, a-t-il dit, c'est une oeuvre.[29] "

Mitterrand aura en effet marqué l'espace français de sa personne comme il en aura imprégné la durée.[30] Sa fameuse affiche électorale de 1981, où l'on voit un village serré autour du clocher au coeur de labours[31] fumants, n'était pas qu'une image mais un programme. Pour cet homme qui fut un véritable maître de la politique, c'est à dire quelquepart entre les pôles de l'opportunisme et de la clairvoyance, il y avait des fidélités.[32] La terre en était une; il sut non seulement l'évoquer dans ses livres mais la chérir par la pratique assidue du jardinage. Contre son itinéraire personnel de provincial monté à Paris[33] et contre presque toute évidence, il évoquait encore dans les années récentes le caractère irrécusablement rural de la France, à l'opposé des grandes villes. En[34] pélerinage à la roche de Solutré ou ailleurs, il faisait cas de[35] ses origines paysannes, en réalité relativement lointaines.

Sens de l'opportunité

Quant au temps, on connaît son fameux aphorisme -il faut laisser du temps au temps[36] - par lequel il ressemble au général de Gaulle et à Mao Tsé-toung, occasionnels amateurs et émetteurs[37] comme lui de sonores platitudes. Par là comme par sa mort si méticuleusement préparée, il manifeste son sens de l'opportunité, de la durée, de la persévérance.[38] Et plus attachant que tout, la fréquentation de la mort[39] l'intéresse de plus en plus, par curiosité autant intellectuelle que spirituelle, à mesure qu'il vieillit. Il décrit la maladie comme un combat honorable à mener contre soi-même. A une époque où[40] rares sont les gens qui savent (ou peuvent) mourir dignement, l'ultime cadeau aux Français de son départ impeccable n'est peut-être pas le moindre.

(Antoine Maurice, *Journal de Genève et Gazette de Lausanne*, 9 janvier 1996)

Guiding Notes

The above article is a representative sample of the journalistic treatment of a news item. It appeared the day after President Mitterrand's death and, being written from a foreign albeit French speaking country's point of view, gives a non partisan tribute to the late head of state. The prose is dense and informative and the vocabulary is non specialized but makes use of "in" phrases and stylistic features which pertain to newspaper writing: this is manifested in the love of nominal groups (i.e le siège du bureau présidentiel, la fréquentation de la mort), the importance of set expressions from the spoken language (la volonté de paraître, cueilli à froid, faire cas de), neologisms which may need defining (l'espace français) and the special use of tenses which have no counterpart in English (here: the futur antérieur: aura dirigé, aura marqué, etc.)

---

[1] **Title**: after translating the article find a title which can best sum up its contents and write it English headline style using verbs.

[2] **Subtitle**: the main problem here is the translation of "tutoyer" a concept which no longer exists in the English language; to help you along the way of a suitable translation ask yourself: is the verb used here in a literal or figurative meaning? What does the use of "tu" to a person imply about the relationship?

[3] **Est mort**: does this verb express a situation or an action here? Consequently is it a present passive or a passé composé?

[4] **Au siège de son bureau**: simplify.

[5] **Près du Champ de Mars**: ask yourself whether this landmark, which is well known to French speakers, is also well known to your audience; if not, substitute a better known landmark.

[6] **Aura dirigé**: the use of the futur antérieur (future perfect) is widespread in journalistic parlance; in regular literary prose its function is to anticipate on the occurrence of a future action or situation (i.e. Demain à cette même heure nous serons arrivés à destination: Tomorrow at this hour we will have reached our destination); here however it is clearly not a future since the former president just passed away: the purpose of the journalistic futur antérieur is to look back upon a whole course of events (in this case Mitterrand's career) and take stock; what tense seems best suited in English?

[7] **Deux septennats**: a "septennat" is a period of seven years; it is generally used to designate the seven year term a French president serves.

[8] **Longévité présidentielle sans précédent**: a modulation will be necessary here; be sure not to overlook all the information contained in these few words.

[9] **L'ancien chef de l'Etat**: the adjective is a false friend.

[10] **Une intervention chirurgicale**: simplify.

[11] **Etait atteint d'un cancer de la prostate**: use a verb and a preposition modulation; watch out for the proper tense in English since this is a continuous situation in the past.

[12] **Son mandat**: what word is used in English for this specific sort of "mandate", a presidential "mandate"?

[13] **Classe politique comprise**: the term "classe politique" is a rather recent one and refers to all politicians, from the left to the right; find a phrase.

[14] **En cette matinée**: use a preposition modulation.

[15] **Auront été cueillis à froid**: a highly idiomatic expression not to be taken literally; look up its meaning in a French monolingual dictionary such as *Le Petit Robert* before deciding on a translation.

[16] **Sportivement**: false friend; "sportivement" has a very specific meaning: in an attitude of fair play.

[17] **Retraite**: false friend in this context.

[18] **Les fêtes de fin d'année**: refers to the Christmas and New Year's holidays.

[19] **Sous le soleil du Nil**: a possible literary allusion to and stylistic reproduction of the title of Georges Bernanos's novel "Sous le soleil de Satan"; modulate.

[20] **Avec ce mélange...qui les caractérise**: analyze all the elements of the sentence and rephrase them in an idiomatic way.

[21] **Tous manifestaient peine et estime**: a change of focus to the passive voice would work best.

[22] **Le plus senti**: the past participle needs some padding in English.

[23] **L'occasion**: false friend.

[24] **Pour rendre un dernier hommage**: both a verb and noun modulation are needed.

[25] **Au *début* de l'après midi**: use an adjective transposition.

[26] **Les proches**: an adjective turned into a noun meaning "ceux qui étaient proches de lui", "ses intimes".

[27] **Dans l'intimité**: one T.U.

[28] **Le président Jacques Chirac**: remember that the translation is from a non French point of view; the nationality of the president needs to be explicited for the target audience.

[29] **Une oeuvre**: refers to one's achievements, whether literary or otherwise.

[30] **Aura marqué l'espace français...durée**: see note 6 for the use of the futur antérieur; "l'espace français": a neologism with no English equivalent. One hears especially nowadays about "l'espace francophone", i.e. all the French speaking countries of the world. The sentence seems rather cryptic at first . It plays on the double factor of space and time and how both were affected by Mitterrand's tenure. It is obvious that no literal translation will do.

[31] **Labours**: champs labourés.

[32] **Pour cet homme...fidélités**: simplify the construction.

[33] *Monté* **à Paris**: the consecrated phrase for French people who leave their native province to make a career in Paris, since most of them come from a more southern position than Paris; can the image be kept for a non-French public?

[34] **En pelerinage**: use a preposition modulation.

[35] **Il faisait cas de**: il se vantait de...

[36] **Il faut laisser du temps au temps**:   work on that formula; what does Mitterrand mean?

[37] **Amateurs et émetteurs**:   the play on words with an internal rhyme for stylistic effect is perhaps best left out of the translation but remain concise in your rendition.

[38] **Par là comme par sa mort...persévérance**:   for the structure of this sentence follow the approach favored by the English language, essential argument first, circumstancial details second.

[39] **La** *fréquentation* **de la mort**:   use a word modulation.

[40] *A* **une époque** *où:*   use a preposition modulation and an adverb-conjunction transposition.

Mitterrand's Death or the End of a Remarkable Struggle against Terminal Illness
He had been living with death too long to fear it

According to official news François Mitterrand died at 8:30 am, Monday the 8th in his Paris office on the Avenue Le Play near the Eiffel Tower. Mitterrand was the fourth president of the Fifth Republic founded by general de Gaulle and led his country for fourteen years, a record of two consecutive terms. The former head of state had been suffering from prostate cancer since 1992 when surgery first brought it to public attention. He had managed to reach the end of his second term in spite of periods of acute pain. The French people, including politicians from all sides, were grateful to him for bearing his illness so gracefully.

Chancellor Kohl pays his last respects

The news took France by surprise on that winter morning. Mitterrand, who, like a good sport, had withdrawn from public life after leaving office, had been seen a few days ago in Egypt where he enjoyed spending the Christmas holidays in the sunny valley of the Nile. Parisians on the street, with their typical mixture of emotional reserve and desire to show off, expressed surprise along with suitable comments on an event which, perhaps, had been anticipated too long to leave any room for spontaneous feelings. Nonetheless sorrow and appreciation were evinced by everyone.

An impressive flow of tributes started pouring from the editorial staffs of newspapers in France and abroad. Among those, chancellor Kohl's was probably the most heartfelt. Already, on the president's retirement, the chancellor had taken the opportunity of writing to convey his best wishes to the man who had proved an unlikely but loyal traveling companion for a decade.

Friends and VIPs immediately crowded the presidential office to pay their last respects to the late president and express sympathy to his family. In the early afternoon it was announced by people close to him that, in compliance with François Mitterrand's last wish, the funeral would be held privately not in Paris but in the small town of Jarnac in south western France where he had his family roots.

François Mitterrand: "A sum of achievements"

Last night on television French president Jacques Chirac paid tribute to his predecessor in a very personal tone. "The life of François Mitterrand, he declared, has been a sum of achievements."

Mitterrand certainly has left his personal mark on France through his long presidency. His famous 1981 campaign poster which showed a village huddling around a church steeple in the middle of misty ploughed fields was not just a picture but a whole program. The man, a master politician who maneuvered between the poles of opportunism and clearsightedness, remained faithful to a few ideals. Land was one of them. Not only did he succeed in bringing it to life in his books, but he was also able to show his love for it through the regular practice of gardening. In recent years in spite of his own personal itinerary (he had gone "up" to Paris as a country lad) and in spite of much evidence to the contrary, he kept alluding to the irrefutably rural character of France, in contrast to the big cities. While on a pilgrimage to Solutré or elsewhere he would emphasize his peasant origins, actually quite remote.

A sense of timeliness

We all know his aphorism on time: "You must let time take its time", done in the tradition of General de Gaulle and Mao Tse-tung, also occasional amateurs and dispensers of resounding truisms. His sense of timeliness, endurance, and perseverance shows through such a pronouncement, as well as in the manner of his death, so meticulously prepared. And more endearing than all the rest, as he progressed in age the proximity of death brought about in him a curiosity both spiritual and intellectual. He described illness as an honorable battle to be fought against oneself. In an age when those who know how to die or can do it with dignity are few, his impeccable departure may be his last but not his least gift to France.

Article 2
Gatt: Pourquoi il faut absolument un accord
Le Mythe de la France seule[1]

Les négociations sur le Gatt arrivent à échéance,[2] et la France paraît un peu seule dans la défense de ses intérêts agricoles et dans la proclamation[3] de son "exception culturelle".[4] Cette double cause[5] rassemble une majorité de Français et, sans doute, le combat actuel[6] du gouvernement ne manque-t-il pas de bons arguments. Moins acceptable, plus inquiétant, est le retour insidieux, au milieu de cette bataille diplomatique, de l'esprit protectionniste.

Celui-ci[7] a dominé notre pays,[8] toutes classes confondues,[9] pendant si longtemps, que ses marques restent indélébiles.[10] Napoléon III avait imposé un libre-échange en 1860 contre sa classe dirigeante:[11] on parla de *"coup d'état[12] douanier"*.

Au début des années 1880, quand la dépression économique mondiale atteignit la France, on n'eut de cesse de[13] vouloir rétablir la protection douanière. Un républicain modéré s'en fit alors le champion[14] et le législateur: Jules Méline, futur auteur d'un *Retour à la terre*, ouvrage dont le titre est à lui seul[15] un vaste programme. Il satisfaisait aussi bien la France des "petits" que la France des "gros":[16] la démocratie rurale des laboureurs,[17] des vignerons et des bûcherons s'alliait[18] aux manufacturiers pour réclamer le cadenassage[19] des frontières.

Ces tarifs douaniers donnèrent sans doute un peu d'air[20] à tous ces petits propriétaires, mais à la longue,[21] ils contribuèrent à maintenir des structures archaïques, donc des coûts élevés, lesquels, par un effet de retour,[22] impliquaient la fermeture. Résultat: une agriculture médiocre sur laquelle vivait mal un monde rural surabondant.[23] La modernisation des années 60 fut d'autant plus brutale. Elle était nécessaire, elle se fit[24] à coups de[25] subventions massives et, pour les paysans[26] transformés en patrons de PME,[27] à coups d'endettements écrasants. La situation actuelle de l'agriculture française est encore tributaire de ce passé protectionniste, quand bien même[28] elle n'a de respiration que par les ventes à l'étranger.

L'exception culturelle est en soi une formule risible. La France est le pays de l'universalisme. J'entends bien[29] qu'on doit défendre le cinéma français et le reste! Mais d'abord par des oeuvres à portée universelle, où la France de Voltaire et de Diderot, où la France de Balzac et de Victor Hugo, où la France d'Auguste et de Jean Renoir[30] s'y reconnaisse.[31] Le reste n'est que bataille corporatiste. La défense de la sub-culture "bien de chez nous"[32] ne présente aucun intérêt, ni pour l'avenir de la France, ni pour celui de l'humanité.

Il y a toujours eu dans notre pays une tendance au repli sur soi.[33] Charles Maurras, en son temps, a fort bien exprimé cete psychologie et cette idéologie de la société close [...] horrifiée par tout ce qui est étranger et qui par définition, altère sa quintessence. Après la défaite de 1940, ce fut le slogan de "la France seule" sous le bâton du Maréchal.[34] L'illusion fut de courte durée.[35]

La France est la quatrième puissance exportatrice du monde: il ne faudrait pas parler du Gatt comme si nous pouvions ruminer sur notre pré carré,[36] derrière des fils barbelés, en attendant l'abattoir.

(Michel Winock, *L'Evènement du Jeudi*, 2-8 décembre 1993)

Guiding Notes

This editorial from a weekly magazine on the occasion of the 1993 Gatt negociations gives a historical perspective of the French position on trade tariffs and like all editorials advocates a certain stance. Although aimed at a general readership, some of its vocabulary may be somewhat arcane from a T.L. point of view and words from the field of business and economics may require the use of a specialized dictionary. The translator will also have to be familiar with some of the commonplace expressions of political discourse (i.e. "la France des petits et la France des gros", "la classe dirigeante"), with neologisms ("l'exception culturelle", "Une bataille corporatiste", "une subculture") and with modern French history, literature and art to recognize some of the less transparent cultural references.

---

[1] **Subtitle**: a nominal title is not a characteristic feature of English headlines; find a more suitable formula which would keep all the elements implied in the original. Remember that a "myth" implies something not quite in touch with reality. It is best to select a title and subtitle after having translated the whole article for a thorough understanding of its contents.

[2] **Les négociations sur le GATT arrivent à échéance**: arrivent à terme; give an adverb transposition for the noun. Notice that the English acronym GATT instead of the French one AGETAC is used.

[3] **Dans la défense et dans la proclamation**: using verbs instead of nouns would be closer to the English stylistic approach; also remember that English simplifies by dropping all prepositions but the first in a list.

[4] **Son "exception culturelle":** the use of inverted commas in the text indicates that the term is new and not yet a household word (it was coined for the negociations). It refers to France's determination not to include the products of her movie and television industry among the business and trade brought to the negociation table and to impose quotas on U.S.-made films in an effort to protect her own culture from Hollywood's overwhelming influence. Since the concept was born in France of a specific situation there can be no English equivalent: use a calque.

[5] **Cette double cause:** give a modulation.

[6] **Actuel:** false friend.

[7] **Celui-ci:** the use of this demonstrative pronoun is frequent in French to refer to previously mentioned persons or facts; "the latter" is often suggested as an English equivalent, but makes the sentence sound too much like a translation; a preferable course of action would be to determine what word the pronoun refers to and simply repeat it.

[8] **Notre pays:** from whose point of view is the article written? some clarification will be necessary for the T.L. public.

[9] **Toutes classes confondues:** toutes classes sociales mélangées.

[10] **Ses marques restent indélébiles:** give a message modulation (a different perspective).

[11] **Sa classe dirigeante:** la classe qui gouverne; a common phrase in political discourse; find an equivalent.

[12] **Coup d'état:** the word has been borrowed in English with a slight modification.

[13] **On n'eut de cesse de...:** an old fashioned expression meaning "on ne s'arrêta pas avant de..."; rephrase the sentence.

[14] **S'en fit le champion:** headed the movement.

[15] **A lui seul:** en soi

[16] **La France des "petits" et la France des "gros":** in this phrase the adjectives are taken as nouns; the antithetical and metaphorical terms designate the two poles of French society; find an English equivalent

[17] **Laboureurs:** false friend.

[18] **S'alliait:** a past perfect seems more appropriate in translation than a past progressive.

[19] **Le cadenassage:** a word coined by the author from "cadenas" (lock) plus suffix -age (which indicates the action of...); use a gerund.

[20] **Donnèrent un peu d'air:** permirent de respirer; the expression is used in a figurative sense; keep the image in English in your search of an equivalent.

[21] **A la longue:** use a preposition modulation and pad.

[22] **Par un effet de retour:** try to visualize the concept by following the author's argument closely to be able to come up with an equivalent.

[23] **Résultat...surabondant**: sentence without a main verb which is not uncommon in French journalism; replace the implied verb in your translation.

[24] **Elle se fit**: false reflexive verb meaning "elle eut lieu".

[25] **A coup de**: avec beaucoup de.

[26] **Les paysans**: this term in French does not carry the pejorative connotation of its English counterpart, it is simply a synonym of "fermiers".

[27] **PME**: an acronym which stands for "Petites et Moyennes Entreprises"

[28] **Quand bien même**: (literary) même si.

[29] **J'entends bien que...**: a not so well known meaning of "entendre". In this context: "je suis d'accord", "j'admets".

[30] **Auguste et Jean Renoir**: the former, one of the major painters of the famous impressionist group, the latter, his son, a movie director who created some of France's great movie classics.

[31] **S'y reconnaisse**: se retrouve.

[32] **La sub-culture "bien de chez nous"**: typiquement française.

[33] **Le repli sur soi**: use a verb transposition for the noun.

[34] **Le Maréchal**: a historical allusion to Marshall Pétain who led the Vichy government during the Nazi occupation of France between 1940 and 1944; obviously this allusion will fail to be clear to a T.L. public; an explanation is therefore necessary in the translation.

[35] **Fut de courte durée**: use a verb transposition for the noun.

[36] **Pré carré**: idiomatic expression meaning "reserved domain". Obviously here the image of the meadow gets lost in translation.

Gatt:
Why an Agreement Is a Must
Can France Really Go It Alone?

Gatt negociations are coming up and France appears somewhat isolated in defending her farming interests and proclaiming her "cultural exception". The French in their majority are behind these two issues and the governement's current battle certainly does not lack for good reasons. But less acceptable and more worrisome is the insidious come-back of the spirit of protectionism in the middle of this diplomatic fight.

Protectionism in France has been prevalent for so long in all strata of society that it has left a permanent impression over the country. In 1860 when Napoleon III imposed a free trade agreement against the wish of the ruling class of the time, it was referred to as a "trading coup".

In the early 1880's, as a world economic depression reached France, a return to customs tariffs was urgently advocated. A moderate republican, Jules Meline, who later was to write "Back to the land" a book whose title is in itself a vast program, became the champion and legislator of this movement. It was an answer to the expectations of both working class and ruling class: the rural democracy of farmers, vintners and woodcutters had concluded an alliance with factory owners to require a tight closing of the borders.

Trade tariffs undoubtedly gave all small landowners a breather, but in the long run, were partially responsible for keeping on archaic structures, therefore high costs, which, through a boomerang effect led to closed borders. The result was an agriculture which left much to be desired and barely managed to feed a rural overpopulation. Modernization in the sixties proved all the more brutal. It had become necessary, was carried out through massive subsidies and turned farmers into small firm owners at the cost of overwhelming mortgages. The present state of French farming is still linked to this protectionist past, even though exports are its only life saver.

Deep down the idea of a "cultural exception" is laughable. France is the land of the universal. Certainly the French movie industry should be protected, along with the rest! But first through works of universal value, which the France of Voltaire and Diderot, the France of Balzac and Victor Hugo, the France of Auguste et Jean Renoir could call her own. The rest is nothing but a corporate fight. The defence of a Gallic subculture offers no interest, either for the future of France, or of humanity.

The country has always had a tendency to look inward. In his day, Charles Maurras was a good exponent of the psychology and ideology of a closed society, a society horrified by anything foreign which by definition would alter its quintessential purity. In the wake of the 1940 defeat came the slogan "France on her own" under the rule of Marshall Petain. It proved to be a short-lived illusion.

France is the fourth largest exporting nation in the world: we should not be talking about Gatt as if we were chewing our cud on our reserved domain behind barbed wire, while waiting for the slaughter house.

Article 3
Sida:[1] Une Découverte française majeure
Une équipe de chercheurs de[2] l'institut Pasteur, dirigée[3] à Paris par le Professeur[4] Hovanessian, met en évidence[5] un mécanisme essentiel de l'infection

Probablement capitale, cette découverte[6] devrait, à terme,[7] permettre aux chercheurs de trouver un moyen d'attaquer le virus. [...] Les résultats complets de ces travaux[8] ont été présentés officiellement mardi 26 octobre lors[9] d'un colloque consacré à la recherche sur cette maladie qui rassemblait les plus grands noms de la recherche mondiale.[10]

Les virologues pensaient jusqu'à présent qu'il existait sur les cellules un seul récepteur, la molécule CD4,[11] qui permettait au virus de pénétrer dans l'organisme. "En fait, nous avons découvert qu'il fallait, non pas un seul récepteur, mais deux, les CD4 et les CD26, pour permettre au virus d'infester cette cellule," a expliqué le Pr. Hovanessian.

Schématiquement,[12] on peut comparer le virus à la cargaison d'un cargo,[13] et la cellule cible[14] au quai de débarquement. Pour que le déchargement du bateau puisse être effectué,[15] il faut, premièrement, une amarre pour immobiliser le navire à quai et, deuxièmement, une grue pour extraire la cargaison de la cale et l'entreposer. Les molécules CD4 qui fixent le virus servent en gros[16] d'[17] amarre et les CD26 représentent la grue. De la même manière que[18] le déchargement n'est possible que si un bateau est immobilisé et si on dispose d'[19] une grue, l'infection ne peut se produire qu'au terme de[20] deux étapes, l'accrochage[21] du virus et l'entrée. "Il s'agit d'[22] un mouvement en deux temps[23] qui fait de ces deux protéines des éléments indissociables,[24]" indique le Pr. Hovanessian. "S'il n'y a pas de CD4 à la surface des cellules cibles, le virus du SIDA ne peut pas y pénétrer et, inversement, si les cellules visées par le virus sont dépourvues de protéines CD26, le virus reste errant autour de la cellule."

Le Pr. Hovanessian et ses collaborateurs ont en outre découvert que les CD26 savent reconnaître, sur une des parties les plus importantes du virus, des "clefs" qui restent constantes[25] chez tous les virus et permettent d'ouvrir la "porte" CD26. Il suffira donc de brouiller la serrure pour empêcher le virus de passer[26] "Même si le virus du SIDA change -ce qu'il fait constamment-, les clefs restent identiques," souligne le Pr. Hovanessian. Selon ce dernier,[27] cette constance, particulièrement importante, montre qu'il existe un point commun à tous les types de virus. Jusqu'à présent, en raison de la versatilité du virus du SIDA et faute de[28] trouver un point commun aux différents virus, les chercheurs n'étaient même pas sûrs de parvenir à créer un vaccin polyvalent.

Ils redoutaient au contraire de devoir lutter au coup par coup,[29] contre le virus africain ou asiatique par exemple, et de devoir adapter leur formule vaccinale en fonction de[30] variations de virus. Au contraire, l'existence d'un dénominateur commun à tous les virus du SIDA devrait donner aux chercheurs un objectif de choix.[31] En théorie, il suffirait de trouver un moyen de bloquer l'interaction entre les clefs et les CD26 ou d'utiliser des molécules bloquant directement l'activité des CD26 pour empêcher le virus d'infecter les cellules. "Ce sera un travail de longue haleine[32] " a estimé le Pr. Hovanessian. "Le rôle du CD26 a été démontré et nous disposons d'inhibiteurs efficaces utilisables comme modèles. Mais il nous faut encore parvenir à augmenter leur activité avant de pouvoir les injecter aux malades, dans deux ans si tout marche bien." [...]

Directeur de recherches au CNRS[33] et chef de l'unité de virologie et d'immunologie cellulaire à l'Institut Pasteur (associé au CNRS) le Pr. Hovanessian a mené ses recherches en coopération avec trois autres chercheurs. [...]"Nous avons gardé nos travaux confidentiels jusqu'à ce que tout ait été démontré de façon irrévocable," a-t-il précisé à l'AFP.[33] [...]Le Pr. Luc Montagnier, responsable de l'équipe française de l'Institut Pasteur qui a découvert le virus de l'immuno-déficience humaine (VIH), a souligné l'importance du travail du Pr. Hovanessian qui constitue une percée nouvelle qui permettra peut-être de mettre au point de nouvelles thérapeutiques ou un vaccin contre le SIDA.

(Reprinted with the permission of the newspaper *France-Amérique*.
Philippe Coste, AFP, *France-Amérique*, 30 octobre-5 novembre 1993)

Guiding Notes

This last article from the medical column of a weekly newspaper does not target specialists in the field but the general public. Its purpose is to vulgarize the latest findings in research medecine on AIDS, that is to say make them understandable to non-experts. Nonetheless its vocabulary is in part specialized, and as such requires the use of a medical or scientific bilingual dictionary. The article also makes frequent quotations, which will provide good practice for the student translator to adapt the phrasing of the sentences leading to these quotations to English usage, interpolated sentences like "indique le professeur", " souligne le professeur", "a-t-il estimé" etc.

---

[1] **SIDA:** acronym for Syndrôme Immuno-Déficitaire Acquis; find the English acronym from which it is a calque.

[2] **De l'Institut Pasteur:** choose a preposition connoting origin.

[3] **Dirigée:** an example of French love of abstract concepts where English prefers concrete ones.

[4] **Le Professeur Hovanessian:** in France, this is the title of a physician teaching at a medical school. May be referred to as Professor or Doctor in English.

[5] **Met en évidence:** one T.U.

[6] **Probablement capitale, cette découverte:** restructure the beginning of this sentence by expanding it into a full clause, and remember that you can use a transposition or a modulation to convey the meaning of "probablement".

[7] **A terme:** (literary) au bout, à la fin (don't forget to make use of a French monolingual dictionary to clarify the meaning of words or expressions you are not familiar with).

[8] **Ces travaux:** i.e. ces travaux de recherche, ces recherches.

[9] **Lors d'un colloque:** a preposition modulation is advisable here, shift from a concept of time to a concept of place.

[10] **De la recherche mondiale:** a nominal group with adjective in French which becomes a compound noun in English; preposition modulation on "de".

[11] **La molécule CD4:** scientific neologisms are almost always calques from the language which made the discovery and first came up with the word. The only difference in English will be one of word sequence: we are dealing with a semantic calque, not a structural one.

[12] **Schématiquement:** an adverb patterned after a noun which is a false friend in English "un schéma", meaning not a scheme, but a diagram, a sketch. There is no equivalent adverb in English; modulate.

[13] **Un cargo:** a false friend; refers to the ship transporting the cargo (Fr. cargaison).

[14] **La cellule cible:** a semantic calque.

[15] **Effectuer un déchargement:** one T.U.

[16] **En gros:** en substance, sans entrer dans les détails.

[17] **D'amarre:** preposition modulation.

[18] **De la même manière que:** one T.U.

[19] **On dispose de:** false friend; means "on a à sa disposition".

[20] **Au terme de :** see note 7.

[21] **L'accrochage:** a noun patterned after "accrocher" (to hook) meaning the action of hooking; use an English gerund.

[22] **Il s'agit de**: an impersonal expression synonymous of "c'est".

[23] **En deux temps**: en deux étapes.

[24] **Indissociables**: the adjective does not exist in English; use a padded expression.

[25] **Restent constantes**: restent les mêmes.

[26] **Il suffira...passer**: transpose on "il suffira" and "brouiller la serrure".

[27] **Ce dernier**: like "celui-ci" a French stylistic idiosyncrasy referring to the last person mentioned; find another solution beside using "the latter".

[28] **Faute de**: par manque de.

[29] **Au coup par coup**: par une suite d'actions séparées.

[30] **En fonction de**: selon.

[31] **Un objectif de choix**: un objectif numéro un.

[32] **Un travail de longue haleine**: literally, "work that will take a long breath", meaning "that will take a long time".

[33] **CNRS, AFP**: acronyms not intelligible to an Anglophone public; shortly explain what they stand for in your translation.

Aids: A Major French Discovery
Headed in Paris by Dr. Hovanessian, a Research Team from the Pasteur Institute Demonstrates One of the Infection's Main Mechanisms

The discovery appears to be of primary importance and should in time give researchers the means to fight the virus. The final results of this undertaking were officially presented on October 26 at a colloquium which brought together the most famous names in world research on the virus.

Up until now virologists thought that only one receptor on the cells, the CD4 molecule, enabled the virus to enter the system. Dr. Hovanessian shed light on his findings: "We have discovered that not one but two receptors, CD4 and CD26, are actually necessary to let the virus take over the cell."

In a simplified illustration of the procedure the virus may be compared to the cargo of a ship and the target cell to a landing dock. For the ship cargo to be unloaded, first, moorings are needed to secure the ship to the wharf, then a crane to remove the cargo from the hold and store it in the warehouse. The CD molecules which fix the virus roughly serve as moorings and CD26 plays the role of the crane. Just as the unloading becomes possible only when the ship is moored to the wharf and a crane is on hand, the infection can take place only after two steps are completed: after the virus has fixed itself onto the cell and after it has penetrated the cell. In the words of Dr. Hovanessian "this is a two-step process by which the two proteins become elements that cannot be dissociated. If there are no CD4 on the surface of target cells, the AIDS virus cannot enter, and conversely if the cells targeted by the virus have no CD26 proteins, the virus is kept wandering outside the cell."

In addition, Dr. Hovanessian and his collaborators have discovered that, on one of the most important parts of the virus CD26 can recognize "keys" which are found in all the viruses. With these keys it is possible to open the CD26 door. Therefore a simple jamming of the lock will prevent the virus from entering. Dr. Hovanessian pointed out that "even if the AIDS virus changes, as it keeps doing, the keys remain the same." In his opinion, this extremely important constancy shows that there is a factor common to the various virus types. Up until now in the absence of a common factor between the different viruses, researchers were not even sure of being able to come up with a polyvalent vaccine due to the ever changing character of the AIDS virus. They were afraid of having to fight the various strains of the virus, such as the

African or Asian strains, one by one, and of having to adapt their vaccine formula to the variations of the virus. Now on the contrary, the existence of a denominator common to all AIDS viruses should provide researchers with a prime objective. Theoretically all that is needed is the means to block the interaction between the keys and CD26 or to use molecules which would directly block the activity of CD26 in order to prevent the virus from infecting the cells.

In Dr. Hovanessian's estimation this will take some time. "The role of CD26 has been demonstrated. We have efficient inhibitors at our disposal to use as models. But we still have to increase their activity before we can inject them into patients, in two years' time if all goes well."

Dr. Hovanessian, head of research at the French National Center for Scientific Research (CNRS) as well as head of virology and cellular immunology at the Pasteur Institute (which is associated with CNRS) has carried out this experiment with the help of three other research assistants. He disclosed to Agence France Presse, the French news agency, that the undertaking was kept a secret until everything could be demonstrated in an irrefutable way. Dr. Luc Montagnier, chief of the French team who discovered the human immunodeficiency virus (HIV) at the Pasteur Institute, has emphasized the importance of Dr. Hovanessian's work as a new advance which may lead to new therapies or to a vaccine against AIDS.

Chapter 18
Guidelines for the Translation of Ads

Ads and cultural references

Next to translating poetry, translating advertisements is perhaps the most creative and the most difficult task a translator can undertake. Creative, because of the impossibility to remain literal, and difficult because of the extensive use the industry makes of cultural references in targeting potential customers.

The use of cultural hints is widespread in French advertising. It is a way of letting the ad reader know that he or she belongs to a sociological group with a common education and common traditions. Many ads read like little riddles which try to appeal to the readers' taste for puzzles while comforting them with a sense of cultural identity.

I will give three examples of French ads making cultural allusions the focal point of their argument. One will quickly see why such ads are on the borderline of translatability.

The first, a recent poster in the Paris metro, reads:
> Carpaccio à volonté: ils sont fous, ces bistros Romains!

The message, flaunting the generosity of a chain of Parisian bistros in indulging their clients with as much carpaccio as they want, seems rather flat and disconnected to an English speaker. To a French person on the other hand, whose education would not be complete without having read the very popular comic strip *Astérix*, the quip evokes the vision of a wily and endearing little Gaul who, with the help of his friends and a magic potion concocted by the

village druid, undertakes to keep Ceasar's Roman legionnaires in check. When faced with some puzzling behavior on their part, he always lets out his leit motiv phrase: "Ils sont fous, ces Romains!"
It is clear that a literal translation of the ad would only yield half of the message and destroy its spirit. The obstacle being a metalinguistic one, only adaptation can rescue some of the original intention. The translator would be well advised to keep to the T.L. cultural field and find a solution in, for instance, one of Charlie Brown's favorite sayings or a catch phrase by some other well known U.S. comic character.

A second ad vaunting a shuttle service goes as follows:
> Orlyval: Paris-Orly en 30 minutes pour que votre avion ne soit pas un mirage.

The pun here revolves around a double entendre on the word *mirage*. The translator has to be aware, first, that Orly refers to one of the two Paris airports, and second, that a mirage, beyond the primary meaning of the word, refers to a certain prototype of French plane well known to anyone with a French background. Even though others may have heard of the plane, the message still is not as clear outside the S.L. when translated literally.

In fact French ads revel in playing on words, making them untranslatable as such. Indeed, how is one to translate the following ad from a restaurant offering each prospective client a pair of sunglasses during the summer months?
> Des lunettes à l'oeil: des lunettes de soleil avec notre menu.

"Sunglasses on the house", which is what is meant, loses both pun and image.

Finally, in *France-Amérique* (10/23-29/93), an ad for AT & T pitching savings on international calls features the picture of a human-looking well-clad and evidently well-nourished ant who is turning away from her doorsteps and into the cold weather a famished looking grasshopper carrying a guitar with the caption:
> Cet automne, chantez comme la cigale à des prix de fourmi.

The ad is an allusion to a very popular fable by seventeenth century beloved fabulist Jean de la Fontaine. Since the cultural apprenticeship of any French school boy or girl entails the memorization of this particular fable, its morality will be present to their mind: in France the hard working and provident ant has long become a symbol of rewarded labor and frugality while the insouciant and fun loving grasshopper is left to die when hard times finally arrive. But the ad cleverly gives a new twist to the story and to its morality by implying that readers can have the best of both worlds: have fun while enjoying the savings offered by the company. A translation into English however is near impossible unless an equivalence of situation can be found in a book more familiar to an English speaker, a tale with overtones of moralization, perhaps Mother Goose or some other nursery rhyme.

Keep in mind the following advice for the translation of ads

- Writing or translating an ad is not unlike writing a title or headline. It is doing a bit of marketing, for you must grab a potential client's attention with catchy phrases, buzz words, striking formulas, and punch lines.

- Concision, short sentences, and going straight to the point are your best bets.

- Since making a point or pitching a product is what matters most, you can take liberties with the wording in your translation. Keep to the ideas but use idiomatic language and clichés, and remember that syntactically French is analytical and English synthetical: where French will say *"Ceci ne prend pas beaucoup de temps"*, English will say *"this is not time-consuming"*.

- You will most likely have to resort to equivalence or adaptation in order to render the spirit of the original message, since cultural barriers will probably stand in the way of comprehension for the T.L. audience.

Ad One

Dans les yeux des enfants brillent les plus belles visions du monde de demain.
Alors nous avons conçu un téléviseur qui transforme votre salon en salle de cinéma.

Avec son format 16/9, ce téléviseur Thomson vous permet de voir les films dans leurs vraies dimensions. Et cela dans les meilleures conditions de confort pour les yeux. Comme au cinéma. Il vous assure une qualité visuelle et sonore tout à fait exceptionnelle. Le système acoustique Cabasse 2 x 50 watts apporte au son des films un relief saisissant.
Ce téléviseur est vraiment conçu pour être à la mesure de votre imagination.

Thomson: autant voir grand.

Notes

In this ad the stylistic emphasis is concentrated on the opening sentence and the closing punchline. Therefore devote most of your attention to their translation for maximum impact on the reader. A modulation direct object-subject in the first sentence will allow you to keep the image. Amplification will also be necessary for the sentence connector *alors* which, in this context, serves to draw a conclusion and just cannot be translated literally as *then*.

The body of the ad merely gives information. Again a modulation object-subject on the verb *vous permet/ you can* as well as a transposition on *visuelle et sonore* will make the message more idiomatic. Some imagination will be required to render the word *relief*, a false friend for which there is no real English counterpart, and which means something like *contrast sharpness*. Find an equivalent for the idiomatic verbal locution *être à la mesure de*.

The eyes of children mirror the most beautiful visions of the future.

That's why we have designed a TV set that will turn your living room into a movie theater.

With the Thomson 16/9 TV screen you can see films true to size and in the best conditions of comfort for your eyes. Just like at the movies. It will bring you an exceptional quality of sound and picture. And Thomson's Cabasse 2 x 50 watts acoustic system gives the sound track amazing reality.

A TV set truly designed to live up to your imagination.

Thomson why not see big?

Ad Two

Avec le four multi-fonctions Dimension 4 la grande cuisine devient enfin accessible à tous.

Un four qui, d'une seule touche, calcule lui-même la puissance, la température ainsi que la cuisson nécessaire, vous connaissez plus simple? Et c'est bon. Très bon même, car le four Dimension 4 est un vrai four, vraiment multi-fonctions: parois en émail, 36 litres, neuf modes de cuisson combinant micro-ondes, convection, chaleur tournante, gril ou gril pulsé pour réussir une cuisson traditionnelle.
Alors, qui a dit que la grande cuisine était difficile?

Panasonic, Quel bonheur!

Notes

A reversal in the order of idea presentation will help with the translation of the first sentence. While French favors the approach: circumstantial details first and essential argument second, English likes to turn things around. Certain concepts such as *la grande cuisine* cannot be translated literally, a modulation is needed to render the same. Also remember to use some cliché expressions such as *cooking time, featuring* etc. A conversion to cubic feet will be necessary to make the capacity of the oven intelligible to your English speaking public, who, most likely, will have no idea of how much one liter is. Use your creativity for the closing formula in the form of a pun, and keep in mind that you do not need to stick to the original.

Now gourmet cooking within everyone's reach with the multiple features of Dimension 4 oven.

An oven which figures out the right power, temperature and cooking time, all at the touch of a button, what could be easier? And with absolutely delicious results, since Dimension 4 is a real oven, featuring enamel walls, a nine cubic feet capacity, nine cooking combinations with microwave, convection heat, turntable, broiler and pulsating broiler, for you to turn out a great traditional dinner anytime.

So, who still says that gourmet cooking is a hassle?

Thank goodness for Panasonic!

Ad Three

Paul-Loup Sulitzer, votre prochain manuscrit, vous l'enverrez en Distingo.

Vous avez certainement déjà constaté que certain courriers sont plus importants que d'autres: un manuscrit original, par exemple. Et dans ce cas, vous aimeriez que tout le monde le comprenne. La Poste comme votre destinataire. C'est pour répondre à ce besoin que nous avons créé un service nouveau: Distingo. En Distingo, votre courrier se distingue:
-Par son traitement particulier: transporté de manière privilégiée dans son enveloppe indéchirable en "Tyvek", Distingo est remis chez votre destinataire. En cas d'absence, le courrier Distingo est déposé dans la boîte aux lettres tandis qu'un avis signalant le passage spécial du facteur est glissé sous la porte.
-Par sa simplicité: selon le volume de votre envoi, l'enveloppe Distingo existe en deux formats prétimbrés (A4 et demi A4). Vous n'avez même plus besoin de la peser avant de la glisser dans la boîte.

Distinguer le courrier important, c'est nouveau, c'est Distingo.
Pas de problème. La Poste est là.

Notes

This is an example of cultural allusion in advertising. If translated literally, the opening sentence would be totally meaningless to an English speaking audience. Who, this side of the Atlantic, has ever heard of Paul Loup Sulitzer? To a French public, on the other hand, the name conjures up the figure of a popular best-selling novelist. Clearly an equivalent has to be found to suit the English speaking culture: someone on top of the best seller list. In addition, some words present a semantic problem: *courrier* and *destinataire* for instance are difficult to translate in this context: English simply does not make use of *mailing* and *addressee* as much as French does.

Keep the parallel construction of the ad to emphasize the dual point of the message: distinctive treatment and simplicity of use. And try to find an attention getter for the closing lines.

Michael Crichton, trust your next manuscript to Distingo!

It's obvious that some mail takes priority, an original manuscript for instance. And if so, you would like everyone to know, the Postal Service as well as the recipient. In response to this need we have created a new service: Distingo.
With Distingo your mail stands out.
It receives special treatment. We deliver it in a special non tearable "Tyvek" envelope. If no one is at home, the carrier will leave it in the mailbox and slip a notice under the door to indicate special delivery.
Distingo is simple to use. Envelopes come in two prestamped sizes (A4 and half size). They don't even have to be weighed before you drop them into the mailbox.

Give priority mail distinction, give it to Distingo.

No problem. We deliver.

Appendix   The Translator's Tools

If, ideally, a professional translator should be bilingual, in practice things tend to be different, and the history of translation has many records of translators actually learning the source language they were translating from as they were doing a particular translation, from Baudelaire deciphering Edgar Allan Poe to Proust interpreting Ruskin.

Thus translators, even professional ones, must rely on a panoply of tools to help them in their undertaking, and, so must, even more so, apprentice-translators.

On top of the list are dictionaries, both mono- and bilingual; the first, to assist you in your comprehension of a difficult and unusual SL concept or to fine tune your mastery of a TL one; the second to bring you the TL counterpart. Next are thesauri, whose importance cannot be stressed enough, for they are "analogy" dictionaries that bring you concepts by semantic fields instead of separately, allowing you to search for just the right word, once you understand the original concept but are not happy with the TL counterparts found in the bilingual dictionary. They offer a wide range of choices not available in even the most detailed bilingual dictionaries.

Of great help also are dictionaries of synonyms, idioms and colloquialisms, false cognates, slang as well as dictionaries of quotations and books on cultural references.

For technical translation resort to specialized glossaries and dictionaries and to encyclopedias: medical, scientific, juridical, financial and so forth. Translators of texts that are on the cutting edge of technology and science will have to turn to experts in the field and specialized reviews for help or resort to borrowings or neologisms, since no dictionary can claim to be up to date in that respect.

Last but not least, in this computer age you can access data bases for files of specific terminologies. And since they are constantly updated, these are even more reliable than dictionaries for technical translation.

Bilingual dictionaries

Considered the most indispensable tool, they can also prove the most frustrating and disappointing. But there are only "bad" bilingual dictionaries insofar as they are misused. Paradoxically, people who are beginning to learn a language tend to use pocket size dictionaries which only give few entries for each word and most of the time not even in context, so that mistakes are easily made by misjudgment of the semantic range of words. Instead, since new learners are not yet aware of the problems involved in translation, they should be the ones using the most detailed bilingual dictionaries, which show the polysemy of words by illustrating their various nuances in context.

The following are some of the very good medium and large size bilingual dictionaries on the market (all are French to English and vice versa).

Atkins, Beryl T., et al. *Webster New World: French Dictionary*. Concise edition. New York: Mac Millan, 1992. (Over 100,000 contemporary words and phrases).

Carney, Faye, general ed. *Larousse: grand dictionnaire français-anglais, anglais-français*. Unabridged edition. Paris: Larousse, 1993. (Over 300,000 references and over 500,000 translations).

_____. *Larousse: Standard Dictionary*. New ed. Paris: Larousse, 1994. (Over 220,000 references and 400,000 translations).

Corréard Marie Hélène, and Valérie Grundy, ed. *The Oxford Hachette French Dictionary*. Oxford, New York, Toronto: Oxford University Press, 1994. (Over 350,000 words and phrases and over 530,000 translations).

Cousin, P.-H., et al., ed. *HarperCollins French Dictionary*. College Edition. London, New York: HarperCollins, 1990.

_____. *HarperCollins French Dictionary*. Unabridged Edition. London, New York: HarperCollins, 1993.

Duval, Alain, Lorna Sinclair Knight, et al., general ed. *HarperCollins Robert Dictionary*. Unabridged. 4th ed. Glasgow: HarperCollins, 1995. (Over 300,000 entries and 550,000 translations. Fully revised and updated "Language in use" section. Comprehensive treatment of current French and English, including thousands of technical, political and business terms).

Duval, Alain, & Vivian Marr, general editors. *Le Robert & Collins Super Senior. Français anglais.* 1 vol. *Anglais-français.* 1 vol. Paris: Dictionnaires Le Robert, 1995. (225 000 translation units).

Duval, Alain, et al. *Le Robert & Collins Junior.* 1 vol. Paris: Dictionnaires Le Robert. (105,000 translation units).

Goldie, Jane, et al., ed. *Harrap's Shorter French Dictionary.* New revised ed. Edinburgh: Harrap, 1991. (Over 235,000 references and 460,000 translations).

Mansion, J.E., revised and edited by D.M. Ledesert and R.P.L. Ledesert. *Harrap's Standard French and English Dictionary.* 4 vols. Edinburgh: Harrap, 1994.

NTC's New College French and English Dictionary. Lincolnwood: National Textbook Company, 1997.

Urwin, Kenneth, ed. *Langenscheidt's Standard French-English/English-French Dictionary.* New York, Berlin and Munich: Langenscheidt, 1988.

On CD-ROM

Let's not forget the most recent bilingual dictionaries on CD-ROM for both Windows and Macintosh which make consulting an entry as expedient and easy as a click of the mouse:

Dictionnaire Larousse bilingue de la langue anglaise (contains a general bilingual French-English dictionary with 90,000 words and expressions, as well as a bilingual business dictionary of 40,000 words and a bilingual computer science dictionary of 30,000 words).

Grand dictionnaire Larousse anglais-français/français-anglais (boasts 350,000 words and expressions, acronyms and proper nouns, historical and cultural articles and the conjugation of the French verbs).

French Monolingual Dictionaries

Guérard, F., et al.. *Hachette: dictionnaire pratique du français.* Paris: Hachette, 1987.

Hachette. *Dictionnaire du français.* Paris: Hachette, 1992.

_____. *Dictionnaire Hachette multimedia.* CD-ROM Windows/Mac. 1997. (New version, 80,000 entries, 4,500 illustrations, 300 interactive cards and 3-dimensional animated videos, sound documents, access by alphabetical order, theme, hypertext or multiple search).

Larousse. *Dictionnaire général pour la maîtrise de la langue française*. Paris: Larousse, 1993. (classical and contemporary culture, 44,000 words and proper names, phrases, synonyms, antonyms, literature, the fine arts, social sciences, science and technology.)

_____. *Le Petit Larousse illustré*. Paris: Larousse, 1996. (84,500 articles, 3,600 illustrations, 288 maps).

_____. *Larousse Encyclopédique*. 4 vols. Paris: Larousse, 1994.

_____. *Dictionnaire Larousse de la langue française*. CD ROM for Windows/Mac.

Rey, Alain, et al., rev. ed. *Le Grand Robert: langue française*. 9 vols. Paris: Dictionnaires Le Robert.

_____. *Le Grand Robert électronique*. CD-ROM Windows. (60,000 quotations, 100,000 articles and 1 million synonyms, analogies, homonyms).

_____. *Le Robert d'aujourd'hui*. Paris: Dictionnaires Le Robert, 1995. (synonyms, analogies, conjugation of verbs, difficulties of the language, phrases and proverbs, sciences and technologies, geographical and historical atlases)

Rey-Debove, Josette and Alain Rey, rev. ed. *Le Nouveau Petit Robert 1*. Paris: Dictionnaires Le Robert, 1995. (2,600 pages, 60,000 articles).

_____. *Le Robert pour Tous: Dictionnaire de la Langue française*. Paris: Dictionnaires Le Robert, 1994.

_____. *Le Robert électronique*. CD-ROM Windows/Mac.

_____. *Le Petit Robert*. CD-ROM Windows/Mac.

Analogical Dictionaries

Berube, Margery S., et al. *Roget's II: The New Thesaurus*. 3rd edition. Boston, New York: Houghton Mifflin Co., 1995.

Boussinot, Roger. *Dictionnaire Bordas des synonymes, analogies, antonymes*. Paris: Bordas, 1988.

Chapman, Robert L., ed. *Roget A to Z.*. New York: Harper Perennial, 1994.

Dictionnaire des termes officiels de la langue française. Paris: Journal Officiel, 1996.

Gove, Philip B., ed. *Webster's New Dictionary of Synonyms*. Springfield: Merriam-Webster, 1984.

Mairé-Weir, Kay, ed., et al. *Webster's Collegiate Thesaurus*. Springfield: Merriam-Webster, 1988.

McCutcheon, Marc. *Roget's Super Thesaurus*. Cincinnati: Writer's Digest Books, 1995.

Niobet, G. *Dictionnaire analogique*. Paris: Larousse, 1992.

Péchouin, Daniel. *Thésaurus Larousse*. Paris: Larousse, 1991.

Urdang, Laurence. *The Oxford Thesaurus*. American Edition. Oxford, New York, Toronto: Oxford University Press, 1992.

Ward-Pitha, Elizabeth, chief ed., et al. *Barlett's Roget's Thesaurus*. Boston, New York, Toronto, London: Little Brown and Company, 1996.

Dictionaries of False Cognates

Colignon, Jean Pierre, and Pierre-Valentin Berthier. *Lexique des faux amis*. Paris: Hatier/Profil, 1985.

Kirk-Greene, C.W.E. *NTC's Dictionary of Faux Amis*. Lincolnwood: National Textbook Company, 1996.

Thody, Philip, and Howard Evans. *Mistakable French: A Dictionary of Words and Phrases easily Confused*. New York: Charles Scribner's sons, 1985.

Van Roey, Granger, and Swallow. *Dictionnaire des faux amis français-anglais*. Gembloux: Duculot, 1988.

Borrowings, English to French

Colpron, Gilles. *Dictionnaire des anglicismes*. Chomedey Laval: Beauchemin, 1982.

Deak, Etienne. *Grand Dictionnaire d'américanismes américain-français*. Paris: Dauphin, 1981.

Etiemble, René. *Parlez-vous franglais?* Paris: Folio-Actuel, 1991.

Leprat, Henri. *Dictionnaire de franglais*. Paris: Livre de Poche, 1980.

Rey-Debove, J., and G. Gagnon. *Dictionnaire des anglicismes: les mots anglais et américains en français*. Paris: Dictionnaires Le Robert, 1990.

Dictionaries on French idioms, colloquialisms and slang

Blum, G., and N. Salas. *Les idiomatics français-anglais*. Paris: Seuil, 1989.

Brunet, François, and Dedan McCavana. *Dictionnaire bilingue de l'argot pour tous: anglais-français/français-anglais*. Paris: Langues pour tous, 1996.

Burke, David. *Street French: How to Speak and Understand French Slang*. John Wiley, 1988.

_____. *More Street French Slang, Idioms and Popular Expletives*. New York: John Wiley, 1990.

Colin, Jean Paul, and Jean Pierre Mével, with the collaboration of Christian Leclère. *Dictionnaire de l'argot*. Paris: Larousse, 1996.

Deak, Etienne, and Simone Deak. *A Dictionary of Colorful French Slanguage and colloquialisms*. New York: E.P. Hutton, 1961.

Denoeu, François, David Sices, and Jacqueline B. Sices. *2001 French and English Idioms*. 2nd edition. New York: Barron, 1996.

Hérail, René James, and Edwin A. Lovatt. *Dictionary of Modern Colloquial French*. London: Routledge, 1984.

Kettridge, J.O. *French Idioms and Figurative Phrases with Many Quotations*. New York: French and European Publications.

Levieux, Michel, and Eleanor Levieux. *Cassell's Colloquial French: a handbook of idiomatic Usage*. London: Macmillan, 1980.

Lupson, Peter, and Michel Pelissier. *Guide to French Idioms*. Lincolnwood: Passport Books, 1987.

Marks, Georgette, and Charles Johnson, revised by Helen Knox. *Harrap's Slang: Dictionnaire d'argot anglais-français/ français-anglais*. Edinburgh: Harrap, 1993.

Books on French cultural references

Bologne, Jean Claude. *Les allusions littéraires: Dictionnaire commenté des expressions d'origine littéraire*. Paris: Larousse, 1989.

Dournon, Jean-Yves. *Le dictionnaire des proverbes et dictons de France*. Paris: Livre de Poche, 1986.

_____. *Le grand dictionnaire des citations françaises*. Paris: Belfond, 1992.

Guterman, Norbert. *The Anchor Book of French Quotations with English Translations*. New York: Doubleday, 1963.

Maloux, Maurice. *Dictionnaire des proverbes, sentences et maximes*. Paris: Larousse, 1992.

Montreynaud, Pierron and Suzzoni. *Dictionnaire de proverbes et dictons*. Paris: Dictionnaires Le Robert, 1993.

Oster, Pierre. *Dictionnaire des citations françaises*. 2 vols. Paris: Dictionnaires Le Robert, 1993.

Rey, Alain, ed. *Le Petit Robert dictionnaire universel des noms propres*. New ed. under Thieri Foulc. Paris: Dictionnaires Le Robert, 1996.

Rhyming dictionaries and books on English and French prosody
Abercrombie, Ascelles. *Principles of English Prosody*. New York: AMS Press, 1976.

Allen, Gay Wilson. *American Prosody*. New York: Octagon Books, 1966.

Espy, Willard R. *Words to Rhyme with*. New York: Facts on File Publication, 1986 (includes a primer of English prosody).

Fergusson, Rosalind. *The Penguin Rhyming Dictionary*. New York: Viking, 1985.

Grammont, Maurice. *Petit traité de versification française*. Paris: Armand Colin, 1966.

Johnson, Burges. *New Rhyming Dictionary and Poet's Handbook*. New York: Harper, 1957.

Packard, William. *The Poet's Dictionary: a Handbook of Prosody and Poetic Devices*. New York: Harper & Row, 1989.

Shapiro, Karl, and Robert Beum. *A Prosody Handbook*. New York: Harper & Row, 1965.

Wood, Clement. *Wood's Unabridged Rhyming Dictionary*. New York: The World Publishing Company, 1943.

Young, Sue. *The New Comprehensive American Rhyming Dictionary*. New York: William Morrow & Co., 1991.

Specialized bilingual dictionaries
Business
Baleyte, Jean, et al. *Dictionnaire économique et juridique*. Paris: Navarre, 1992.

Harrap's Business French. Englewood Cliffs: Prentice Hall, 1991.

Bernard, and Colli. *Vocabulaire économique et financier*. Paris: Seuil, 1989.

Collin, P-H., et al. *Dictionary of Business*. Teddington: Peter Collin, 1990.

Duvillier, Fabienne. *Dictionnaire bilingue de la publicité et de la communication*. Paris: Dunod, 1990.

Echaudemaison, C.D. *Dictionnaire d'économie et de sciences sociales*. Paris: Nathan.

Kettridge, J.O. *French-English and English-French Dictionary of Commercial and financial Terms, Phrases, and Practice*. London: Routledge, 1992.

La Rocque, G. de, and Y. Bernard. *Dictionnaire de l'anglais des affaires*. Paris: Livre de Poche, 1988.

Lenoir, Robert. *Dictionnaire commercial et économique bilingue français-anglais et anglais-français*. Paris: Editions Economica, 1989.

Marcheteau, Michel, et al. *NTC's French & English Business Dictionary*. Lincolnwood: National Textbook Company, 1996.

Péron, Michel, et al. *Le Robert & Collins du management: commercial, financier, économique et juridique*. Paris: Dictionnaires Le Robert, 1995.

Ritchie, Adrian C. *Newspaper French: A Vocabulary of Administrative and Commercial idiom with English Translation*. Cardiff: University of Wales Press, 1990.

Computer science

Collin, S.M.H., et al. *Dictionary of Computing and Information Technology*. Teddington: Peter Collin, 1991.

Dictionnaire de l'informatique. Paris: Afnor, 1989.

Fisher, Renée. *Dictionnaire informatique français-anglais*. Paris: Eyrolles, 1986.

Ginguay, Michel. *Dictionnaire d'informatique français-anglais*. Paris; Masson, 1993.

Harrap's Data Processing French Dictionary. Englewood Cliffs: Prentice Hall, 1986.

Hildebert, Jacques. *Dictionnaire de l'anglais de l'informatique*. Paris: Presses Pocket, 1992.

Larousse. *Dictionnaire de l'informatique*. Paris: Larousse, 1996.

Pyper, T.R. *French Dictionary of Information Technology*. London: Routledge, 1989.

Virgatchik, I. *Dictionnaire bilingue d'informatique*. Paris: Marabout, 1990.

Wiard, A., and I. Virga. *Dictionnaire bilingue d'informatique*. Paris: Hachette, 1995.

Legal

Baleyte, Jean, et al. *Dictionnaire économique et juridique*. Paris: Navarre, 1992.

Hachette. *Dictionnaire de l'anglais économique et juridique*. Paris: Hachette, 1996.

Herbst, Robert, and Alan G. Readett. *Dictionary of Commercial, Financial and Legal terms*. English, German, French. Bergh Publishing, 1990.

Kahn-Paycha, Danièle. *Lexique d'anglais juridique*. Paris: Ellipses, 1993.

Le Docte, E. *Legal Dictionary in four Languages: English, French, German, Dutch*. Maklu, 1988.

Medical

Delamare J, and T. Delamare-Riche. *Dictionnaire des termes de médecine*. Paris; Maloine, 1992.

Gladstone, William J. *English-French Dictionary of Medical and Paramedical Sciences*. 4th ed. Edisem, 1996.

Lepine, P. *Dictionnaire des termes médicaux et biologiques*. Paris: Flammarion, 1974.

Lexique médical anglais-français/français-anglais. 2nd ed. Paris: Masson, 1991.

Sciences and engineering

Bucksch, Herbert. *Dictionnaire pour les travaux publics, le bâtiment et l'équipement des chantiers de construction*. Paris: Eyrolles, 1982.

Chapin, Marie Madeleine. *Dictionnaire technique du français et de l'anglais*. Paris: Marabout.

Collin, P.H., and M. Schuwer. *Dictionary of Ecology and Environment*. Teddington: Peter Collin, 1992.

Ernst, Richard. *Dictionnaire général de la technique industrielle français-anglais*. Brandsletter, 1982.

Forbes, J.R. *Dictionnaire des techniques et technologies modernes*. Paris: Lavoisier, 1993.

Lydersen, Aksel L. *Dictionary of Chemical Engineering: English, French, German, Spanish*. Chichester, New York: John Wiley, 1992.

Malgorn, Guy. *Dictionnaire technique français-anglais*. Montrouge: Gauthier-Villars, 1975.

Michel, J.P., and R.W. Fairbridge. *Dictionary of Earth Sciences*. Chichester, New York: John Wiley, 1992.

Piraux, H. *Dictionnaire des termes relatifs à l'électronique, l'électrotechnique et l'informatique français-anglais*. Paris: Eyrolles, 1984.

The following are suggested readings on the problems of French to English translation:

Bensimon, Paul, chief ed. *Palimpsestes*. Number 1: *Traduire le dialogue, traduire les textes de théâtre*. Paris: Presses de la Sorbonne Nouvelle, 1987.

_____. *Palimpsestes*. Number 2: *Traduire la poésie*.Paris: Presses de la Sorbonne Nouvelle, 1990.

_____. *Palimpsestes*. Number 3: *Traduction/ Adaptation*. Paris: Presses de la Sorbonne Nouvelle, 1990.

_____. *Palimpsestes*. Number 8: *Le traducteur et ses instruments*. Paris: Presses de la Sorbonne Nouvelle, 1993.

_____. *Palimpsestes*. Number 10: *Niveaux de Langue et registres de la traduction*. Paris: Presses de la Sorbonne Nouvelle, 1995.

Chuquet, Hélène, and Michel Paillard. *Approche linguistique des problèmes de traduction anglais-français*. Gap: Ophrys, 1989

Delisle, Jean. *L'Analyse du discours comme méthode de traduction*. Ottawa: Ottawa University Press, 1980.

Gallix, F., and M. Walsh. *Pratique de la traduction: la presse économique, versions et thèmes anglais*. Paris: Hachette, 1993.

Gile, Daniel. *Basic Concepts and Models for Interpreter and Translator Training*. Philadelphia: John Benjamins, 1995

Gouadec, Daniel. *Le traducteur, la traduction et l'entreprise*. Paris: Afnor, 1990.

Guillemin-Flescher, J. *Syntaxe comparée du français et de l'anglais: problèmes de traduction*. Gap: Ophrys, 1981.

Kussmaul, Paul. *Training the Translator*. Philadelphia: John Benjamins, 1995.

Lefevere, André. *Translating Literature: Practice and Theory in a Comparative Literature Context*. New York: The Modern Language Association of America, 1992.

Mounin, Georges. *Les problèmes théoriques de la traduction*. new ed. Paris: Gallimard, 1976.

_____. *Linguistique et traduction*. Bruxelles; Dessart and Mardaga, 1978.

Thompson, Jean-Max. *From and Into English*. Paris: Dunod, 1993.

Vinay, J.P., and J. Darbelnet. *Stylistique comparée du français et de l'anglais*. new edition. Paris: Didier, 1977.

_____. *Stylistique comparée du français et de l'anglais: cahier d'exercices/workbook*. Chomedey Laval: Beauchemin, 1990.

Watson Rodger, Valentine. *Apprendre à traduire*. Toronto: Canadian Scholar's Press, 1993.

Index

DATE DUE
